"I'M TIRED ALL THE TIME . . . DEPRESSED . . . BORED."

Sound familiar? You hear it every day. And you think it's all in their heads. Only maybe it's not. In fact, there's an illness that's more widespread than anyone has ever dreamed, and it produces anxiety, depression, and tension. The illness is hypoglycemia. Millions of people have it without knowing it. This book offers immediate help—a diet that's easy to follow and may make millions of lives happier and healthier in a matter of weeks!

DIET AWAY YOUR STRESS, TENSION AND ANXIETY

THE FRUCTOSE DIET BOOK

J. DANIEL PALM, Ph. D.

INTRODUCTION BY DAVID R. HAWKINS, M.D.

PUBLISHED BY POCKET BOOKS NEW YORK

POCKET BOOKS, a Simon & Schuster division of
GULF & WESTERN CORPORATION
1230 Avenue of the Americas, New York, N.Y. 10020

ISBN: 0-671-82979-3

First Pocket Books printing May, 1977

10 9 8 7 6 5

Trademarks registered in the United States and other countries.

Printed in the U.S.A.

Contents

APPENDICES

Introduction

This is the first book to be published in the United States on the subject of fructose. Dr. Palm explores thoroughly the whole phenomenon of stress and the mechanisms whereby stress eventually results in pathologic conditions. He then documents the biochemical and physiologic changes in the body in response to stress as originally outlined by Cannon and later amplified by Selye. In this treatise, Dr. Palm concentrates on the relationship of stress to altered carbohydrate metabolism and how the stress-induced abnormalities of carbohydrate metabolism eventuate into such common disorders as hypoglycemia, migraine headaches, hyperkinetic syndromes and other symptoms or disease states.

Dr. Palm points out how stress-induced hypoglycemia can be ameliorated by the dietary use of fructose, commonly known as fruit sugar. The book not only provides sufficient details of physiology and chemistry to satisfy the scientist, but it goes on to such practical applications as providing diet plans and recipes designed to introduce fructose into the diet.

Dr. Palm's theory is that when fructose is provided in a dietary regimen to supply a sufficiency of sugar to maintain normal nervous system activity, the distress of a deficiency of intracellular sugar and the subsequent stress response which normally is initiated to correct this condition are eliminated. The theory was developed as an extension of the data in a well-controlled research program which he describes. Some of the benefits of a diet including fructose are a decrease of demand for alcohol among alcoholics, the elimination of the craving for food among those who tend to overeat, a decrease of premenstrual tension, the reduction of symptoms in psychiatric disorders such as schizophrenia or the hyperkinetic syndrome in children, and a reduction of frequency and magnitude of migraine headaches. He also includes a discussion of the use of fructose in the management of diabetes.

One impressive piece of evidence which Dr. Palm presents to support his theory is the demonstration in controlled research that the fructose diet significantly decreases the stress response as indicated by a reduction of stress hormones (catecholamine derivatives) in the urine.

Americans are unfamiliar with fruit sugar in the form of purified fructose. However, fructose itself is a normal constituent of sucrose, which is ordinary table sugar. It also occurs naturally in many fruits and constitutes half the content of honey. For many years, fructose was expensive and unavailable because its manufacture was by an extensive, slow, complicated method. In the last few years, however, new industrial technology has been developed which will result in fructose becoming much less expensive and more widely available. Over the years, it has been available in Europe and its commercial production was such that all available fructose was used by Europeans and none was available for export to the United States.

At the North Nassau Mental Health Center on Long Island, we have been doing research on hypoglycemia and the part that it plays in emotional and mental disorders. Our own research and that of many other investigators interested in the problem has demonstrated that hypoglycemia plays a decisive factor in a large percentage of patients with alcoholism, schizophrenia, depressive disorders, anxiety neurosis and hyperkinetic syndromes. We reported on this research and devoted several chapters, because of the importance of the subject, in the book *Orthomolecular Psychiatry,* edited by myself and Professor Linus Pauling. In addition, hypoglycemia can mimic any emotional or psychiatric disorder and can, at times, be the sole cause of the entire symptom picture. It is one of the most frequent causes for irritability, tension, temper outbursts, insomnia. Hypoglycemia can result in lowering of the convulsive threshold so as to result in epileptic seizures, as well as more minor symptoms such as dizziness, faintness, confusion and fatigue. Many clinicians recognize that undetected hypoglycemia can lead, by conditioning, to excessive alcohol consumption which then develops into alcoholism. Similarly, the frequent eating of carbohydrates as a result of hypoglycemic episodes can lead eventually to obesity. Many children develop hyperkinetic behavior in response to their hypoglycemia, and hypoglycemia contributes to decrease in learning and controlled behavior. Hypoglycemic episodes are a common precipitating cause of migraine headaches. Clinically, in hundreds of cases, we have found that correcting the hypoglycemia brought about an amelioration and, at times, a complete cure of these stressful clinical conditions.

Our treatment included placing the patient on a sugar-free and caffeine-free diet, elimination of refined starches such as white bread and bolstering the body defenses by the use of vitamins. We knew that fructose could be substituted for ordinary sugar because fructose does not induce an insulin response. Patients with an abnormal glucose tolerance test curve in response to eating sucrose will show a normal glucose tolerance test after eating fructose. Many patients found it difficult if not impossible to stay on a sugar-free diet because their eating patterns had become so habituated to large amounts of sweets. Fructose turned out to be a boon to these people who have learned to cook with it the same as one would with ordinary sugar and, so long as it is used in moderation, they have benefited often to a marked degree.

There is much public interest in hypoglycemia, and

the public seems to be ahead of the medical profession in understanding not only the incidence, but the importance and manifestations of this widespread and frequently undiagnosed condition. There is even opposition to the concept by certain academic segments of the medical profession. This opposition seems to stem primarily from a lack of clinical experience because it can be easily demonstrated that a sizable percentage of patients respond dramatically to elimination of ordinary sugar from their diet. Similarly, many normal people experience considerable benefit from such a diet change and report that they experience less fatigue, irritability, sleeplessness and variation in their daily energy level. Fructose is widely used, especially in Europe, for sustained energy by athletes prior to competitive events.

Several years ago, there was an unexplained plane crash. The pilot was experienced, weather conditions were ideal, the aircraft was in perfect condition. The reason for the crash defied investigators until it was discovered that the pilot had hypoglycemia. This cast light on several other plane crashes and resulted in the publication of scientific papers in the *Journal of Aerospace Medicine* in which they reported the investigation of hypoglycemia among pilots and recommended fructose-containing foods and the elimination of sucrose. This eliminated plane crashes due to this disorder. Since becoming acquainted with these facts, I have brought them up in discussions of hypoglycemia with medical colleagues who are skeptical of the importance of hypoglycemia. It is amazing how fast the concept of hypoglycemia is accepted when several million dollars' worth of aircraft and the lives of several hundred passengers depend on its recognition. I often wonder how doubting colleagues would feel about flying to a convention if they knew that the pilot had had two jelly doughnuts and a cup of coffee with two spoons of sugar a few hours before take-off.

This book is an important work in that it demonstrates a practical means for the alleviation of enormous amounts of human suffering. Inasmuch as that is also the goal of my own lifework as a physician, I recommend this book to those who have similar goals.

David R. Hawkins, M.D.
Medical Director
North Nassau Mental Health Center

DIET AWAY YOUR STRESS, TENSION AND ANXIETY

THE FRUCTOSE DIET BOOK

CHAPTER ONE

New Ideas from Old Information

Many relationships between good diet and good health are very well known. To function properly the cells of the body must be provided with adequate and appropriate energy supplies in addition to various minerals, vitamins, and certain specific substrate molecules which the cells require for synthesis of a variety of necessary biochemicals. Much research data has been accumulated about the minimal requirements necessary to prevent known vitamin- and mineral-deficiency diseases. It is unlikely that any new major discoveries will be made in this area of health care. However, a different kind of focus is necessary to understand the problems of the proper provision of energy and substrate supplies to the cells.

Health is more than just an absence of infection and a control of growth processes. Health is a state of being in which the cells are functioning in effective harmonious balance. A healthy person is free of diseases. Some diseases leave telltale signs of the ravages of cells. In some diseases so many cells die that major organs cannot continue to function adequately. In certain disorders abnormal biochemicals accumulate while in others essential molecules are deficient, so various identifying symptoms are demonstrated. These signs of physical damage and different symptoms of disorders aid the physician in his diagnosis and treatment.

Many of our health problems do not produce distinguishing signs or symptoms which identify particular diseases. Without a distinct diagnosis and an understanding of the mechanisms of the health problem effec-

1

tive treatment is difficult. Some people just don't feel well. They don't have a focus to their disorders. They complain of fatigue but are unable to sleep through the night. They experience unexplained nausea and headaches. Others have abdominal gas and heartburn while some feel chilly even though the room is warm. Many of these people recognize that they are irritable while others may develop various kinds of abnormal social behavior. They say that they are under stress. They are anxious and tense. Such diffuse symptoms don't give the physician much diagnostic help. The diagnosis must be as imprecise as the symptoms, but the symptoms do focus on the stress component of the problem.

Stress disrupts lives. It comes in many forms and arises from many causes. Any change in our lives that threatens our physical and emotional stability or challenges our continued well-being is a stress. Stress causes a variety of symptoms. It therefore follows that if you reduce stress you can enjoy a better and possibly longer life. You have a better chance for good health, both physical and mental.

Stress has many faces. It can come either from the inside or from the outside of our bodies. Fear, worry, apprehension, and severe frustration are stresses which arise within the brain. These stresses may be real or imagined. A job of snow shoveling is a stress. A bacterial or viral infection is a stress. Burns, fractures, and severe cuts are all stresses. A chill of the body is a stress. So are the deficiencies of the metabolic requirements for certain of our cells. All of the little stresses are additive. A collection of several small stresses can be as damaging as a major and continuing stress. Some stresses we recognize. Some we don't. It is the magnitude of the accumulated stress which is the problem.

It is impossible to escape from all of the stresses which impinge on our lives. Some stress is unavoidable. In order to maintain ourselves, both physically and mentally, we learn to compensate for these stresses.

We must also learn to reduce or avoid other stresses or we'll suffer the consequences. It is commonly accepted by physicians, scientists, and statisticians that a stress-filled life can lead to an early death. Death can result from the stress of a ruptured artery or the toxins produced by microorganisms. Sometimes it is not the initial stress which directly causes death; instead the effects of our response to stress conditions lead to a variety of physical changes which detrimentally affect our lives.

All varieties of stress, regardless of origin, result in an immediate and automatic onset of the stress response, a biochemically controlled set of physiological changes which regulate a variety of systems in the body. Everyone is acquainted with the most obvious immediate effect of the stress response. Just after a very harrowing experience a person's face is drained of blood so that he is "white as a sheet." The blood vessels of the neck and temples pulsate visibly with each contraction of the heart. The pupils of the eyes are dilated. The muscles of the jaw and face are tense. Cold sweat pours down the inner sides of the arms. The palmar surfaces of the hands are clammy. The mouth is dry. The breathing is fast and shallow. All of these changes are consequences of the stress response. The stress-response changes, not the stress itself, are the bases for anxiety and tension.

Tranquilizers and depressant drugs cannot reduce stress. These drugs are intended to lower the stress response, to diminish its most obvious effects. Drugs can be given to decrease the blood pressure and heart rate directly. They can be given to reduce tension and anxiety. Yet they do not eliminate the actual stress which caused the increase in heart rate, or blood pressure problems, or anxiety, or tension. The use of drugs to lower the stress response is somewhat analogous to bandaging an infected wound. The bandage may prevent some new infection. It may also just cover the mess so the defect is not obvious but the actual problem may remain obscured and untreated. Drugs are not the answer to the plaguing problem of stress. Drugs can be used to stimulate particular cells to provide their unique secretions. They can be used to inhibit the growth of microorganisms or to deactivate toxins. But unless the stress is identified and corrected the drugs which block normal responses to stress can cause more problems than they were expected to alleviate.

Although the mental and emotional stresses have attracted the most public attention, other kinds of stresses may be much more dangerous. Physiological stresses can be more persistent. Because such stresses come from within the body we do not recognize their existence until they initiate a stress response. We may then misinterpret the origin of the problem. There is considerable evidence to support the idea that the most repetitive, continuous, and widespread stress condition is a deficiency of usable sugar to maintain the regulatory functions of the nervous system. We cannot measure the actual amount of sugar in these cells. Instead of a direct determination we can only measure the availability of sugar in the blood stream. If a deficiency of blood sugar exists the cells of the nervous system will be deprived of the sugar they require. It seems that this may be the most dominant and detrimental stress in the lives of many persons.

A new and exciting theory about the effects of this stress and the control of the stress cycle is presented in this book. The theory, in brief, states that an insufficiency of sugar in the blood supplied to the brain is enough of a detrimental condition, and therefore a stress, to initiate physiological responses and behavioral changes which develop into a variety of disorders. A deficiency of blood sugar which is known to be associated with a variety of disorders is seen not as a consequence of the disease but as a primary and original physiological stress. Behavioral changes may be inadequate or inappropriate attempts of the stress-affected persons to compensate. It is believed that if the stress of an insufficiency of blood sugar can be prevented various kinds of abnormal behavior can be controlled.

To eliminate this stress of a deficiency of blood sugar a new dietary program is offered here. This diet is based on the metabolic characteristics of fructose (fruit sugar) and its advantageous use when it is exchanged for glucose or other carbohydrates which are digested to glucose and then absorbed.

The ideas presented in this book are quite simple and straightforward. They are new, fresh, logical, exciting, and unconventional. They do not resolve all of the uncertainties about diet, disease, and behavior which abound in our society. Instead they provide a radical shift of focus from the usual mode of interpretation of the symptoms and initiators of different disorders, both physical and psychological. The ideas are technically sound, easily understood, simple to apply, usually effective, and completely safe.

The book is addressed to the layman. It is also intended to provide ideas and information to physicians, biochemists, physiologists, and students who have not been able to take the necessary time to investigate the ramifications of the stress response in humans. Most of the language is quite non-technical. In the instances in which a simple technical discussion is necessary, an attempt has been made to keep the scientific terms to a minimum. It is desirable to include all the information needed for a complete understanding of these new theories, to identify their implications, and to describe the research which supports it. The specifics in biochemistry and physiology which might not be of primary interest to the layman are included in the Appendices.

Stress and the effects of the stress response reach into all our lives. No one is so isolated that he is unaware that alcoholism, drug dependencies, severe overweight, psychotic behavior, excruciating headaches, continuing fatigue, and depression are common in our society. Such other problems as coronary or other circulatory diseases, ulcers, hyperactivity in children, and colic in babies are also well known. We all know someone who has been troubled with one or more of these problems.

Although we may not have experienced these disorders ourselves, we know that we have had periods of anxiety, tension, insomnia, and irritability which we have ascribed to the pressures of modern life. Perhaps we called it stress. Our reactions to these pressures, both from within ourselves and from the outside, are the subject of this book.

The research which led to its being written did not begin as an investigation of the metabolism of food carbohydrates. It was initiated to investigate some biochemical relationships involved in the general and accepted recognition that some people who are exposed to stress are unable to maintain their previous equilibrium and live effectively while others, exposed to apparently similar stresses, are able to cope. If the stresses are the same, the people must be different. If the people are not biochemically different, the stresses or the control of the stress response must be the basis of the problems of some people.

Much that is presented here as applications of the basic theory is actually an extension of commonly accepted ideas which permeate our culture. As an example, if you ask any adult how to sober up a drunken friend you will probably be told to give him several cups of strong black coffee. Caffeine in the coffee will not directly decrease the alcohol in the blood supplied to the cells. Alcohol must still be metabolized by the cells. Yet someone discovered that the effects of alcohol were decreased when coffee was provided. You could ask, Why coffee? Why should it be black? Is it okay to have sugar? It is unlikely that you will get acceptable answers, not because the logic for this remedy is unavailable—we know a lot about the effects of coffee and the metabolism of both sugar and cream —but because most people don't bother to inquire. The advice is good. There is no better way known to sober up a person than to reinforce the sympathetic nervous system with coffee. Cream is fat. Fat and alcohol are both converted to the same intermediate molecules and use the same enzymes. Cream is slowly digested and would not rapidly accumulate in the blood stream but it does not provide any help in the sobering-up process. The drinker may have begun his drinking because of stress, perhaps that of a deficiency of blood sugar. The provision of sugar in the coffee may seem initially advantageous but if it triggers off the release of insulin this effect may be short-lived and may initiate another period of low blood sugar. If the coffee does its job it should raise the blood sugar level by influencing some liver cells to convert stored glycogen to glucose. Common dietary carbohydrates are not only unnecessary, they may trigger other unfortunate changes. Thus, an explanation of the biochemical logic for using black coffee to sober up someone who has drunk too much alcohol does require extensive information. Similar information is also involved in explaining much that is included in this book, since the relationships among low blood sugar, the sympathetic nervous system, the metabolism of fat, and the effect of dietary sugars are paramount in the explanation of the logic of the new ideas.

If you ask another question, What will happen to a person's weight if he quits smoking? the answer undoubtedly will be that when some people try to stop smoking they tend to gain weight. This piece of information may have come from the experience of the person who answers your question or from the observation of others. Your informant may also suggest that when some people quit smoking they replace one bad habit with another. Such psychological explanations for behavior are widely known and frequently proffered. They are difficult if not impossible to test, but they persist because they cannot be disproved. Some people apparently do exchange smoking for overindulgence at the table, although people have not tried to analyze from a physiological or biochemical standpoint the relationships between the elimination of the smoking habit and the apparent increase in eating or drinking. Everyone just seems to know that smoking, drinking alcoholic beverages, and overeating are habits that are partially interchangeable. People do have all three—they smoke too much, drink too much, and eat too much. Such behavior is directly associated with our stress responses and is therefore a part of the subject of this book.

It may not be initially obvious to the reader that questions about sobering up a drunk and about the increased consumption of food by those who try to quit smoking are closely related, but they deal with the same general topic, the stress response. The control of the stress response and the behavior related to this bio-chemical adjustment are involved in the reasons why some persons overeat, others drink too much, and still others develop miscellaneous other habits or kinds of behavior.

Many other pieces of information related to the stresses we encounter and the effects of our reactions are popularly subscribed to. Some are so widely held that they automatically affect the way we interpret some problems, and thus regulate our behavior. Occasionally we can use this general information to aid in our adjustment to stress conditions. In other circumstances we may recognize the basic problems without being able to do much about them.

It would be advantageous to know how valid are many of our general beliefs as well as to recognize their scientific basis. A number of interesting implications can be derived from such knowledge as that hangovers frequently result from alcoholic beverages containing large amounts of carbohydrates (e.g., sweet mixed drinks, wines, and beer) but are less frequent and less drastic after alcoholic drinks which contain few or no carbohydrates. Another truism states that people who try to quit smoking or "go on the water wagon" usually crave candy. Migraine sufferers can verify that when a person is recovering from a migraine headache he frequently craves salt. All psychiatrists agree that stress can make a man impotent, and many large-scale treatment projects have been designed to reduce this stress. Many magazine articles and news stories support the contention that nervous people are prone to develop ulcers or coronary problems. Anyone can verify that smokers seek the effect of a stimulant, nicotine, when they wish to relax. Every mother knows that if her children eat candy before meals it is difficult to get them to eat the foods they need.

This list could go on and on. Some of this common knowledge has been verified in well-controlled scientific research programs. Some is generally accepted even without scientific scrutiny. The research reported in these pages shows that the fundamental basis of much of our common knowledge is related and therefore somewhat interdependent. When you analyze the implications of all of these separate pieces of information, you are immediately led to the formulation of new ideas. Such are the ideas that are here introduced.

This book is not intended just to verify some of our common beliefs. It is intended to apply our knowledge about the stress response and its control to a wide variety of circumstances. It therefore includes the implications of certain general information commonly accepted by laymen and verified by professionals who work in the problems related to stress. Since excess stress is conceded to be detrimental, the ideas presented here provide a system to reduce or eliminate one stress, that of cellular sugar deficiency, also called hypoglycemia.

The basic information about various stress situations and the stress responses is old information. The new ideas introduced here are based on this well-known series of relationships. I believe them to be of special interest because they present a wholly unique method of reducing the stress of blood sugar deficiency. That method is based on the dietary use of fructose.

CHAPTER TWO

The Dietary Logic
for Stress-Response Control

Every large library has numerous shelves devoted solely to diet books. There are diets for losing weight, for gaining weight, for diabetics, for children with hereditary enzymatic problems, for people with ulcers, allergies, gout, and arthritis, and several diets for hypoglycemics. Many of these diets are well conceived. Some of them may be downright dangerous because they are deficient in the dietary requirements to provide sufficient energy or in the essential materials for maintaining good health.

In this chapter and in Chapter Three you will find another new diet and some capsule explanations of its requirements. The remainder of the book presents in detail the logic for the fructose diet and why it works to alleviate certain specific disorders. Briefly, the diet's effectiveness depends on the periodic ingestion of fructose. Although it is possible to achieve some of its benefits by eating honey or dates instead of fructose in exchange for other carbohydrates, it is much more difficult to get completely satisfactory results. Since glucose is so rapidly transferred from the digestive tract into the blood and is so effective in triggering the release of insulin, it is an ideal food only for those who have no problems with hypoglycemia. A partially satisfactory result can be expected if a high-protein, low-carbohydrate diet is followed and dates are eaten between meals to aid in maintaining an adequate blood sugar level. Dates contain nearly equal amounts of fructose and glucose as the simple sugars. The sugars are not combined into the double sugar sucrose. Since we ordinarily do not chew our foods enough to rupture all of the cell membranes and cell walls, these sugars are contained in natural "time-release" form which makes them advantageous in the regulation of the blood sugar concentration.

Fructose is a food. It is not a drug. Like all other carbohydrates, it is oxidized in the cells of the body to create energy for such uses as synthesis of new molecules, the contraction of muscles, nerve cell activity, and the housekeeping duties of the kidney and liver and to provide the raw materials from which cells can synthesize required molecules. Since it is a carbohydrate, it provides 4 calories of energy per gram of weight. Although the terms "calories" and "grams" are common words, most people don't really know their meanings. A calorie is the amount of heat required to raise 1 c.c. of water 1 degree Centigrade, a definition that isn't much clearer than the word "calorie" itself. A calorie is an international measure of energy. It is specified in the metric units. No equivalent in ounces of water and Fahrenheit degrees is given. It is a convenient measure of energy content, but it does have its limitations.

It would not help to devise new words for the energy content of food. It might be easier to use some common reference that is part of everyone's experience, but no satisfactory alternative has been proposed. Some authors have converted the energy content of foods to what they call carbohydrate equivalents, but even then it is necessary to carry a table of food values in your pocket. For this reason the food contents given in the eating plans in Chapter Three do not individually specify the total energy content available to the body before digestion and conversion into molecules that can be used on sugars, fats, and proteins.

Table 1 in this chapter lists a large variety of foods in caloric value for energy use. Although this designation indicates the amount of energy each food supplies, such information is insufficient to indicate the total nutrient value of each food. Good nutrition comes from good food. It is now known that 50 or more nutrients are required for good health. The greater the variety of the foods in the diet the more likely that the requirements for health will be provided without the necessity of additional food supplements.

The nutriment requirements can be divided into six main groups of materials—carbohydrates, fats, proteins, vitamins, minerals, and water. Only the first two are primarily energy sources. Occasionally they are substrates for synthesis, but usually they are cellular fuels which are "burned" ("oxidized") to free the energy contained in their chemical bonds. Although they both provide energy, they require different enzymes (organic catalysts which allow the "burning" of the compounds to occur at body temperatures). Fats and carbohydrates enter different metabolic pathways. Sugars can be completely oxidized to carbon dioxide, water, and energy without any contribution from fats. Yet fat is mobilized from storage cells as a part of the stress response which may be regulated by the presence of sugar in the blood. Sugars can be converted into fats, but the body is unable to convert fats to sugars. Without sugar to prevent the stress response, the fats will be mobilized (freed from their storage sites inside of cells) faster than they can be oxidized. If fats are incompletely oxidized, the intermediate molecules called ketones accumulate in body fluids. These compounds can lead to acid-alkali problems in the blood.

Our bodies can, and do, oxidize proteins to obtain energy, but proteins are not good energy sources. Before a protein can be oxidized at all, it must be digested into its individual component amino acids. Then the nitrogenous portion of each of these amino acids must be removed and excreted from the body as urea, creatinine, or other nitrogenous compounds. The cellular work necessary to obtain energy from proteins has not been accurately measured, but there is good reason to believe that in many cases it is almost equal to, and may exceed, the amount of energy that the proteins provide.

We have obtained our general information about the energy content of various foods by actually burning a weighed amount of it in pure oxygen. The amount of heat given off (in calories) under these conditions does not subtract the energy required in the body to "burn" this material. The caloric value of the foods given in Table 1 includes the caloric contribution from the protein portion of the food. This may be in slight error but is more correct than considering proteins as providing 0 calories per gram. It is admittedly a compromise, but a necessary one, and it is preferable to err on the side of conservatism.

Proteins are not needed to provide energy in the diets of most persons in the world. Carbohydrates and fats do a much better job of that. Proteins are needed instead to provide amino acids, which our cells can recombine into other proteins necessary for our health. Proteins are also required for the nucleoproteins of our hereditary materials which provide the instructions for the activity of the cells. Proteins are necessary for cell membranes and other structural units within cells. Proteins are necessary for some of our amino acids which are made into necessary hormones. All of our enzymes require their protein components. Proteins in the blood are essential as antibodies for our immune response. Proteins, in short, are so uniquely required for our health that they should not just be burned for their chemical bond energies. (In the absence of a sufficient amount of blood sugar, however, it certainly is to our benefit that many proteins provide amino acids which can be made into sugar or can directly supply the body with essential molecules that are necessary for the regulation of the nervous system.)

Vitamins do not provide energy. They are necessary for the regulation of energy release from our cellular fuels and for many other metabolic actions. They are

not needed in quantity and are usually available in
sufficient amounts in every good, varied diet which
contains fruits, vegetables, dairy products, and meats.
No single food contains all of the necessary vitamins,
so any diet that relies on a single type of food will
eventually result in a vitamin deficiency. Such deficiencies can cause the development of a large variety
of human diseases with such symptoms as behavioral
problems, degeneration of skin, bone, muscle, nerve,
and sensory organs, and a whole host of malfunctions
of many organs in the body.

Some of our required vitamins are made by bacteria
we harbor in our lower digestive tracts. We provide
these cells with a home and with food, and they provide us with vitamins which they synthesize. To get
some of these vitamins into our blood it is necessary
that some fats be provided in the diet. The bacteria do
not make the vitamins from the fat we eat, but the
vitamins are fat soluble, not water soluble, and dietary
fat is necessary to transport these newly synthesized
vitamins. It should be provided in small amounts
throughout every day. Some bile salts which are made
from cholesterol must also be available from the liver
to enable the cells to absorb the vitamin-fat complexes.
After the vitamins have been transferred into the body
cells, the fats are then oxidized for the energy they
contain.

Alcohol can be and is oxidized for the energy it
contains. Even though it, like simple sugars, does not
require digestion before absorption, it, like fat, cannot
be made into sugar. Although alcohol may depress the
nervous system, it cannot provide for the synthesis of
essential nerve regulator molecules.

The best estimates suggest that a minimal but complete diet should contain at least 65 to 100 grams of
carbohydrate daily, primarily for the synthesis of GABA
for the nervous system, and at least 25 grams of fats.
Each gram of carbohydrate contains 4 calories of fuel
energy, so if 100 grams is taken as a safe minimum

this would amount to 400 calories. Each gram of fat provides between 8 and 9 calories. With these restrictions it is impossible to devise a safe diet, even for persons who are desperately trying to lose weight, without requiring an intake of at least 600 calories. Some of those calories can be obtained from proteins so that there is considerable latitude in choosing foods if the diet contains a sufficient amount of proteins above the amount needed to provide the required amino acids.

The proper functioning of the body also requires a rather large array of minerals. Iron is required for the blood. Calcium is needed, together with other minerals, for bones and teeth as well as for several other necessary cell products. Potassium and sodium are needed to regulate a variety of cellular functions. Iodine is required in small amounts to act as one of the components of the secretion of the thyroid gland, which regulates the cell metabolic rates. Other minerals are needed in trace amounts but generally are supplied in the diet without the need for supplements. It is because we do not know exactly which kinds of minerals are needed that it is usually considered best to obtain these materials from natural foods rather than to rely on synthetic diets which might inadvertently neglect some trace material that we need but do not recognize. Different combinations of natural foods can be included in a diet so that all of the necessary materials are provided without requiring us to eat foods which we find to be unpalatable or unavailable.

Some people will, because of specific problems, require mineral and vitamin supplements to their diet. Many persons will prefer to include synthetic vitamins to insure that they do not become deficient even though their diet includes what is thought to be sufficient vitamins and minerals. Fortunately, overdoses of most vitamins usually do not cause harm. Additional vitamins and minerals may not do any good for most persons, but they do injustice primarily to the pocketbook.

The dietary suggestions given here provide a sufficient amount of carbohydrate, fat, vitamins, minerals, and proteins to maintain good nutrition. The diet is specifically designed also to decrease the problems of blood sugar control for those who have such problems. In essence, the diet is a complete high-protein, low-carbohydrate diet which provides—by substituting fructose for most of the carbohydrate—a means by which the blood sugar can be maintained at optimal levels.

The effectiveness of the diet depends on some changes in the types of foods consumed and the timing of the dietary intake. Some foods should be avoided by everyone who has trouble with blood sugar control. They are not "forbidden" but are troublemakers. These foods are those which include any significant amount of sucrose. Therefore most candies, jams, jellies, marmalade, syrups, pie, cake, cookies, pastries, soft drinks, sugar-coated cereals, and foods high in starch should be avoided. Starchy foods include such near staples as macaroni, noodles, spaghetti, potatoes, and rice. Rice and potatoes, however, may not be as offensive as the milled products because the digestive action necessary to precede absorption may make these something like timed-release carbohydrates. They may therefore be considered as restricted carbohydrates and included with the vegetables if eaten in small amounts occasionally to provide some variety to the diet.

Milk should also be restricted in a diet for hypoglycemic control. Although milk is a good food which provides some protein and fat, its primary content, except for water, is lactose sugar. Like glucose, this milk sugar induces the release of insulin. The minerals in milk can be obtained by eating cheeses and yogurt, the preparation of which eliminates much if not all of the lactose but retains the advantageous minerals and proteins.

Fructose will not be able to provide its primary benefit of remaining available for cellular use for extended periods of time if insulin secretion has been initiated by glucose or lactose provided in the restricted foods. Candies, syrups, gelatine, jellies, Kool-Aid, and other prepared foods using fructose as the only sweetening agent should be included in the diet. This provides a way to get the necessary carbohydrates and at the same time to repress the stress response.

Fat little girls are not just sugar and spice and everything nice. They contain a lot of water. This is not all excess water that can be safely eliminated. Some water is needed as the main component of the blood. Some water is needed in the fluids which bathe the cells, since foods and wastes must travel between the blood stream and the cells in a fluid medium. Most of the inside of all cells is water. Much of this is called "bound water." This water is essential. We also require water for perspiration to regulate the body temperature by evaporation, and some water is needed to eliminate waste products removed from the blood stream as it passes through the kidneys. Dehydration is a dangerous condition. It is assumed that every person who follows this dietary program will drink enough fluids to insure the necessary tissue requirements.

Retention of water is based on the reabsorption of sodium salts from the kidney tubules under the influence of steroid hormones secreted by the adrenal cortex cells. If this suggested dietary program is followed, there is likely to be a reduction in the steroid hormones and thus a decrease in the reabsorption of water which normally causes edema. The loss of this water is desirable. It is very temporary if the steroid hormones are secreted at a later time to adjust to the stress of a low blood sugar or any other stress. Only as long as the fructose and other carbohydrates keep the blood sugar level above that which initiates the stress response will the unnecessary water be excreted in the urine. If the stress is reinitiated, the weight of the retained water may be more than the oxidized fat which was expected to decrease the weight of the person. For persons who use this dietary program to achieve weight loss it is this fat reduction that is important. Differences in body weight between night and morning weighings are frequently two pounds or more. This difference is the amount of water lost in the urine which is voided in the morning as well as that lost from the lungs and by perspiration.

The variability of water retention has frustrated many a good diet program. Since any stress can affect this water accumulation to some extent, it is the weight loss over the period of a week or month that should be considered; one should not expect that each and every day there will be a measurable decrease in poundage.

This dietary program which uses fructose as the primary carbohydrate was designed on the premise that if a complete and satisfying minimal diet is provided it is unwise to attempt to "con" the body into requiring metabolically useless drinks and foods. That is, it is unnecessary and ill-advised to use sugar substitutes in drinks or candies. Sugars are good foods. For the hypoglycemic, fructose seems to be the best answer that nature has provided. When you feel as if you need a dietary soft drink or a snack, follow your instincts and provide the body with the one food which will provide energy but does not require digestion, induce insulin release, or require insulin.

Fructose should be taken with and between meals to avoid the onset of the stress response initiated by a low blood glucose condition. Some persons who have been unable to obtain pure fructose have found that the dietary suggestions work quite well if natural honey is used instead of fructose. It may, however, be difficult to get enough honey in one's diet to prevent hypoglycemia and still avoid the secretion of insulin by honey's glucose component. Honey and dates are better in this respect than most other foods, but they are potentially difficult to regulate. Their glucose content will also provide the necessary nutrients for bacterial growth in the mouth, which could lead to extensive plaque and cavities. Although fructose is not so apt to cause plaque deposition as glucose, one should brush his teeth more often if he frequently eats fructose candies.

The design of the diets suggested in this book allows each person individually to tailor his needs and preferences to a sensible diet. The diet is easy to follow. The foods are generally available, both for home preparation and when eating out. The diet allows one to measure rather than weigh food. Thus you can maintain your proper food intake just as easily away from home as when you fix your food in the kitchen.

The foods are divided into seven basic types: (1) "free foods" which can be eaten in any amount since they contain negligible amounts of carbohydrates, fats, or proteins, (2) meat, (3) fat, (4) milk, (5) vegetables, (6) fruit, (7) flour products. The foods are listed in amounts normally supplied as an "average serving" in addition to the conventional specification of grams of carbohydrates, fats, and proteins. The caloric value of the protein component of the foods is specified and included in the total amount of calories of each of the foods. When these foods are taken as recommended, they will supply ample amounts of essential proteins, fats, carbohydrates, vitamins, and minerals.

The combinations of the various foods into different types allow a person to select a variety from each food group. For example, you may replace one serving of fat from List 3 with a piece of fried meat or eat a few potato chips if you substitute the potato for one of the vegetables in List 5. It is best not to omit the suggested amount of any of the food types. A balanced and complete diet requires each variety of food in proper relationship. Slight deviations will not produce any disaster if the over-all balance is maintained.

This diet is intended for people who have functional hypoglycemia, for those who wish to lose weight without feeling hungry or irritable, for those who wish to reduce their craving for alcohol, for people who wish to avoid the onset of migraine headaches or premenstrual tension, for hyperactive children, and for persons with certain psychotic tendencies. For this reason provision is made to adjust the diet in many ways. If a person needs to lose weight, the diet should contain fewer calories than are demanded by his daily activities. If the weight is to be maintained, the total diet should include enough calories so that reserves are not mobilized to maintain the body. Some people want to gain weight, but because of the tension and anxiety which accompany their hypoglycemia their dietary intake and absorption have been inadequate. The diet can be used here too. Such adjustments are outlined in Chapter Three, and additional variations designed for people suffering from the specific disorders listed above are given in the individual chapters on those ailments.

This diet can also be used by some overweight diabetics who do not require insulin. The majority of the carbohydrate is fructose. The slow absorption of the fructose will inhibit the hunger that is experienced by diabetics just as it does for those who are hypoglycemic but do not accumulate sugar in their urine. However, since fructose is chemically different from glucose, the normal glucose urine test is not as applicable. The slow absorption of fructose is of value here since the concentration in the blood rises so slowly that it does not exceed the reabsorption capability of the kidney tubules. The concentration of glucose which normally "swamps" the kidney is 160 mg% ml. To reach this concentration with fructose it would be necessary to consume the major portion of a daily allotment at one time.

The presence of glucose in the urine prevents the reabsorption of water from the kidney tubules. The amount of urine excreted is increased by this loss of water, which dehydrates the diabetic person. If fructose is eaten faster than it can be absorbed in the upper portion of the digestive tract, it will cause water retention in the intestines and a soft bowel condition. To prevent this minor inconvenience and to make effective use of all of the ingested fructose, it is recommended that the dieter increase his consumption of leafy green vegetables and other, non-digestible foods. The presence of these fibrous foods will delay the movement of the food mass through the upper digestive tract and thus allow enough time for absorption of the fructose. If a soft bowel condition continues, it means that too much fructose is being consumed at one time.

The amount of fructose required to provide the 75 to 100 grams of necessary carbohydrate each day may seem excessive to a person who has not stopped to consider the alternatives. A teaspoon of fructose weighs 4 grams. It provides 16 calories. Commercial fructose tablets usually are prepared in 2-gram sizes. Thus they contain 8 calories of energy. An ordinary slice of un-buttered bread contains between 12 and 13 grams of carbohydrate. Even if we go by the lower value of 12 grams of carbohydrate for 48 calories, a slice of bread is equal to three heaping teaspoons of crystalline fructose or six commercial tablets. One slice of unbuttered bread just doesn't go far when you are hungry because it takes time for its digestion and may cause insulin release. That many calories in the form of fructose will supply the necessary sugar for two to four hours for most people.

The fructose diet program differs from most other diets since it will work at any time if the amount of "insulin-inducing" carbohydrates is kept to a minimum. To avoid premenstrual headaches and cramps the diet can be restricted to just a few days before the onset of menses. For those who get migraine headaches on weekends the diet will work if followed from, say, Thursday through Sunday. The fructose-exchange diet plan is the most variable diet plan available.

Most people will discover that after they have regu-lated their weight and behavior problems they can keep in good shape with a less restrictive diet than given here if they use fructose between meals and es-pecially early in the evening as a food and not as a restricted drug. A single tablet of fructose is not enough to do much good between meals, but three or four may be sufficient to avoid the stress response.

TABLE 1
DIETARY FOOD LISTS

List 1—Foods that are free of carbohydrates or fats—"free foods."

Bouillon (fat free)	Mustard (dry)
Clear broth	Pepper and other spices
Coffee	Pickles (unsweetened)
Cranberries (unsweetened)	Rennet tablets
Gelatine (unsweetened)	Salt
Horseradish	Seasonings
Lemon	Vinegar

List 1A—Vegetables eaten raw need not be measured. If these vegetables are cooked (which makes them more easily digestible) a 1-cup serving may be exchanged for any one serving of the vegetables in List 5.

Asparagus	Peppers, green or red
Bean sprouts	Pimento
Broccoli	Radishes
Brussels sprouts	Rhubarb (without sugar)
Cabbage	Sauerkraut
Cauliflower	Spinach
Celery	Squash, summer
Cucumber	String beans, young
Eggplant	Tomatoes
Lettuce	Tomato juice, ½ cup
Mushrooms	Zucchini
Parsley	

List 2—Meats, fish, cheese, peanut butter, and eggs. These are the high-protein foods. Each serving provides 7 grams of protein and 5 grams of fat. 73 calories per serving.*

---

* Caloric content given for usable energy content. Carbohydrates=4 calories per gram. Fats=8 calories per gram. These computations include caloric content contribution from the proteins in the food.

Lean meat and poultry
  Beef, lamb, pork, veal,
  liver, chicken, turkey, ham,
  etc. (Visible fat removed
  at the table.) Cooked size
  3"×2"×½". 1 slice
Hamburger patty, 1 small
Cold cuts (4" round, thin
  slice), 1 slice
Wiener, 1 small
Fish
  Flounder, halibut, trout,
  whitefish, salmon, tuna,
  etc. (2"×2"×1"), 1 slice

Salmon, tuna, lobster,
  canned, ¼ small can
Sausage (3"×⅛"), 2
Oysters, shrimp, clams, 5
  small
Sardines, 3 medium
Cheese
  Cheddar, American
  (1½"×¼"), 1 slice
  Cottage, Parmesan,
  Roquefort, etc. ¼ cup
Egg, 1
Peanut butter, 1
  tablespoon

List 3—Fats. Each serving provides approximately 5 grams of fat. 45 calories per serving.

Avocado (4" diameter), ⅛
Bacon, crisp, 1 slice
Butter, margarine, 1
  teaspoon
Chocolate, unsweetened,
  melted, 2 teaspoons
Cream, light (sweet or sour),
  2 tablespoons
Cream, heavy, 1 tablespoon
Lard, drippings, 1 teaspoon

Cream cheese, 1 tablespoon
French dressing, 1
  tablespoon
Mayonnaise, 1 teaspoon
Nuts, 6 small
Oil or cooking fat, 1
  teaspoon
Olives, green or ripe, 5
Shortening (vegetable),
  1 teaspoon

List 4—Milk and milk products. Carbohydrates, 12 grams; protein, 8 grams; fat, 10 grams per serving. 170 calories per serving.

Milk
  Whole, 1 cup
  Evaporated, ½ cup
  Skim, 1 cup
  (add 2 servings from List
  3 if fat free.)

Yogurt, 1 cup
Ice cream, vanilla, ¼ cup
Ice milk, ¾ cup

List 5—Vegetables. All servings ½ cup. Carbohydrates, 7 grams; protein, 2 grams. 37 calories per serving.

Beets	Squash, winter
Carrots	Turnips
Onions	Tomato puree, canned
Green peas	Vegetables, frozen, mixed
Pumpkin	Catsup, 2 tablespoons
Rutabagas	

List 6—Fruits. All the fruits are fresh or canned without sugar. At least one serving of citrus fruits, carrots, or pumpkin each day will provide the vitamin A requirement of a good diet. Carbohydrates, 10 grams. 40 calories per serving.

Apple (2″ diameter), 1	Grape juice, ½ cup
Applesauce, ½ cup	Honeydew melon
Apricots	(7″ diameter), ¼
Fresh, 2 medium	Figs, fresh, 2 large
Dried, 4 halves	Figs, dried, 1 small
Banana, ½ small	Nectarine, 1 medium
Berries (blueberries,	Orange, 1 small
raspberries, strawberries),	Peach, 1 medium
1 cup	Pear, 1 small
Cantaloupe (6″ diameter),	Pineapple, ½ cup
½	Pineapple juice, ⅓ cup
Cherries, 10 large	Plums, 2 medium
Cider, ½ cup	Prunes, dried, 2
Fruit cocktail, ½ cup	Raisins, 2 tablespoons
Dates, 2	Tangerine, 1 large
Grapefruit, ½ small	Watermelon (3″×1½″), 1
Grapes, 12	slice

List 7—Flour products and starchy vegetables. Since all of these products are converted into glucose in the digestive tract they should be included in the diet sparingly and never more than one serving per meal for a person who has trouble regulating the blood sugar

level. Protein, 2 grams, carbohydrates, 15 grams. 68 calories per serving.

Bread, 1 slice
Biscuit, roll
   (2" diameter), ½
Hamburger bun, ½
Wiener bun, ½
Muffin (2" diameter, 1
Cereal
   Cooked, ½ cup
   Dry flakes, ¾ cup
Crackers
   Graham, 2
   Saltine, 5
   Soda, 3
Flour, 2½ tablespoons
Spaghetti, ½ cup
Macaroni, ½ cup
Noodles, ½ cup

Pretzels (ring, medium), 6
Sponge cake, 1½" cube
Baked beans, ¼ cup
Beans, lima, navy, ½ cup
   dry cooked
Corn, ⅓ cup or ½ ear
Parsnips, ½ cup
Peas, dry cooked, ½ cup
Potatoes
   Baked or boiled,
   1 small
   Mashed, ½ cup
   Fried, 6 small strips
Potato chips, 15 (omit 2 fat
   servings)
Sweet potatoes, ½ cup

CHAPTER THREE

Now Design Your Own Diet Program with New Recipes

Each of us is an individual. No one diet will suit everyone. Even identical twins may like different foods. Generalized diets should be considered only as guidelines and should provide many possible substitutions so that the diet you design does not become a bore. Eating is a social activity for most of us. If you must forgo some of your favorite foods to achieve metabolic regulation of your blood sugar, it isn't necessary to portray yourself as making such a sacrifice that you inflict misery on those around you. Take the time to assess your personal problems. Then with the help of the diets given here and the food lists in Chapter Two and in Appendix 4 learn what you will have to do to meet your objectives.

The general eating plans included here allow each person to tailor his needs and likes to a sensible diet. Your metabolic requirements may be well above 3000 calories each day if you are doing heavy labor or if you are a nursing mother. Another's demand may be considerably below 2000 calories each day to prevent a weight gain. No single diet can be proposed for such a spread in caloric demand. You must adjust the diet to your problem and to your own satisfaction or you will not continue to follow it and to gain its benefits.

The general rule requires that every diet provide each day at least 50 grams of protein, 65 to 100 grams of carbohydrate (preferably as fructose to prevent the stress of low blood sugar), and a minimum of 25 grams of fat. These foods should be provided in a diet with an adequate intake of vitamins, minerals, and some non-digestible bulk.

Many people are overweight and many people would gladly shed their excess pounds if they could be free of the stress which caused them to overeat. They know that they don't eat just to maintain the body's activities. Excess weight is the direct consequence of a higher intake of calories than are used by the body at that time. One of the diets given here, called the *Minimal Diet Eating Plan* (Diet No. 1), provides fewer calories than are required to keep the body going. The necessary functions of the body will be maintained by using the stored fat supply. Each pound of fat represents 3500 calories of energy. It took the equivalent of 218 teaspoonfuls of sugar over the energy required to maintain the body to accumulate each pound of fat. This is over 4 cups of sugar, since a cup contains 48 teaspoonfuls. To eliminate this hoard, it is necessary to subtract an equivalent amount of sugar and fat from the dietary intake. This reduction in calories must be a reduction in carbohydrates and fats without sacrificing the essential proteins, vitamins, and minerals. Some fat must be included to absorb those bacterial-produced vitamins, and a minimum of carbohydrate must be kept available to provide the brain and the remainder of the nervous system with their requirements.

If we assume that an average person (actually no person is "average" because one day he is active and the next he isn't) requires 2000 calories per day, the Minimal Diet is almost 800 calories deficient since this eating plan provides only 1200 calories of carbohydrates, fats, and proteins. A deficiency of this amount of energy from that necessary to supply the body will result in a desirable weight loss. This decrease in the dietary intake will account for almost 2 pounds of fat loss per week. In addition, there will be a decrease in body water.

In order to achieve the best results from this diet, fish and meats should be broiled, baked, or boiled. Do not use fried food unless you use only the amount of fat you are allowed in your meal. The vegetables can be prepared in any fashion. Avoid smothering them with butter or flour sauce unless you subtract this fat and carbohydrate from the allowance for that meal.

If one is engaged in strenuous physical activity, the amount of fructose consumed can be increased to prevent hunger between meals. At such times it is almost mandatory that more fructose be eaten, or adrenalin will be released and initiate the hunger signal. There is sufficient flexibility in the individual diets to allow adding 5 teaspoons of fructose without upsetting the dietary applecart. This is equal to 10 of the commercial fructose tablets. It is best to save half the fruit allowance from the meals for a snack between meals. Since many of the fruits are quite high in glucose, they may precipitate insulin release if the entire amount is eaten at one time. This is especially true if the carbohydrates from vegetables are available because these foods were cooked.

Remember, you cannot have your cake and eat it too. Some people expect that a diet can be devised which will allow them to lose weight but at the same time permit them to eat an entire day's allowance at one sitting and then go without eating anything for the remainder of the day. Others want to be able to drink any amount of alcoholic beverages and still lose weight. Heavy drinking or gorge eating will sabotage any well-designed weight-loss diet. A drink before a meal or in the evening will not make it impossible for you to lose weight, but it may slow down the rate of weight loss to some degree. If you are going to drink, you should not waste good fructose by having beverages which are loaded with carbohydrates. Beer, wines, brandies, and sweetened hard-liquor mixed drinks will induce insulin release and make fructose unavailable to the cells.

The *Sustaining Diet Eating Plan* (Diet No. 2) provides a well-balanced diet for a person who does not need to lose weight but may suffer from any of the symptoms associated with the stress response initiated by a low blood sugar condition. This diet provides just over 1800 calories in the meals and fructose, but it is much higher in protein than the Minimal Diet. Because hypoglycemic persons are unable to regulate their blood sugar concentration effectively, this diet provides more fat than is included in the Minimal Diet.

The *Venture Diet Eating Plan* (Diet No. 3) is for those rare individuals who, although they have the symptoms associated with hypoglycemia when they eat glucose-providing carbohydrates, need to gain weight. This diet includes more fat but less protein than the Sustaining Diet. High amounts of proteins can require so much energy for their digestion and for the removal of the nitrogenous portion of the amino acids that they may subtract from the normal energy-providing foods. The provision of fructose supplies a sufficient carbohydrate source to insure that no stress response to a condition of a low blood sugar will interfere with the storage of the excess calories. It is the excess fat and fructose, over the amount necessary to maintain normal body functions, which will provide for a desirable weight plan.

At the end of this chapter are a few recipes which use fructose as the primary carbohydrate. The amount of glucose provided in a serving of these foods is low enough that it is unlikely it will initiate insulin release. The desserts are not provided only to top off the meal but as a good way to provide the necessary fructose for that meal. And for a pleasant-tasting drink, see the egg nog recipe given on page 150. Any good cookbook will provide other possible foods which are primarily protein, contain a minimum of milk and starch, and allow fructose to be substituted for the sucrose. A variety of salad dressings can be devised with sour cream and any number of cheeses. But it's hard to beat the Sweet-Sour Dressing suggested here.

The main dish recipes are provided to indicate the interesting varieties of foods to provide the meat protein and the bulk needed in the diet in cost-cutting meals.

The possibilities are almost endless. Use your imagination and common sense. Avoid foods that contain anything more than a very minor amount of carbohydrate if you want to regulate your diet to prevent the stress response to a cellular sugar deficiency. You'll know within a day or two whether your stress, tension, and anxiety can be controlled by this simple diet. Then you can experiment and still keep things under control.

It is at this time impossible to specify the exact dietary consequences of many of our high-carbohydrate foods. Their caloric value has been measured by determining the amount of heat produced when a measured amount of such foods is burned in pure oxygen inside a bomb calorimeter. This burning process consumes all the material, both that which is digestible and that which is not. Only termites can digest the cellulose fibers. Some of the bacteria of the lower digestive tract can digest and use a group of carbohydrates called oligosaccharides, but humans cannot do so. Even if the bacteria digest these complex carbohydrates, the sugar molecules cannot be absorbed from the lower digestive tract. If the bacteria do not completely use these carbohydrates, the remainder are lost in the feces.

The bran portion of our grain products and the cell walls of all our plant foods show up as caloric content in the tables of food calories although they actually provide nothing in our diet but needed bulk and roughage. It is unlikely that we chew our food well enough to break the cell walls of foods like whole grains and rice. The digestive action may complete this rupture and eventually free all of the easily digested starches, but the process certainly will delay the glucose accumulation in the blood. Such whole-grain products can serve as natural time-release foods which are not expected to trigger the massive insulin release and storage of the glucose as glycogen that might be expected from readily available starches made from milled grains or from foods containing large amounts of sucrose or glucose.

One can and should experiment with his diet. He can learn to recognize rather subtle differences in the way he reacts to different foods. If a food seems to delay the onset of fatigue, tension, and anxiety, this should serve as a signal to prefer such foods to others. Some may find that they actually feel better when they eat average servings of brown rice, in a variety of dishes, than when they eat foods made from rapidly digested grain flour. The chief reason for testing brown rice against milled-starch foods is that the hardened cover of the rice kernels may delay the digestive and absorptive processes. You also get the benefit of the vitamins and minerals that are lost in the polishing process. A few years ago it would have been impossible to purchase brown rice on the commercial market, but now, because of the proliferation of "health food" stores across the country, it is readily available to most of us.

Rolled oats and rolled wheat can certainly provide as much energy and other nutrients as the flaky and puffed-up breakfast cereals made from milled grains. Maybe our mothers were right when they contended that such foods "stuck to the ribs"—in other words, were more slowly digested and stored—better than prepared cereals. The current acceptance of farina and granola may also be due to their "stability" in addition to their palatability.

Breakfast is the best meal to provide additional carbohydrates. If cereal with milk and fruit is provided, insulin will be released to store some of this sugar. In this way the liver will have glycogen which can be mobilized by the glucagon, or if this action is insufficient, the blood glucose can be raised by adrenalin. Don't miss breakfast. It can be the most important meal of the day.

Minimal Diet Eating Plan—Diet No. 1

Servings	List 1 FREE	List 2 MEAT	List 3 FATS	List 4 MILK	List 5 VEGE-TABLES	List 6 FRUIT	List 7 FLOUR
Breakfast	FREE	1	1	—	—	1	1
Lunch	FREE	1	—	½	1	1	1
Dinner	FREE	2	1	½	1	1	—

PLUS the equivalent of 15 teaspoons of fructose.
(15 teaspoons=30 commercial fructose tablets.) Fructose can be eaten as candy, used to sweeten beverages or fruits, or as the sugar in Sweet-Sour Dressing for crisp lettuce or cabbage. Fructose should be eaten between and before meals to insure the prevention of hypoglycemia.

Sustaining Diet Eating Plan—Diet No. 2

Servings	List 1 FREE	List 2 MEAT	List 3 FATS	List 4 MILK	List 5 VEGE-TABLES	List 6 FRUIT	List 7 FLOUR
Breakfast	FREE	2	1	1	—	1	1
Lunch	FREE	3	1	1	1	1	1
Dinner	FREE	3	1	1	2	1	—

PLUS the equivalent of 15 teaspoons of fructose. Fructose should be eaten each hour. It is best that the allowable fruit and flour products be eaten as between-meal snacks to reduce the chance of insulin release.

Venture Diet Eating Plan—Diet No. 3

Servings	List 1 FREE	List 2 MEAT	List 3 FATS	List 4 MILK	List 5 VEGE-TABLES	List 6 FRUIT	List 7 FLOUR
Breakfast	FREE	2	2	½	—	1	1
Lunch	FREE	3	2	½	2	1	1
Dinner	FREE	3	3	1	2	1	1

PLUS the equivalent of 20 teaspoons of fructose each day. Fructose can be eaten at any time, but it is suggested that it not be eaten within one half hour of the beginning of the meal, since it will reduce or eliminate hunger and thus may depress the appetite. Fruit and flour products should be staggered between the meals to decrease the possibility of triggering a hypoglycemic episode by initiating insulin release when the blood glucose concentration rises because of these foods.

NOTE: The severe reduction in flour products and starchy vegetables in the diet program for the Minimal, Sustaining, and Venture Diets, necessary to reduce the insulin release, decreases the content of non-digestible bulk fibers contained in most diets. This reduction in bulk together with the inclusion of slowly absorbed fructose may result in loose stools for two or three days until the bacteria of the lower digestive tract adapt to the available foods. The inclusion of additional servings from the free food list will usually eliminate this problem.

TESTED FRUCTOSE RECIPES

Many of the following recipes call for fructose syrup. It may be made by boiling ¾ cup granular fructose in ½ cup water.

Sweet-Sour Dressing

½ teaspoon plain gelatine   1 teaspoon paprika
1 tablespoon water   ½ teaspoon salt
½ cup lemon juice   ½ teaspoon onion powder
½ cup fructose syrup   ½ teaspoon dry mustard
2 tablespoons salad oil   Pinch of white pepper

Dissolve gelatine in water. Mix remaining ingredients and bring to a boil. Remove from heat and add gelatine. Celery seed, sesame seed, or caraway seed may be added to taste. Refrigerate.

Stay-Crisp Cole Slaw

2 tablespoons water
1½ teaspoons plain gelatine
⅓ cup vinegar
⅓ cup fructose syrup
2 tablespoons salad oil
¼ teaspoon dry mustard

½ teaspoon salt
¼ teaspoon pepper
1 teaspoon celery seed
4 cups shredded cabbage
1 cup shredded carrots

Mix all ingredients except cabbage and carrots. Heat to dissolve gelatine. Do not boil. Cool until slightly thickened. Beat well and pour over cabbage and carrots. Mix lightly until coated. (Minced onion, celery, or green peppers may be added if desired.) Refrigerate.

8 servings

Hot Slaw

2 eggs
¼ cup water
3 tablespoons vinegar
½ teaspoon salt
¼ teaspoon dry mustard

2 tablespoons granular fructose
1 tablespoon butter
½ teaspoon celery seed
2 cups finely shredded cabbage

Beat eggs, add water, vinegar, spices, and fructose. Cook until thick. Add butter and celery seed. Stir in the cabbage. Mix thoroughly. Cover and heat a few minutes.

Sweet-Sour Beets

2 tablespoons vinegar
1 tablespoon water or beet juice
1 tablespoon butter or margarine

2 tablespoons cornstarch
½ teaspoon salt
¼ cup fructose syrup
2 cups diced or sliced cooked beets

Mix all ingredients except beets. Cook slowly until thickened. Add sauce to beets.   *4 to 6 servings*

Swedish Cheesecake

2 eggs
⅓ cup fructose syrup
12 ounces creamed low-fat
  cottage cheese

3 tablespoons water
1 teaspoon vanilla
1 teaspoon flour

Beat eggs well. Beat in remaining ingredients. (If using a blender, fold in the cottage cheese by hand to give a chewy consistency to the cheesecake.) Bake in 8×8-inch pan or medium-sized casserole for 55 minutes at 350° F. or until inserted knife comes out clean.

NOTE: ½ cup granular fructose can be substituted for syrup by increasing water in recipe to ½ cup.

6 servings

Lemon Custard Topping or Dressing

2 eggs
¼ cup fructose syrup

¼ cup lemon juice
1 tablespoon water

Beat eggs; slowly add fructose syrup. Fold in lemon juice and water. Cook over boiling water until thickened. Cool. Use on cole slaw or cheesecake.

NOTE: ⅓ cup granular fructose may be used by increasing water to ⅓ cup.

Cherry Topping

1 16-ounce can sour pie
  cherries

2 teaspoons plain gelatine
½ cup fructose syrup

Drain cherries and dissolve gelatine in juice. Add fruc-

tose syrup and heat to dissolve gelatine. Pour over
cherries. Chill. Use on cheesecake.

Basic Pudding Dessert

1½ teaspoons gelatine
2 tablespoons cold water
¼ cup granular fructose
Dash of salt
½ cup cottage cheese
½ cup water
Choice of flavoring

2 egg yolks
1 tablespoon butter or oil
  (omit for weight-loss diet)
2 egg whites
⅛ teaspoon cream of tartar
¼ cup granular fructose

Dissolve gelatine in 2 tablespoons water. Blend ¼ cup
fructose, salt, cottage cheese, ½ cup water, egg yolks,
and butter in blender until smooth. Bring to a boil and
cook, stirring constantly, 2 minutes. Remove and add
gelatine and flavoring. Cool. Beat egg whites and cream
of tartar; add ¼ cup fructose and continue beating
until stiff. Fold into custard. Pour into dessert dishes
and chill.   *4 servings*

Black Bottom Pudding

Use recipe for Basic Pudding Dessert. Spoon off ½
cup of hot custard. Add 1 square unsweetened chocolate and ½ teaspoon vanilla. Pour into sherbet dishes
and chill. Stir 1 tablespoon rum or ¼ teaspoon rum
flavoring into remaining custard. Cool. Fold in beaten
egg white mixture and spoon over chocolate layer. Chill.
                                              4 servings

Lemon Custard Pudding

Use recipe for Basic Pudding Dessert. Substitute 3
tablespoons lemon juice for 3 tablespoon of water.
                                              4 servings

Chocolate Pudding

Use recipe for Basic Pudding Dessert. Dissolve 1 square unsweetened chocolate in hot mixture. Add ½ teaspoon vanilla. Chill.   *4 servings*

Peanut Butter Candy

½ cup peanut butter   ½ cup fructose syrup
About 1 cup dry skim milk
  powder

Mix peanut butter and fructose syrup together. Add milk powder until mixture holds its shape. Form into a roll or pat into pan. Chill. Cut into 24 pieces.

Basic Candy Recipe

1½ cups granular fructose   Flavoring
½ cup water   1 tablespoon butter

Boil ½ cup fructose and ½ cup water or ⅓ cup fructose syrup to 260° F. Add butter and flavoring (vanilla, peppermint, spearmint, coconut, rum, etc.). One tablespoon cocoa can be boiled with the syrup for chocolate flavor. Let stand about 15 minutes. "Powder" 1 cup granular fructose by putting it in a blender for a short time. Add to warm syrup. Work in more fructose if needed until candy holds its shape. Spread in buttered pan or cookie sheet. Cut into 50 to 60 pieces. Cover. Keep at room temperature.

Rhubarb Dessert

1 egg   1 teaspoon nutmeg
¾ cup granular fructose   2 cups cubed rhubarb
1 tablespoon flour

Beat egg. Beat in fructose, flour, and nutmeg. Fold in
rhubarb. Turn into buttered small casserole. Bake 45
minutes at 350° F.   *6 servings*

Coconut Macaroon Haystacks

3 egg whites
⅛ teaspoon salt
1 cup granular fructose

1 teaspoon vanilla
1¼ cup shredded coconut

Beat egg whites and salt until stiff. Add the sugar
slowly, beating constantly. Fold in vanilla and coconut.
Drop batter by teaspoon onto a greased and floured tin.
Bake at 250° F. for 35 minutes. Makes about 50 hay-
stack cookies. Store in tight container.

Peanut Butter Cookies

2 eggs
1 cup granular fructose

1 cup crunchy peanut butter
1 teaspoon vanilla

Mix all ingredients thoroughly. Drop by teaspoon on
cookie sheet. Bake 15–18 minutes at 250° F. until top
springs back to touch. Makes about 30 cookies. Store
in tight container.

Lemon Sponge

⅔ cup fructose syrup
½ cup cottage cheese
3 eggs, separated
¼ cup flour

¼ cup water
2 tablespoons butter
⅓ cup lemon juice
⅛ teaspoon salt

Mix fructose syrup, cottage cheese, water, and butter
in blender. Heat to lukewarm. Beat egg yolks and blend
in flour, juice, and heated mixture. Beat egg whites
with salt until stiff. Fold into lemon mixture. Turn into

8×8-inch buttered pan. Set in another pan containing 1 inch water. Bake at 350° F. about 1 hour or until set.

NOTE: 2 tablespoons cocoa and ⅓ cup water may be substituted for lemon juice.   *4 servings*

LOW-CARBOHYDRATE
MAIN DISH SPECIALTIES

Cabbage Casserole

1 pound ground beef
1 medium onion, chopped

1 head cabbage, coarsely shredded
1 can cream of tomato soup

Sauté beef and onion (do not brown). Layer half the cabbage in casserole. Cover with beef mixture. Put other half of cabbage on top. Pour undiluted soup over top. Cover and bake 1 hour at 350° F.   *6 servings*

Beef-Cabbage Rolls

8 large cabbage leaves
1 pound ground beef
3 tablespoons chopped onion
1 egg

¾ teaspoon salt
Dash of pepper
Dash of thyme
Butter
½ cup stock or bouillon

Drop cabbage leaves in boiling water for 3 to 4 minutes. Drain. Rinse with cold water and wipe dry. Trim thick center rib. Combine ground beef, egg, onion, salt, pepper, and thyme. Divide into 8 parts. Place one portion on each cabbage leaf. Fold in sides and roll up leaf. Secure with toothpick and place in buttered baking dish, open end down. Dot each roll with ½ teaspoon butter. Pour hot stock or bouillon over and bake about 1 hour at 350° F. until leaves are very tender.

4 servings

Cabbage-Hamburger Casserole

1 small head cabbage
2 teaspoons salt
1 pound ground beef
1 small onion, chopped
¼ teaspoon pepper

1 cup sour cream
¼ cup milk
½ cup grated Cheddar
    cheese

Cook shredded cabbage in 2 cups water seasoned with 1 teaspoon salt for 7 minutes; drain thoroughly. Brown beef and onion; season with remaining salt and pepper. Drain. Place cabbage in casserole; cover with beef mixture. Thin sour cream with milk; pour over casserole. Top with cheese. Bake at 350° F. until cheese melts.   *6 servings*

Stuffed Peppers

4 or 5 green peppers
1 pound ground beef
1 onion, chopped
1 egg

Salt and pepper
2 8-ounce cans tomato
    sauce

Cut stems off peppers and hollow out. Mix beef, onion, egg, salt, and pepper. Stuff peppers with meat mixture. Place upright in pan. Pour tomato sauce over and simmer 1 to 2 hours, or until tender and meat is done.

4 to 5 servings

Eggs Foo Yung

1 onion, chopped
1 stalk celery, chopped
1 cup shrimp
6 eggs

Salt and pepper to taste
2 cups drained bean sprouts
Butter
Soy sauce

Sauté onion, celery, and shrimp in oil until vegetables are translucent. Drain on paper towel. Beat eggs. Add all ingredients and season to taste. Make small omelets. Brown both sides in butter. Serve with soy sauce.

6 servings

Bran Cakes

½ cup 100% Nabisco Bran
2 eggs
½ cup cottage cheese
2 teaspoons fructose syrup

⅛ teaspoon salt
¼ teaspoon baking powder
½ teaspoon oil
2 tablespoons water

Mix bran in blender to make fine crumbs. Add other ingredients and blend until smooth. Fry dollar-sized pancakes in Teflon-coated pan or lightly oiled fry pan. Serve with warm fructose syrup flavored with maple flavoring.

2 servings

Zucchini Casserole

6 medium zucchini
1 pound ground beef
1 onion, minced
1 teaspoon oregano
½ teaspoon garlic powder
⅛ teaspoon pepper
½ teaspoon salt

1 teaspoon rosemary
1 6-ounce can tomato paste
1 8-ounce can tomato sauce
¼ cup red wine
1 4-ounce can grated
Parmesan cheese

Cook zucchini in salted water about 10 minutes, until tender. Cut lengthwise into 3 strips each. Brown beef and onion; add seasonings, tomato paste and sauce, and wine. Simmer 10 minutes. Place half of zucchini in 9×12-inch pan; sprinkle on half of cheese; add meat mixture; cover with another layer of zucchini and remainder of cheese. Bake at 350° F. for 15 minutes. May be served over hot boiled rice.   *4 to 6 servings*

CHAPTER FOUR

An Introduction to the Stress Response

Having seen the fructose diet—or at least its major components—and what its special requirements are, let's return in greater detail to why fructose works, and for whom, and why it should be preferred over other carbohydrates. What follows answers those questions and others, beginning with the point most centrally at issue—stress and how the human body deals with it.

Stress is a simple concept that is difficult to define. The word is used in engineering, psychology, and biology. The engineer uses it to include a force or a condition which distorts, perturbs, or modifies a situation. A biologist or a psychologist uses it somewhat differently because his stress condition is not so easily identified or measured as the stresses encountered by the engineer, but in all cases stress requires a response or counteraction to re-establish the original conditions. In the health sciences stress can be defined as a threat to the continuation of the regulated stable life.

One of the most productive contributors of new ideas about the effect of stress on human lives has been Dr. Hans Selye, a Canadian physiologist-physician. A quarter of a century ago when Dr. Selye recognized the interrelationships between stressful conditions and the onset and progress of many illnesses, he introduced a powerful set of concepts to the scientific community. Many research programs have been conducted to investigate his propositions about the stress induction of disease. No informed challenges to them have developed, and each new research extends rather than limits or rejects his observations, now recognized as some of the greatest contributions to the understanding of symptoms and diseases that have been developed in this century.

Dr. Selye's suggestion was that all of us respond to stressful conditions with an integrated set of physiological changes. He has since been chiefly concerned with the effects of such sets of changes in diseases of the circulatory system.

Late in the last century an astute French physician, Claude Bernard, introduced what he called "homeostasis" to express the relationships of the regulatory functions of the body. In Greek, homeo=similar+stasis=continuation. Homeostasis, therefore, is the tendency of a living animal to maintain an internal stability. It means that an organism modifies its chemistry in a co-ordinated response to any stimulus or distinct change in the environment so as to preserve itself. It is a fundamental principle of modern animal biology.

An understanding of homeostasis is necessary to explain the body's response to any of a variety of stressful situations. The body changes its biochemistry and thus minimizes the effect of any environmental change which would otherwise disturb its usual function or physical condition. In some situations the changes may be very slight. In others they may be drastic.

Health is dependent on homeostasis. It can continue only if the major homeostatic systems remain fully operational. If any of them become inoperable or unrepairable, the person is soon in an alarming physical condition and may die.

The defense mechanisms which counteract the effects of the invasion of disease-producing microorganisms are a common complex of homeostatic systems. They include the production and activity of the white cells of the blood, which are normally able to engulf and destroy the pathogenic (disease-producing) organisms. Some of the other blood cells form antibodies to preserve the tissues by neutralizing the effects of bacteria and viruses in different ways.

The process of knitting of broken bones, the development of scar tissue, the regeneration of damaged liver cells, the replacement of the lining of the digestive tract, the regulation of the menstruation cycle in the human female, the control of body temperature by providing for evaporative cooling by perspiration and by increasing the metabolic rate to raise body heat, the adjusting of the viscosity of the blood, the release of hormones and appropriate enzymes, the excretion of waste products are other examples of homeostatic actions.

It is not necessary, nor is it usually possible, for us consciously to initiate the actions of the homeostatic regulators. The homeostatic systems are innate. They are hereditary biochemical adjusters and instinctive regulators, provided us in the genetic material we received in our biological inheritance from our ancestors. We inherited thereby the ability to maintain ourselves, to survive, to adjust to the rigors of existence.

Dr. Selye was the first to recognize that the response to stress of any type was a general homeostatic set of biochemical changes. He defines the homeostatic stress-response mechanism as the non-specific response of the body to any of several demands upon it. That response is the same for all stresses and begins with the activation of an alarm system. That is, the nervous system recognizes deleterious changes and immediately initiates a group of biochemical activities to stimulate, in turn, a set of protective body reactions. All of these responses are automatic, and all of them develop on each occasion of stress, even though some may not seem entirely appropriate.

If the stress is an invasion of microorganisms, for example, the body is adjusted by an increased circulation of bacteria-fighting white blood cells. It doesn't initially seem that the process of digestion needs to be inhibited also. Yet this occurs.

If the stress is a broken bone, the body accumulates fluids in the surrounding tissues to form a splintlike support provided by the swelling. Yet simultaneously there is an increased circulation to the head.

If the stress is a burn, the steroid hormones which counteract infection and regulate healing are available, but there is also an increase in the concentration of free fatty acids in the blood.

If the stress is a severe cut, the body is soon ready with extra blood coagulants, and yet the heart rate and the general circulation of the blood are increased to the major organs of the body but decreased to the skin.

If the stress requires extreme physical exertion, the muscles are already tensed and provided with extra energy-producing compounds. A general part of the stress response requires an increased metabolic rate. This increase in metabolic demand requires an increase in the fuels provided to the cells. To provide this extra energy the stress response includes a means of increasing the available energy-providing molecules, the fats and sugars. It also includes a system to provide amino acids for repair of damaged tissues.

In the days of our caveman ancestors the stress situation which initiated all of these integrated responses was probably the appearance of a predatory beast. The stress responses were those that allowed him to flee, or fight, and then to repair his wounds.

Now this same stress response is initiated not only by the tissue-damaging stresses listed above but also by a domestic quarrel, a threatening interoffice memorandum, or a traffic incident.

When the threat is over or is effectively counteracted, the original stability returns. Some of the biochemicals which regulated the stress response are deactivated and excreted from the body. Certain of the excess hormones are reabsorbed into storage cells where they can be held until the next stress situation is encountered.

When a stressful situation is prolonged or repetitious, the homeostatic system of the stress response deteriorates. Like a mechanical device that is constantly abused, the defense system gradually wears out. The homeostatic regulators are no longer completely effective. The body is no longer able to repair or adjust to stress.

Medical research is largely concerned with disorders which cause the deaths of great numbers of persons. The number of coronary or other circulatory system disease cases is increasing each year. They are now the most prevalent causes of death of persons under sixty-five years. Much heart disease research has been focused on the stress conditions thought to be the prime contributors to circulatory system disorders. Many investigators believe that heart disease is a predictable end for a stress-filled life. It is generally accepted that stress increases the aging process, additional stress can be a killer. It may, however, show up either as a stroke or as susceptibility to pneumonia or some other infection; the system cannot cope with all of the stresses to which it is exposed.

We inherited our capability to withstand stress. Some of us can adjust to stresses which overwhelm others, but in everyone there is some yet undefined limit of ability to adapt the body to stress. The adjustment system eventually wears out. Once we have used up our reserve of this adjustment resource, we cannot replenish it for all of the appropriate responses. It is now a part of the medical dogma that if a person chooses a high-stress career he runs the risk of expending his stress-adaptation capability. If this happens, he ages rapidly. In the meantime he will probably be afflicted with other stress-related physical or mental problems.

The body systems used to counteract the stresses imposed by environmental changes are used for all other stress conditions. Even though the stress may come from the pressure of a job or emotional conflicts within the home or society, our homeostatic responses are the same as if our lives were threatened. Every time, our stress-response system mobilizes every one of the defense mechanisms which our far distant ancestors developed to keep themselves alive in their confrontations with the wild beasts.

This may seem as if we are using a sledge hammer to swat a mosquito, but the genetic instructions we received were those which co-ordinated the responses to the stress of fear with flight. Although we have changed our external environment since the days of the caveman, we have kept, programmed in our genes, his ability to respond to stress.

All stresses are detected by some portion of the nervous system. Sometimes the stress is a change in the external or physical environment. Such changes are detected by the sense organs. Other stresses are emotional. They originate within the brain. Still others are physiological threats caused by infections or toxins. And one of the primary stresses of the body is an insufficiency of cellular fuel and of raw materials required to continue normal metabolic activities. Fortunately, the general stress response includes an increase in the concentration of fat and sugar in the blood supplied to all of the cells of the body.

Since a deficiency of blood sugar initiates the stress response in all its complexity, we know it to be a stress. It is a threat to the continuation of the normal activities of the body. It is, however, a hidden stress. It is internal. We are usually unaware that it exists or that this stress is added to all other stresses which we recognize in the environment.

The body responds to changes in the external and internal environment by biochemical adjustments that are primarily regulated by the autonomic nervous system. This portion of the nervous system is divided into two parts. One portion is called the sympathetic nervous system and the other the parasympathetic system. One system causes an increase in the heart rate while the other's action is to slow it down. One type of nerve causes the dilation of a blood vessel while the other constricts it. While one system is able to raise the blood pressure the other causes its lowering. Nevertheless, it is inaccurate to regard the two portions of the autonomic nervous system as acting out a "tug of war." A teetertotter serves as a better analogy. When one sys-

tem is in control the other is quite inactive. In some
situations the parasympathetic system may be in control in one portion of the body while the sympathetic
system is in control in another.

The parasympathetic nerves are primarily connected
to the brain through the vagus nerve. Parasympathetic
nerve cells secrete a chemical compound called acetylcholine which is used to trigger reactions by other cells.
Acetylcholine can be called a transmitter which stimulates other cells into action. In turn, acetylcholine is
chemically deactivated by an enzyme called acetylcholine esterase which is secreted by other cells associated
with the nervous system. When acetylcholine is released
from parasympathetic nerve cells into the spaces around
the nerve endings, the enzyme is able to convert acetylcholine into biologically inactive molecules. This prevents the acetylcholine from causing a continuing
stimulus which otherwise might improperly affect unrelated nerve endings.

The sympathetic nervous system cells secrete two
different chemicals to regulate the tissues of the body.
These two hormones, noradrenalin and adrenalin (some
call these two hormones norepinephrine and epine-
phrine), are biochemically very similar although they
do have slightly different actions and sites of control.
Sympathetic system cells can convert noradrenalin into
adrenalin. All adrenalin is made from noradrenalin in
specific cells. Noradrenalin is primarily secreted by
cells which are directly connected to the brain by a
series of interconnected nerves and ganglia. Adrenalin
is primarily found in the medulla (central) portion of
the adrenal gland. The body uses a sequence of actions
of other hormones to cause the release of adrenalin
from these adrenal gland cells.

Whenever a stress occurs, information about it is
transmitted to the hypothalamus portion of the brain.
The hypothalamus is a mass of brain tissue at the lower,
central portion of the brain just above the pituitary
gland above the roof of the mouth. Like a switchboard,
the hypothalamus co-ordinates the strees responses to

changes in the body. Whether the information about the stress is detected by the sensory nerves from the external environment or from chemical changes in the blood, that information is co-ordinated by the hypothalamus to initiate the stress response.

From the hypothalamus some nerve signals travel rapidly to the noradrenalin-secreting cells of the sympathetic nervous system. In this way the response to a stress condition is initiated almost immediately when a stress is detected. You know how fast you shiver when you step out of a warm shower into a cool bathroom. That chill was detected by nerves in the skin. The information was then transmitted to the hypothalamus, which triggered the sympathetic cells to cause contraction of certain small muscle cells just below the skin even before you can reach for the towel.

If the stress is continued, the hypothalamus then activates the pituitary gland to provide for a continuation of the sympathetic nervous system response as well as to provide for the release of other hormones of the general stress response.

The regulation of the pituitary by the hypothalamus results from certain secretions within the latter's cells. These hypothalamic cell products are carried by a series of small blood vessels directly to the pituitary gland, which lies just below the hypothalamus, and cause the pituitary to secrete the necessary trophic hormones to control other glands. One such hormone is ACTH, a shorthand way of saying adrenocorticotrophic hormone. It is carried by the blood from the pituitary to all parts of the body.

ACTH does not affect most of the cells of the body. It acts principally on its target organ, the adrenal cortex tissues. The adrenal cortex is the outer layer of the adrenal glands, walnut-sized organs, one on top of each kidney. The adrenal cortex cells respond to the presence of ACTH by releasing certain steroid hormones, particularly hydroxycortisone (cortisol).

Although these steroid molecules are larger than most other molecules in the body, they cannot be identi-

fied just by looking at them. The body makes a variety
of steroid hormones. They all have a unique chemical
structure made of several rings of carbons, which identify their relationship to cholesterol, from which they are
synthesized.

Steroid hormones are not rapidly destroyed by enzymes. Instead they are eventually passed through the
tubules of the kidney and are excreted in the urine.
Sometimes it seems unfortunate that we cannot rid ourselves of excess cholesterol in the same way, but only
the biologically active hormones pass into the urine.

Steroid hormones regulate many actions of the body.
Their passage in the blood from the adrenal cortex
through the adrenal medulla causes these cells to release their stored adrenalin and to secrete more adrenalin. When the steroids then pass to the liver, they cause
the release (mobilization) of fragments of fat molecules,
fatty acids, and triglycerides, to provide the energy
necessary for many stress responses. They also free
some amino acids from proteins. Although these amino
acids can be oxidized to obtain energy, their primary
job is to allow the formation of new proteins which
might be necessary for the stress response.

When adrenalin from the adrenal medulla gets into
the blood stream, it is carried throughout the body, even
to those tissues which are not supplied with individual
sympathetic nerve system cells. Both noradrenalin and
adrenalin are involved in the behavioral changes associated with the general stress response.

The responses of the body to the sympathetic system hormones, noradrenalin and adrenalin, are purpose-
ful and comprehensive. If some engineer wished to design a system to protect the body from harm, he
couldn't devise a better complex than the one we received from our ancestors. This system provides for
an immediate and continuing response until the threat
has passed. The system is then deactivated until another stress requires the set of appropriate responses.
Unused sympathetic hormones are reabsorbed into
storage cells. The hormone molecules which caused re-

actions are biologically deactivated by enzymes and excreted in the urine. Since the blood vessels of the brain are impermeable to these hormones no adrenalin can escape into the brain cells, but the noradrenalin formed in the nerve cells of the brain can be closely regulated.

Most of the responses of the tissues to sympathetic system hormones begin immediately. It may be helpful to list the responses and explain why the tissues act as they do.

The blood vessels of the skin are contracted. This action has two primary results. It forces more blood to pass through the liver, kidney, major muscles, heart, and to the head. It also reduces the loss of body heat.

The increased flow of blood through the major vessels allows for an increased rate of return of blood to the heart. As more blood returns to the heart, this pump of the circulatory system is stretched. At the next contraction more blood is forced out and the blood pressure rises. This forces more blood through the vessels of the major organs.

When the muscular walls of the heart and the associated vessels which return the blood to the heart are stretched, they stimulate the pacemaker of the heart, causing an increase in the rate of heart contractions. When the heart rate is increased, there is less time to fill the heart. The blood pressure does not continue to rise. This reflex response of the heart prevents an ever increasing blood pressure, which could otherwise burst the walls of the arteries.

The adrenalin in the blood going through the liver initiates a series of chemical changes which cause the conversion of stored glycogen (animal starch) into glucose. This conversion of stored fuel into circulating glucose is particularly important, since the cells of the nervous system require sugar from the blood for some of their syntheses. Nerve cells apparently do not use fats. They do not have the necessary enzymes to convert fats into usable energy molecules. They normally rely on sugar but can use as energy sources some amino acids, which are derived from proteins.

It is the ineffectiveness of glycogen conversion that is believed to be the primary initiator of the anxieties and tensions considered in this book. If the glycogen supply has been depleted because no insulin has caused previous storage of glucose as glycogen, or if for any reason the adrenalin release does not initiate the increase in blood glucose concentration, the secretion of additional adrenalin will be continued.

The understanding of the mechanism of adrenalin action on the reconversion of glycogen to glucose was the basis for the Nobel Prize awarded to the late Dr. Earl Sutherland. His insights into the mode of adrenalin action, particularly in this aspect of controlling the blood glucose level, are integral to the ideas on which this book is based. (A complete explanation of this adrenalin activity is included in the Appendices; its logic is somewhat complex and may not be of interest to all readers.)

Adrenalin acts on the digestive tract to stop its normal churning activity. Digestive action is an energy-requiring process. By temporarily stopping it, the blood sugar can be saved for the immediately essential acts of other tissues.

The motility of the foods through the digestive tract and the entire digestive activity will be resumed automatically as soon as the stress has passed and the adrenalin disappears from the blood stream. The cessation of digestive activity and its resumption as required following the stress response are good examples of interaction to restore homeostasis. The inhibition of the peristaltic activity of the digestive tract provides an opportunity for digestive enzymes to cause ulcers by digesting away the covering of the cells lining the digestive tract. This is a detrimental action. On the other hand, it prevents what could be called social disasters. Adrenalin relaxes the anal sphincter. (This is the drawstring-like muscle which closes the lower end of the digestive tract.) If the peristalsis of the digestive tract continued while the muscles which inhibits spontaneous defecation was relaxed, the result would be an unregulated and unintentional passage of fecal material.

Adrenalin dilates the bronchi. These tubes are the air passages which lead to the thin-walled cavities of the lungs, where oxygen from the air is exchanged for the carbon dioxide in the blood. The dilation of the bronchi insures that the rate of exchange between the air and the blood cells is maximal. This provides the oxygen necessary to maintain the increased metabolic rate demanded by the stress response.

Adrenalin dilates the pupils of the eyes. This increases the amount of light that can pass to the retina. For most stress conditions this activity is superfluous, but it did allow our caveman ancestors to see better under adverse light conditions. And even if we don't need this adrenalin-controlled action, we have no means of stopping it.

Adrenalin causes contraction of the spleen, a sponge-like organ containing many blood cells which are then added to those already in the circulating blood. This contributes to the blood pressure, provides more hemoglobin for the transport of oxygen, and increases the number of other cells for the many other actions of the blood. Some of the cells in the spleen are those white blood cells which are able to engulf and to neutralize pathogenic invaders. This action is particularly beneficial if the stress condition was the invasion of some infective agents, yet this same response occurs even if the stress is emotional in origin.

Adrenalin increases the secretion of chemicals which control coagulation of the blood. If the stress was a severe wound, these materials and the constriction of the blood vessels in the area of the damage can often prevent the excessive loss of blood. There even is a protective system in the blood cells to prevent coagulation of the blood in the capillaries and veins, which could otherwise allow a clot to form and to be carried back to the heart. It is the failure of this system of the stress response which leads to phlebitis and the retention of fluids in the extremities.

Adrenalin relaxes the urinary sphincter (the muscle which serves to regulate the retention of urine) and causes the contraction of the urinary bladder. For adults this is not a major concern except in times of severe fright, but it is certainly an inconvenience and embarrassment to children who wet their beds. Other children at summer camp and similar outings are awakened in the night by the necessity to urinate because they do not keep warm enough in their sleeping bags. Chill is a stress. Adrenalin is released to retain body heat and to replace the blood sugar which was expended in the attempt to keep the body warm but even if it is released for one reason and adjusts that stress it causes other changes too.

Adrenalin increases the tonus (tautness) of voluntary muscles. The tremor of one's hands after a harrowing experience such as a near automobile accident or the morning after a drunk is due to the high concentration of adrenalin in the blood. The same effect on a less drastic scale can be noticed if meals are delayed and the adrenalin release system is activated to raise the blood sugar level. Many people use the term "tension" to indicate this slight muscle spasm. (The word "anxiety" is a term that actually should be applied to the intellectualization of tension. Anxiety, therefore, is not a stress but the recognition that a stress response has occurred.)

The release of adrenalin to accomplish all of these homeostatic adjustments depends on the secretion of the steroid hormones produced in the adrenal cortex. The adrenal cortex makes several different steroid hormones, each of which has distinct effects as well as certain general effects. All steroid hormones are synthesized in the body from cholesterol. Cholesterol is not water-soluble. It is not excreted in the urine, yet each of the biologically active hormones made from cholesterol is water-soluble. They can and do leak across the kidney membranes. Those which pass into the urine are not reabsorbed. They are excreted. To maintain the necessary amounts of the steroid hormones, they must constantly be synthesized so that they can be used for the homeostatic regulation systems.

The steroid hormones which trigger the adrenalin release from the adrenal medulla also have several other actions. The presence of any biologically active steroid hormone causes the fat-storage cells (adipose tissues) to release some of their stored fuels into the body fluids. The fat molecules are broken into smaller segments, the fatty acids and glycerol. (Actually the glycerol is present with three fatty acids to form molecules which are called triglycerides.) The body can use these fragments of fat molecules for energy for most cells of the body. Fat is not made into sugar. The smaller pieces are oxidized (burned) properly only when the rate of mobilization from the storage cells equals their enzymatic use as fuels for cellular activities. If the fat-mobilization system were not available to provide the fuel for most cellular activities, the glycogen supply would be used up within half a day. The cells would then begin to break down cellular proteins to get amino acids which could be converted to sugars or oxidized directly for energy. The availability of dietary sugars or glycogen which can be converted to sugar prevents the stress response from over-mobilizing fats and proteins. When sugars are present, they are used for energy and for supplying needed substrate materials. This spares the proteins from being used as energy-providing fuels. Normally this is an excellent homeostatic system. It is usually adjusted to get the greatest good for the longest time.

Some of the steroid hormones which are released from the adrenal cortex by the ACTH stimulus (or by other pituitary hormones) cause the cells of the kidney to reabsorb water, an easily explained activity. One of the primary effects of the steroid-released adrenalin is to increase the blood pressure. When the blood pressure is increased, more fluids spill over from the blood into the kidney tubules. If these fluids are not reabsorbed but are allowed to pass into the urine, the blood pressure will fall because of a decrease in blood volume. To prevent this loss of water from the blood the steroids from the adrenal cortex cause the kidney cells to reabsorb sodium salts, promoting the retention of water so that the blood pressure is maintained. The adrenal cortex hormone which brings about this specific action is called ADH (anti-diuretic hormone). The reabsorption of the sodium salts does, however, allow the loss of potassium salts into the urine, a loss which has some detrimental effects on the body; nevertheless the immediate problem of maintaining a high blood pressure is satisfied.

Changes in the physical and emotional environment can reduce the stress situation which initiates the response. This cannot be accomplished with drugs. Various medications have been prescribed to depress the stress response, as if these drugs were regulating the stress itself. Some tranquilizers and depressants work directly on the nervous system so that it does not recognize the stress or is unable to react to the stress.

The magnitude of the stress response is usually related to the magnitude and duration of the stress condition. The responses are homeostatic regulations, which normally adjust the chemistry of the body to react adequately to the stress condition. Modern man may have learned to repress his external response to stress in one way or another. He might not have to flee or fight to preserve himself. But the stress is still there. Now it's bottled up. Stresses and the responses to stress still affect the way we feel and the way we live. They are mostly hidden. They do their damage in secret.

Most people are quite unaware of the stresses in their lives. They are continuously responding to stresses of one variety or another but they do not recognize the signals. If we are aware of the physical manifestations of the stress response, we can more fully appreciate the magnitude and the repetitious nature of the stresses we encounter.

When some change in the environment, either from the outside or from within ourselves, requires some counteraction or physiological accommodation, we know this to be a response to a stress. One of the most obvious but least appreciated stress-response signs is the clenching of the teeth. This may come not only in anger but also when one is doing something physically difficult. Some people awaken during the night and recognize that they have their jaws firmly clamped. Perhaps they were cold or their blood sugar level was low, but this clamping of the jaws is a sign of high adrenalin activity, one expression of an increase in muscle tonus and tension; others are "pill rolling" of the fingers and clenching of the fists. The adrenalin so decreases the blood flow to the skin that the palms of the hands get cold and clammy. The mouth is dry when adrenalin is present. To some people this serves as a trigger to chew gum, have a drink, or get something to eat. When adrenalin raises the blood pressure, the arteries in the neck and at the temples pulsate and the heart pounds against the ribs.

If the stress is neither eliminated nor accommodated, the adrenalin-regulated reactions give way to fatigue, irritability, insomnia, and defiance. But these are just some of the stress-response-induced behavioral changes.

CHAPTER FIVE

At the Threshold
of Biochemical Regulation

Throughout all time mankind has been burdened with a scourge of illnesses and disabilities. Many of the oldest historical records contain descriptions of diseases whose symptoms are so distinct that it is possible to diagnose a disease or identify the cause of death of some person who died centuries ago. Included in such diagnostic records are accounts of epilepsy, tuberculosis, gallstones, migraine headaches, malaria, polio, smallpox, dysentery, cholera, gangrene, diabetes, typhoid, nutritional deficiency diseases, allergies, schizophrenia, alcoholism, arthritis, gout, obesity, and many other maladies.

Many of these disorders caused the deaths of the affected persons. Medical science has since identified their causes and has devised effective treatments and preventive measures to control them.

Some of the other sicknesses are not primary causes of death. Maladies such as schizophrenia, migraine, alcoholism, and obesity are important because they make the victim a less effective member of society. Medical science has only learned to treat their symptoms. Their causes, or etiologies, remain obscure.

But we do now know that stress is their common denominator. And if the stress can be identified and eliminated, the conditions can be alleviated or prevented. Instead of using drugs to interfere with the response of the body to stress, the stress can be eliminated

58

by satisfying the demands of the body, particularly the requirements of the nervous system.

This book suggests that many of these stress-initiated disorders are related to problems which originate in the regulation of the blood sugar level. Normally we expect the body to adjust the blood sugar concentration by releasing insulin from the pancreas when the sugar concentration is high and by releasing glucagon, another pancreatic secretion, when the blood sugar level is low. If the glucagon action is insufficient to adjust the required blood sugar level, the body recognizes this stress and releases adrenalin. A deficiency in insulin secretion or action results in diabetes. We know that these systems do not always work as well in some persons as they do in others.

When the blood sugar level is below that required by the body, the condition is known as hypoglycemia. Hypoglycemia (hypo=low, gylc=sugar, emia=blood) is not a distinct disease. It is a condition found among both diabetics and non-diabetics. It is a descriptive term. Hypoglycemia is a condition of an insufficiency of sugar in the blood supplied to the cells of the nervous system. Virtually every normal person experiences short daily episodes of hypoglycemia. The body then readjusts the blood sugar level by converting stored glycogen into sugar by the action of the glucagon and adrenalin. Sugar is an energy-providing fuel. It is also a material from which the brain makes essential molecules. In some persons this system to convert glycogen to sugar is deficient. Such a person is called a hypoglycemic. Actually we would like to know how much sugar is available inside the cells which require it, but we have no way to determine this. We must be content with information about the availability of the sugar in the fluids which serve the cells.

Many different physical conditions are known to cause hypoglycemia. In turn, hypoglycemia and the effects of the hormones necessary to correct it lead to a variety of symptoms. Not everyone responds in the same way. In some people the symptoms are of a physical disorder, particularly fatigue. In others the symptoms encompass a large variety of behavioral changes or even psychiatric conditions such as severe depression, manic state, and schizophrenia. In some the symptoms are the direct results of the insufficiency of sugar supply for the nervous system. In others the symptoms develop from the multiple actions of the hormones released to raise the blood sugar.

In all cases, the prevention of hypoglycemia leads to a reduction, or even complete remission, of symptoms. A simple laboratory test can be done to determine the amount of sugar in the blood at the time the sample was taken.

Unfortunately there is no test that is able to identify the specific reason for most low blood sugar conditions. None of the present tests is designed to identify the hormonal concentrations or the symptoms which develop from the body's responses to a hypoglycemic condition which has existed for a prolonged time. The disorders which seem to be directly associated with hypoglycemia, which develop simultaneously with or as a consequence of hypoglycemia, have long been an enigma. The diversity and irregularity of the symptoms in different people obscure the search for the physiological mechanisms involved.

It is very important to remember that symptoms are not the disease. Such a caution is particularly pertinent when one is considering problems related to a low blood sugar and the attempt of the body effectively to adjust this deficiency. Symptoms are signs that something is wrong.

Symptoms do not indicate what is amiss. They do not indicate which organs or systems are not functioning properly. Drugs and treatments used to reduce the severity of the symptoms do not deal with the cause of the original problem.

An analogy may be helpful to illustrate this difference between symptom and disorder. Certain types of heart disorders are accompanied by severe pain in the upper left arm. "Referred pain" is the name given to such a symptom of a heart problem. The symptom, the pain in the arm, could be relieved by narcotics. Such medications for this condition would be very dangerous for a person whose blood vessels of the heart wall are not supplying the cells with adequate oxygen and cellular fuel. A common medication for such a heart condition is nitroglycerine. The drug acts not on the nerves of the arm but on the cells of the coronary blood vessels. The pain is eliminated by treating the cause of the pain, not by anesthetizing the nervous system.

Behavioral symptoms associated with severe and continued hypoglycemia can also be repressed by the administration of drugs which depress the nervous system. Such drugs do not correct the deficiency of sugar in the blood. They actually mask the true physiological problem of the hypoglycemia which prevents the cells of the nervous system from obtaining their sugar requirements. They reduce the symptoms as if the fundamental defect were in the brain. Drugs of this variety prevent the normal homeostatic responses. In some cases they can actually increase the problem by suppressing the body's own readjustments of the blood sugar concentration.

A prolonged and persistent hypoglycemia is a very dangerous condition. It is especially detrimental to the regulation of the nervous system. The brain in particular requires glutamic acid, which is primarily made from sugar. Although the body is able to store excess sugar as fat, it is unable to reconvert fat to sugar. Sugars can be made available to the body only from carbohydrates in the diet, by conversion of stored glycogen to glucose, or by the metabolic conversion of some amino acids obtained from proteins.

There is good reason to believe that various human disorders are precipitated or influenced either by a low blood sugar situation or by other physiological conditions which require the same stress responses. The primary thesis of this book is that everyone's physiological ability to regulate the hormones involved in adjusting or correcting low blood sugar is predetermined. That is, each of us has a genetic, and therefore biochemical, limit for responding appropriately to hypoglycemia.

Most people accommodate hypoglycemic episodes without any disruption in their lives. Their genetic mechanisms are adequate to readjust appropriately the deficiency of sugar in the blood supplied to the cells. Such people are usually unaware of the biochemical changes which have occurred within themselves. They are physiologically adjusted. Their behavior is stable. Their blood sugar concentration varies only a small amount above and below the optimal amount. They are the "normal" members of the population. They experience neither the physiological high which accompanies high adrenalin levels nor the depression which develops from a prolonged deficiency of blood sugar or may come as a consequence of extreme mood elevation.

Unfortunately, there are many persons who are unable to so adjust. The symptoms they can develop because of a continued and drastic hypoglycemia are many and varied. Such symptoms include behavioral characteristics which initially seem unrelated to the condition of a deficiency of sugar in the blood.

It seems that, if the body systems are unable to correct the blood sugar deficiency, the brain responds by changing the behavior and personality as a part of the readjustment. The behavioral changes are not the direct result of a cellular energy deficiency, or of an insufficiency of substances for synthesis, or of the presence of abnormal biochemicals. They are instead direct attempts of the body to adjust to the deficiency of the sugar and to the hormones which are released because of the stress of hypoglycemia. Such adjustments are usually inadequate and often detrimental in other ways.

An example of such behavioral changes can illustrate this situation. Problems of low blood sugar are frequently found in conjunction with alcoholism and also among people with cirrhosis of the liver. Such liver damage may be an effect of excessive drinking. It is quite possible that a damaged liver is unable to store glucose as glycogen even if insulin is provided. Without a reserve of glycogen which can be rapidly converted to glucose by the glucagon and adrenalin, one would certainly be hypoglycemic. On the other hand, many research programs have identified low blood sugar conditions in alcoholics with no evidence of liver damage. Hypoglycemia might certainly be expected among persons who have virtually restricted their diet to alcoholic beverages: alcohol is intracellularly converted to acetate and then to fat for storage, and it cannot be converted to sugar. Yet a large proportion of Alcoholics Anonymous members who have been on the wagon for years are also hypoglycemic. That is, the concentration of sugar in their blood is insufficient to prevent the onset of the stress response. That concentration is neither some arbitrary amount nor necessarily the average blood sugar concentration of a large population.

Similarly, many severely overweight people suffer from the effects of low blood sugar although their diet is high in the carbohydrates which are converted into glucose and then to glycogen. Excessive eating and excessive drinking are frequently associated with lower than optimal blood sugar levels. In many of these people the measured deficiency of blood sugar is not so severe that the diagnosis of hypoglycemia is obvious and distinct. Yet it is low enough to trigger the stress response.

It is not just academic to question whether the hypoglycemia was present before the alcoholism or overweight condition developed. Perhaps a deficiency in the regulation of the blood sugar level is involved in their development. They could result from attempted compensation for hypoglycemia and for the presence of higher than normal concentrations of the hormones released to reduce this stress. (Such a proposition is considered in detail in the following chapters.) A convincing argument can be made that such behavior developed as learned responses to symptoms accompanying the stress response which is initiated by a low blood sugar concentration. Even though one may recognize that either excessive drinking or excessive eating can be dangerous to one's health, the excesses may have had their genesis in problems with the maintenance of the blood sugar concentration. Instead of correcting or relieving the actual problems, such behavior becomes a complicating factor: excessive drinking and excessive eating can actually reinforce the initial hypoglycemia.

Frequently it has been found that persons who suffer from migraine headaches are hypoglycemic. Apparently these unfortunate people cannot try to make do with changing their behavior; none seems to have discovered any behavioral pattern which will even temporarily relieve the headache. On the other hand many hyperactive children show low blood sugar levels despite their manic behavior. Their near-constant activity may be related to the continuously released adrenalin which is part of the stress response to hypoglycemia. The activity of these children demands a high energy input to satisfy their metabolic requirements. Trying to specify whether the metabolic demand lowered the blood sugar level or whether the adrenalin was released to increase the blood sugar concentration is like arguing which came first, the hen or the egg. Actually these two characteristics cannot be separated. In hyperactive children it has been found that depressive drugs have not been effective in eliminating their behavior problems. Until now the most effective treatment has been the use of a stimulant, amphetamine, which raises the blood sugar concentration as one of its actions of mimicking adrenalin.

Both participants in and spectators of winter sports are exposed to severe stress-response requirements because of chill. The athletic activity involved can require rapid conversion of glycogen to glucose to supply energy, but at the same time the control of body temperature may necessitate an increase in metabolic rate, regulated by the thyroid gland. This additional demand for cellular fuel may surpass the conversion of glycogen to glucose potential. The emotional component of the activity can also raise the concentration of adrenalin in the blood stream. If these adrenalin-release situations happen to coincide with dietary intake of carbohydrates, which trigger the release of insulin from the pancreas, neither the adrenalin nor the insulin will be able to accomplish its normal regulatory function of blood sugar control. Hypoglycemia would be expected to develop as a consequence. If for some reason a person was unable to maintain a high adrenalin release under such situations of high sugar demand, hypoglycemic fatigue would soon be evident.

The various stress responses are also involved in suppressing the secretion of growth hormone from the pituitary and in disrupting the cyclic regulation of the gonadal hormones which regulate the menstrual cycles in the human female. In experimental animals the injection of ACTH into the ventricles of the brain or into the spinal fluid elicits yawning and a characteristic stretching but also increases sex drive. Increases in the ACTH or the adrenal steroid hormones inhibits the action of some enzymes and promotes the synthesis of other quite unrelated enzymes. Some of these enzymes affect the conversion of known nervous system transmitters. One of these enzyme systems changes the concentration of a compound called serotonin in the brain while another increases the conversion of noradrenalin into adrenalin. The exact function of serotonin is not known but it is assumed that it is a biochemical controller of nerve cell activity. The implications of all of these changes as components of the response to stressful conditions are not known or understood. Yet they can be expected to modify behavior in any of several ways.

Persistent hypoglycemia is also found in persons who are not obese, not alcoholic, not subject to migraine headaches, not unable to concentrate. In them the symptoms of hypoglycemia and the effect of the hormones which normally correct the situation are also varied. In some the major symptom is that of near-constant fatigue. Others are emotionally depressed. Still others are hyperactive or hypomanic, often with periods of manic behavior as well as others with the more characteristic schizophrenic symptoms of hallucinations, delusions, catatonia, and depersonalization. Unfortunately such symptoms and the disorders they represent are not uncommon.

It is not the intent here to ascribe all psychoses or other abnormal or socially unacceptable behavior solely to the condition of hypoglycemia. It is irrational, however, not to recognize the contribution of recurrent hypoglycemia in these diseases.

Hypoglycemia is a severe stress to the body. In some people it may be the initiating stress of an abnormal physiological and psychological state. In others it may be a reinforcing stress which, when added to the other biochemical and environmental stresses, exceeds the biochemical regulation of some stress-response mechanisms.

Pathological behavior is a symptom that something is wrong. Behavioral problems are symptomatic of underlying problems. Because such symptoms develop in some persons without any demonstrable physical defect, they have presented severe problems to investigators. Even the names for these behavioral disorders change from time to time and from place to place, an indication of the lack of precision inherent in most research on them.

Everyone has ample evidence from his own experience to recognize that behavior is influenced by the physiological responses to stress. Temper tantrums in children, extreme nervousness at times of severe emotional pressures in adults, phenomenal physical acts of endurance and strength sometimes evident at times of catastrophe are known to everyone. These are all stress-related. Hypoglycemia is a stress. It is normally corrected by the physiological changes initiated by the hormones of the stress response. Hypoglycemia is added to all other stresses. It is quite possible that it is the initial stress which so loads the system that other stresses become the "straw which breaks the camel's back."

Hypoglycemia is an unnecessary stress. Maintaining one's optimal blood sugar level can be effectively managed by most intelligent persons who understand the problem and follow the suggested diet. And the elimination of the hypoglycemia stress and the responses to this stress can be expected to eliminate the onset of many stress-initiated disorders, including the behavioral problems that have been diagnosed as psychotic disorders. Hypoglycemia lowers the threshold of behavioral regulation. Its elimination provides an opportunity to accommodate other stresses without disruption of one's life.

The Metabolism of Foods

Living requires energy and a constant input of certain kinds of molecules which we ourselves cannot make and must obtain in our diet. Every cellular action— synthesis of compounds, contraction of muscle cells, transmission of information by nerves, conversion of complex compounds into simpler usable molecules, etc. —either requires the immediate expenditure of energy or required it previously to make the structures and enzymes that carry out cellular actions.

The energy for all the life processes comes from the chemical bonds present in food. Some foods that contain primarily starches and sugars provide large numbers of such bonds per unit of weight. That's all many such foods provide—energy. The foods that contain fats are also good sources of energy. In fact, the amount of energy in an ounce of fat is twice that of a carbohydrate. In addition to its use as an energy source, dietary fats are necessary to enable us to absorb some fat-soluble vitamins from the digestive tract. Various vitamin deficiency problems develop if no dietary fat is provided, since the necessary vitamins are lost in the feces.

Proteins, on the other hand, provide only a few chemical bonds which can be used for energy by the cells. Proteins have nitrogen-containing complexes which do not provide energy. In fact, before a protein can be used as a source of energy, the molecule must first be fractured into many smaller pieces, the amino acids. Then the nitrogen complexes of these amino acids must be removed and excreted. This is cellular work. It requires energy. It may take as much energy to make use of the energy-containing bonds of a protein as is recovered from the protein itself.

Proteins are necessary in our diet because they are made up of amino acids which contain nitrogen atoms. Amino acids are the building blocks for the formation of new tissues and non-tissue proteins. Enzymes, cellular structures such as membranes, ribosomes, and mitochondria, and such chemical compounds as hemoglobin and molecules that are necessary for initiating the coagulation of blood are primarily synthesized from dietary protein materials. Such structures of the cells and the biochemicals wear out. They must constantly be repaired or replaced. Repair and synthesis require amino acids and energy. Many cells in our body have the ability to make many of our necessary amino acids if these cells are provided with the necessary materials. No cell, however, can make amino acids from carbohydrates and fats alone. The nitrogen must be provided from other sources. We cannot even make all of the necessary varieties of amino acids ourselves. They must be provided in the diet as parts of the proteins we eat.

In addition to energy and amino acids, cells require vitamins which we cannot synthesize. They also require a variety of minerals. The vitamins are necessary as parts of many essential molecules involved in using energy in the cells. The minerals are necessary for making bones, for the enamel and dentine of teeth, for transporting oxygen, for making enzymes, and for many other applications.

Some foods provide energy, amino acids, vitamins, and the required minerals. Other foods contain only one dietary requirement. Sugar is one of them It is concentrated energy. There are no vitamins, amino acids, or minerals in sugar.

Sugar contains no non-digestible bulk; it is just a good-tasting source of energy, a carbohydrate made of carbon, hydrogen, and oxygen. One can live without carbohydrates in his diet. Many generations of Eskimos survived without any carbohydrate at all. They obtained their energy from fat and protein in blubber. But for most people carbohydrates are the primary components of the diet. One would starve to death if the diet contained only carbohydrates, but when they are combined with proteins, some dietary fats, and all the necessary minerals and vitamins, the diet is complete.

All plant products are primarily carbohydrate. Some of it takes the form of sugar and starches that are almost immediately used as energy sources. Some sugars can pass directly into cells, whereas others, and the starches, require only slight modifications before they can pass from the digestive tract into the blood as sources of energy for the cells of the body. Some carbohydrates from plants are undigestible and cannot be used to provide energy. Cellulose (the woody fibers and cell walls of all our plant foods from grains, rice, vegetables, and fruits) cannot be converted into water-soluble molecules which can pass into the blood. The dextrins, a group of similar carbohydrates of which the pectin of our fruit jellies is best known, are also undigestible. We cannot derive energy from celluloses or dextrins. They are, however, valuable components in our diet, since they provide bulk that is advantageous for some of the actions of the lower digestive tract, even though we do not use the bond energy trapped in the molecules. The only organisms that can use woody carbohydrates are the termites: they alone harbor some bacteria in their digestive tracts that have the necessary enzymes to free the bonds of these complex carbohydrates.

All of the energy-providing carbohydrates of the diet, regardless of their source, are converted into sugars while these fuels are still in the digestive tract and before they are absorbed and transferred into the circulatory system. This has been known for a long time. Most carbohydrates in our diet come from starch. In plant cells starch is the storage form of those carbohydrates that the plant can use. The other carbohydrates are incorporated into the plant's structural parts as the woody fibers of cellulose.

Most of the digestible carbohydrates are converted into the simple sugar glucose by digestive enzymes. Some of the carbohydrates are made up of other simple sugars. The simple sugars are called monosaccharides, the simplest form of sugars that exist. Although glucose, which is another name for dextrose or grape sugar, is the most common of the simple sugars, fructose, also called levulose or fruit sugar, and galactose, a monosaccharide component of milk, are also normal parts of our diet. All three of these monosaccharides contain the same amount of energy. They are just different arrangements of exactly the same components. These different arrangements of the atoms of these sugars account for the biochemical characteristics which distinguish each of them.

Some of our sweet-tasting foods contain free monosaccharides—water-soluble sugars that require no digestion or conversion before absorption. Usually the simple monosaccharide sugars are combined to form larger molecules. When two monosaccharides are joined together by the action of cellular enzymes in plants, they form disaccharides (two-sugar molecules). One molecule of glucose joined to one molecule of fructose forms our familiar table sugar, which we call sucrose. Two molecules of glucose joined together form maltose, or malt sugar. One molecule of glucose and one of galactose combine to form lactose, the disaccharide of milk.

When many glucose molecules are joined together, they are called polysaccharides ("many sugars"). The most common of these multiglucose molecules in our diet is starch. When we eat starch, the enzymes of the digestive system break up the large molecules into individual glucose molecules. Starches are convenient storage forms of glucose for plants. Sugar molecules are water-soluble. Native starch molecules are not. The plant has enzymes which can convert the starch to sugar and then back to starch, but the normal flow of water in and out of the plant cells does not affect the starch. Sugars absorb and hold water in physical combination with the molecule. The chemist says that sugars are osmotic. Starches are not osmotic. An osmotic substance is one which causes water to move into cells so that they swell. The plants make sugars by the process of photosynthesis but then combine the simple sugars into starches, dextrins, and the cellulose for storage or for structural parts of the plant.

Animals cannot make or store starch. The polysaccharide of animals is slightly different from that of plants. It is called glycogen, or animal starch. This type of "polyglucose" is stored in the liver and in some muscle cells. A few varieties of plants combine fructose into a storage form called inulin. This is a "polyfructose" and, like starch and glycogen, is not sweet-tasting. Inulin is a well-known molecule to the chemist and biologist, but it is not a common constituent of our diet.

Figure 1 graphically displays the way in which our bodies convert the carbohydrates of our diet into smaller usable molecules. No energy is immediately provided when the enzymes convert starch into simple glucose molecules or when the disaccharides are broken into the constituent monosaccharides.

Energy is made available to the cell only when the simple sugars are broken into the smaller, but now no longer sweet-tasting, sugar fragments. As each of the simple sugars is cleaved, the chemical bond energy is made available for use by the cells. The energy doesn't just escape into the cell fluids but is trapped by a highly complex set of carriers which can then be used to provide energy for the cell's requirements. These energy carrier molecules do not pass from one cell to the next. Whenever energy is moved from one tissue to another, it is transferred as a sugar or fat molecule or as some other similar material which can be oxidized by the cells.

Regardless of which simple sugar provides the beginning material, the eventual fates of the different simple sugars are the same. Yet the pathways of the conversion to the final products, carbon dioxide and

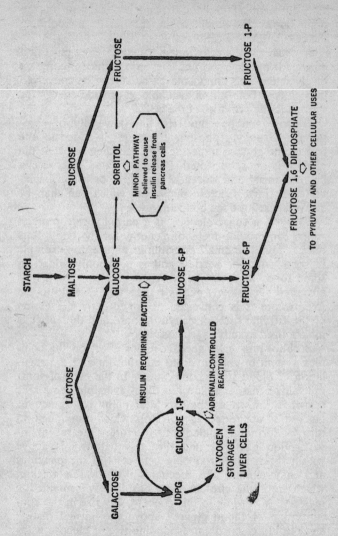

Figure 1 Metabolic Pathways of Common Sugars

water, are not the same for all of the simple sugars. The biochemical choices depend on the type of the other molecules available in the fluids surrounding the cells and in the cellular fluids.

In order for the cells to use galactose, they must first convert it by means of enzymes into a glucose complex or glycogen. This animal starch must then be converted into glucose before it is available to provide energy for the metabolic activities of the cells.

Glucose can be converted into a variety of compounds. Usually a phosphate complex is added to one end of the glucose molecule. We can then say that the glucose is phosphorylated. Phosphorylated glucose can be rearranged and stored as glycogen, or it can be inverted to form fructose phosphate which can then be cleaved to release the bond energy.

Sorbitol, a sugar alcohol, is a carbohydrate product which can provide metabolic energy for the body. Sorbitol is found in small amounts in nature, for example in some fruits or berries, and is commonly added to some foods as a stabilizer. When it is consumed it is absorbed very slowly and is transported directly to the liver where it is converted to fructose by the action of the enzyme sorbitol dehydrogenase and thereafter is metabolized exactly as fructose is.

Sorbitol may have another major effect on the complex system of carbohydrate metabolism and the regulation of blood sugar homeostasis. In the cells of some specialized tissues a specific non-reversible metabolic sequence known as the "sorbitol pathway" is active: glucose is converted to sorbitol, which may then in turn be further modified into fructose. One recent investigation has indicated that this pathway is active within the insulin-producing beta cells of the pancreas and may explain the mechanism of insulin release, which until the present time has largely remained a mystery. According to this concept, any rise in the concentration of blood glucose above the normal fasting level would cause a corresponding rise of glucose within the pancreatic beta cells which, unlike the cells of adipose and muscle tissues, are freely permeable to the glucose without the assisting action of insulin.

The rise of glucose in the beta cells would in turn activate the sorbitol pathway. Since the beta cell membrane is not permeable to the sorbitol molecule its concentration within the cell would rise. This sorbitol in turn, by some as yet undefined reaction, would stimulate the release of insulin from the cell into the blood stream. Since the sorbitol pathway is a one-way street in which fructose cannot be converted "back" into sorbitol, a corresponding rise in the level of fructose in the blood will not cause an increase of sorbitol in the pancreatic beta cells. This in turn would explain why dietary fructose does not stimulate insulin release.

Both dietary fructose and glucose are phosphorylated. However, there are several essential differences in the way these two simple sugars add the phosphate complex. In cells of the muscle or adipose tissues both simple sugars are phosphorylated through the action of an enzyme called hexokinase. However, glucose is not able to enter these cells without the assistance of insulin, whereas fructose can. In liver cells, on the other hand, which are freely permeable to both glucose and fructose, the sugars are phosphorylated by different enzymes. The conversion of glucose into glucose-6-phosphate (glucose-6-P) is facilitated by glucokinase, which is activated by and dependent upon the presence of insulin. Fructokinase, which phosphorylates fructose into fructose-1-phosphate, however, carries out its function completely independent of insulin. In the absence of insulin, as in severe uncontrolled juvenile diabetes, the phosphorylated fructose can be rearranged through the action of cellular enzymes by the process of gluconeogenesis to glucose phosphate and then to glucose. (Gluconeogenesis is the name of the process by which glucose is formed from other molecules such as fructose or amino acids.) In the presence of insulin, which suppresses gluconeogenesis, it is probable that this conversion of fructose phosphate to glucose does not occur to any significant degree.

The singly phosphorylated derivatives of both fructose and glucose are further modified and, through the addition of another phosphate, converted into the double phosphate molecule, fructose, 1,6 diphosphate. It does not matter if this molecule was derived initially from glucose or from fructose. Fructose 1,6 diphosphate is an intermediate form of both these simple sugars. It is the bond energy, released to carriers when fructose 1,6 diphosphate is cleaved into two smaller pieces, which provides the usable energy for the cells from either simple sugar molecule.

Insulin has the other, better-known action which is related to the phosphorylated forms of the simple sugars. It facilitates their storage as glycogen, which then serves as the precursor for glucose formation to readjust the hypoglycemic state.

Glucose and fructose differ significantly in another metabolic aspect. Glucose is transported across the membranes of the digestive tract cells by means of a carrier molecule. The biochemist says that the transport of glucose is "facilitated" in its movement into the blood stream. The actual mode of action of this carrier molecule is quite complex but it is known that this action requires the expenditure of a small amount of energy. The involvement of an energy-requiring action to move the glucose is not a wasteful action by the body. The advantage of the carrier comes from the increased speed of such a transport system. Thus as soon as glucose is present in the digestive tract it rapidly accumulates in the blood. This in turn stimulates the release of insulin by whose action glucose is made available to all the cells in the body.

The absorption of fructose from the digestive tract, on the other hand, is much slower than glucose transport. Only recently has much information about fructose absorption been known, and it has yet to be fully elucidated. While it was thought for a long time that fructose was primarily absorbed by simple passive diffusion, several recent studies have indicated an active mechanism for fructose as well. However, it is quite certain that the mechanism for fructose is distinct from that of glucose and even from that of the fructose half of the sucrose molecule. When fructose is taken in the pure form without any glucose present it is absorbed much more slowly than is either glucose or the glucose-fructose moieties when sucrose is eaten.

The liver stores approximately 100 grams of glycogen, enough to provide up to twenty-four hours' worth of carbohydrate. This glycogen can be reconverted to glucose, which is metabolized in the same enzymatic pathways as the glucose obtained in the diet. Liver glycogen is used for the support of the other cells of the body.

Adrenalin is the primary initiator of the conversion of glycogen to glucose when the stress of hypoglycemia develops. Adrenalin is a hormone, not an enzyme. Hormones are chemical messengers. Adrenalin acts as a messenger to the liver cells to trigger the chemical changes in these cells which cause the stored glycogen to be converted into glucose phosphate.

Many investigators now assume that insulin works in the opposite way from adrenalin on the same system. Simply, insulin causes the conversion of glucose into liver glycogen so that it can be stored for later use while adrenalin causes the reconversion of glycogen to glucose to provide the cells with immediately usable energy. It is these opposing actions of adrenalin and insulin in the liver and muscles that are important in the regulation of the blood sugar concentration. These two hormones do not act directly against each other. They are like a pair of two-way switches at opposite doorways. One turns the reaction on and the other turns it off. Both cannot be "on" at the same time. Neither can accomplish much of anything if both are present simultaneously.

Both insulin and adrenalin are deactivated by cellular enzymes. The deactivation of adrenalin by these cellular enzymes is particularly affected by one called COMT (catechol-O-methyl transferase). The discovery of the action of this enzyme was the basis for a Nobel Prize to Dr. Julius Axelrod. In addition to this specific enzyme, noradrenalin and adrenalin can be modified and deactivated by enzymes of the MAO variety (monoamine oxidase). The addition of the methyl complex by COMT or the removal of the nitrogenous amino fraction by MAO both change the adrenalin, a catecholamine compound in its chemical structure, into biologically inactive compounds excreted in the urine.

Usually both enzyme systems are involved in the deactivation of noradrenalin and adrenalin from the blood. Determining the concentrations of adrenalin's residual end products from a urine sample provides a quantitative measure of how much adrenalin was mobilized (secreted into the blood stream) in the unit of time during which the urine sample was collected. The end products do not completely accumulate in the urine until about four hours after the release of the adrenalin from the adrenal gland. The methodology to determine these products is relatively new, and the laboratory system is not available in most clinical laboratories. If all the products are accurately measured, they provide the investigator with an approximation of the actual stress response. Such a technique will not, of course, identify the stress condition which elicited the response. It does measure the accumulation of the hormone end products of the biochemical response and thus provides a measure of the magnitude of the stress.

The regulation and the storage of excess sugar also involve the synthesis and regulation of cellular fat deposition. Fat droplets do not float in the fluids outside of cells. Fats accumulate in specific cells as the most concentrated form of stored energy. Most of this stored fat was synthesized from excess glucose in the diet. As soon as the glycogen storage spaces are filled, the remaining sugars are converted to fat. Most of the fats in the diet are not the right type for immediate storage. Some come from plants, others from animal sources in our diet. All the dietary fats are broken into smaller pieces, the fatty acids and glycerol, by enzymes of the digestive tract before absorption or are divided into minute droplets by the detergent action of bile salts. The fatty acids and triglycerides pass into the blood. The milklike fat droplets are absorbed into different vessels called the lacteals, which bypass the liver and are then delivered into the blood at the level of the heart.

The dietary fats, digested by the lipase enzymes, are usually used by the cells for energy requirements at that time. Although it is possible for the cells to re-assemble the dietary fats for direct storage, most evidence indicates that the majority of body fat is synthesized from sugars.

The body can use only a small amount of fat at any time to provide the energy for metabolic activities. This fat use saves the sugars as new fat and as a group of related molecules, the sterols. Some triglycerides and fatty acids are normally present in the blood in small amounts. The sterol cholesterol is included in the lipid group (fat) of molecules since it, like fat, is not soluble in water but is soluble in the fat solvents, ether and benzene. The accumulation of cholesterol in the blood of some people has led some nutritionists to recommend restrictions in the diet to reduce its intake. No one has ever demonstrated that the body absorbs any significant amount of cholesterol from eggs or meats in the diet. The best information indicates that we synthesize our own cholesterol from dietary sugars and fats.

The other main constituent of the diet is protein. Proteins, or the amino acids from which they are formed, cannot be stockpiled and stored for later use. Only a small pool of amino acids is kept available. If more protein is included in the diet than is needed for immediate use the excess amino acids are converted, by removal of the nitrogen portion, into smaller molecules which eventually are further converted into sugars or directly oxidized for their energy content. Proteins are not an efficient way to get energy, but they do serve as a possible source of sugar and glutamic acid, which is required for the regulation of the nervous system.

The high-protein, low-carbohydrate diet prescribed

for hypoglycemia is intended to provide amino acids which can be used in place of sugars. The proteins must first be digested to free the amino acids. This requires both time and some energy. In the meantime the hypoglycemic person experiences the early symptoms initiated by the glucose deficiency. A very high-protein diet also puts a minor strain on the liver since the nitrogenous portion of the amino acids must be removed before these molecules can be used to provide energy. Pure amino acids could be included in a diet to provide energy. They would not require digestion, but they would still require the removal of the nitrogenous portion of the molecules. Amino acids are not very palatable. Their use as energy foods has very little to recommend it.

Both fats and alcohol can be used to provide energy. It is necessary, however, to provide some carbohydrates or amino acids to promote complete use of these molecules. If the body is deficient in glucose, the stress response will be initiated. This includes the mobilization of additional fat materials from the adipose cells. The amount of fat that can be oxidized in any given time is regulated by the activity of cellular enzymes. If too much fat is mobilized, the acetate portion of the molecule will be converted to acetaldehyde, which is also an intermediate in the metabolism of alcohol. As acetaldehyde temporarily accumulates, some of it is converted to ketones and organic acids which lead to the excretion of these incompletely oxidized fat fragments. This actually is the basis of one fad diet program suggested by some physicians for weight loss. The intent of this diet is to disrupt the regulated metabolism of fat and thus promote ketosis and the loss of these molecules in the urine. Such a diet can lead to acidosis, a condition developing from an imbalance of the acid-alkali concentration in the blood.

Carbohydrates provided in the diet in a "natural time-release form" (i.e., enclosed in cell membranes inside of cellulose cell walls) are more slowly digested than sugars. The glucose from such starchy foods is provided in small amounts over a long period of time. The blood glucose does not rise so rapidly. Not so much insulin is liberated. The rate of conversion of the glucose into glycogen is slowed down. A constant replenishment of the blood glucose from additional dietary starches or sugars from fruits prevents the onset of the stress response.

Nature has provided us with such materials. Rice and other whole grains are digested more slowly than disaccharides or even milled flour products. Dates are excellent high-carbohydrate foods that provide sugars over an extended period of time. They have nearly equal concentrations of glucose and fructose as monosaccharides enclosed in cell membranes. If dates are eaten each hour, the addition of the simple sugars to the blood supply tends to repress the onset of the stress response. No hypoglycemia symptoms develop. Most fruits are primarily glucose in a watery syrup. Since an apple, an orange, or a banana each contains approximately 16 grams of sugar (compared to a teaspoon of table sugar, which is 4 grams), it is apparent that an excessive intake of fruits can also induce hypoglycemia by promoting too rapid absorption of the glucose and the subsequent insulin release. Fruits with a high content of water are more easily digested than are dried fruits like figs and dates.

Certain diet food manufacturers have recognized that a potential market exists for candies or other snacks that contain no glucose or sucrose. They have devised and sold these products with sorbitol as the sweetener and energy source. Sorbitol is slowly absorbed from the digestive tract into the blood. After its absorption it is transported via the portal vein to the liver where it is converted immediately to fructose. Like fructose, sorbitol which is eaten does not stimulate insulin secretion. It is only that sorbitol which is produced via the sorbitol pathway within the beta cells of the pancreas which may be responsible for the release of insulin. The only caution which should be taken with sorbitol is that if it is eaten in amounts of more than 40 grams per day it is likely to cause diarrhea. It is so slowly absorbed that some may pass into the large bowel and cause the retention of excess water. Small amounts of sorbitol should not cause any problem whatsoever. Sorbitol has been accepted by the USDA as a substitute sweetener for glucose in diet products. Its advantage over the artificial sweeteners is that it is a food which provides some energy rather than just a chemical which stimulates the taste buds that respond to sweet-tasting molecules.

CHAPTER SEVEN

Hypoglycemia,
the Stress of a Low Blood Sugar

An insufficiency of sugar to maintain the regulation of the body, particularly that of the nervous system, is a stress. The general name of this condition is hypoglycemia. Many physicians have used that term as if it were a diagnosis of a distinct disease and have arbitrarily defined the condition. It is more appropriate to say that hypoglycemia is the name given to a condition in which the concentration of sugar in the blood supplied to the cells of the brain is so inadequate that the stress response is initiated. Many of the initial symptoms and later complications of hypoglycemia may develop even though the concentration of the blood sugar has been raised by the homeostatic system to well within the normal range.

In some persons the symptoms of a hypoglycemic condition can be detected when the concentration of the blood glucose is not much below 80 milligrams per 100 milliliters of blood (80 mg%), which some physicians consider to be at the low end of the normal fasting state. Obviously, when you wish to measure the blood sugar concentration accurately, it is necessary to take a blood sample. Unfortunately, most of us respond to the sight of a needle and syringe with a bit of fear and apprehension. The body responds to fear by secreting adrenalin, which in turn converts glycogen to glucose. Almost all of our blood sugar determinations are therefore somewhat higher than was true just moments before. The actual difference between the previous level and the partially adjusted concentration is not known. There is no way to prevent this usual slight error from affecting the statistics unless the person is unconscious.

Normally one cannot rely exclusively on a single laboratory test of the blood sugar level to identify a condition of hypoglycemia. If we wish to prevent the onset of the stress response by adjusting the diet, we must rely on recognizable symptoms.

Initially the hypoglycemia symptoms are fatigue and sleepiness. There is no specific focus to such symptoms. If someone afflicted with hypoglycemia remains inactive he tends to doze. He just can't seem to keep his eyes open. This seems to be the problem of sleepy church-goers on a Sunday morning. Even though they had plenty of sleep, they doze off when they sit quietly. The same is true of the college student sleeping through a lecture at midmorning or midafternoon. Hypoglycemia causes yawning at the theater and the concert. It shows up as a drowsy feeling at sales meetings. For many people some physical or emotional activity may activate the adrenalin release. The blood sugar level may then return to the normal 91–100 mg% that is our measured average concentration just after a full night of sleep. If the blood glucose concentration is not increased by the action of the adrenalin, the symptoms of hypoglycemia become more exaggerated. Some people continuously must contend with a blood glucose level near 50 to 60 mg% except during the time when the glucose is being absorbed from the digestive tract. They are continually tired. They are both physically and mentally depressed.

The symptoms of a low blood glucose level are not restricted to people with laboratory-verified hypoglycemia. They occur almost daily in the most healthy adults, and are symptoms of temporary deficiencies of glucose, which are normally corrected by glucagon and adrenalin. When the concentration of glucose falls below 60 mg%, we all experience a vague sense of uneasiness. People get fidgety, tempers flare. Smokers light up and inhale deeply. Somehow our bodies have learned that nicotine, just like adrenalin, acts as a stimulant. A cigarette or pipe can help to raise the blood sugar level. At a low blood sugar level the typist makes more errors than usual. The carpenter's hammer misses the nail. The baby wakes up and begins to cry. Industrial accidents occur more frequently in midmorning and midafternoon, when the blood sugar tends to be at its lowest point. Normally this is the time just between the glycogen storage action of insulin and the readjustment of the blood glucose by glucagon and adrenalin. Nearly everyone recognizes the midmorning and midafternoon slump, and we have built the coffee break into our culture. The caffeine of coffee and the sugars of the sweet rolls restore our blood sugar levels to the optimum for efficiency of our work and activity.

More drastic symptoms develop if the glucose concentration is not corrected. The type of symptoms depends on the rate of the decrease of the blood sugar concentration and on the magnitude of the stress response to this low sugar level.

If the blood sugar concentration is slowly decreased over several hours, the symptoms of blurred vision, double vision, severe headache, mental confusion, and eventually coma may develop. Not everyone develops all of the symptoms, but all show the initial weariness and progressive fatigue. Accompanying this set of symptoms may be a clenching of the teeth, a nervous tremor of the hands, a flexing of the fingers, and a rather distinctive dry feeling of the mouth as adrenalin is released to readjust the blood sugar level.

If the decrease in the blood sugar concentration is rapid, the most frequent symptoms are those which accompany the increased adrenalin secretion, with the new symptoms superimposed on the previous symptoms. The effect of the massive release of adrenalin is an initiation of sweating, cold clammy hands, hunger, pounding of the blood vessels in the head, a type of inward trembling, irregular heartbeat, distinct tremor of the hands, and a tenderness of the upper left-hand quadrant of the abdomen just under the rib cage due to the contraction of the spleen, stoppage of the digestive tract peristalsis, and increased tonus of the abdominal wall musculature. These latter effects in their more exaggerated form account for the "side ache" experienced by hungry but physically active children.

High adrenalin concentration also heightens anxiety. The lack of sufficient sugar interferes with some functions of the nervous system. Together with an increase in muscle tonus; tremor of the hands, slight spasm of the abdominal muscles, tightening of the muscles of the shoulders and neck, these reactions are commonly termed "tension."

If the blood sugar concentration is not raised by adrenalin and the hypoglycemic condition persists, various psychiatric and nervous system malfunctions may develop. Outbursts of temper, extreme depression, motor deficits, hallucinations, and all of the symptoms of certain psychotic illnesses may develop. The symptoms may occur individually or in any changing set or combination.

Behavioral changes are also superimposed on the different physiological symptoms. The nervousness which accompanies the first mobilization of adrenalin leads to compulsive eating in some persons, compulsive drinking of alcohol in others, hyper- or manic activity in some, and psychological withdrawal in others. Such behavioral characteristics seem to support the contention that the victim is attempting to accommodate the deficiency of the blood sugar and the high concentration of adrenalin by changing his mode of behavior and social interactions. Many of our habits seem to reinforce these conclusions. At times of stress smokers increase their consumption of cigarettes. When we recognize that nicotine mimics the action of adrenalin, we know that nicotine is a stimulant drug. Yet most people use this stimulant to relax. The same is true for those people who drink prodigious amounts of coffee. They are not the depressed persons who would seem to need a stimulant but usually are the active individuals who have learned that in some way they feel better adjusted if they get the stimulation of the caffeine which, like nicotine, supports the action of adrenalin. Both nicotine and caffeine produce the other effects of adrenalin as well: increased blood pressure, increased heart rate, induction of slight spasms of the digestive tract, trembling of the hands, etc. It is very peculiar that coffee after a meal has become such a common part of our lives. At the end of the meal, when the sugars are accumulating in the blood from the digestive tract and the release of insulin to store the glucose is expected, adding caffeine and its attendant physiological action seems to oppose common sense. The caffeine will cause the diminution or cessation of the peristaltic activity of the digestive tract just when it would seem to be the most beneficial. This seems to be one of the enigmas of our way of life.

It has been just over fifty years since Banting and Best isolated insulin from pancreas glands and applied their discovery to the treatment of diabetics. They were able to accomplish their feat by preventing the digestive enzymes of the gland from destroying the insulin. Since diabetes results from a deficiency of insulin action, either an actual deficiency of insulin or the synthesis and release of an inactive insulin-like molecule, the insulin supplied by Banting and Best gave diabetics a chance to regulate their blood sugar levels. The provision of insulin as an injectable hormone allowed diabetics to convert glucose to glycogen so that they had a supply of material which could be reconverted to glucose by glucagon or when the stress response caused adrenalin to be secreted into the blood stream. The insulin provided an opportunity to move glucose into cells and thus reduce the blood glucose concentration so that it would not spill over into the urine and increase the water loss from the body by its osmotic effect.

Hypoglycemia was first recognized in persons who were given too much insulin. A few years later some cases of hypoglycemia were discovered to result from tumors or lesions of the pituitary, adrenal, and pancreas glands. Such anatomical effects can cause difficulties in mobilizing glucagon and adrenalin or distinct hyper-insulinism. The disorder which develops when too much insulin is released to regulate the sugar concentration accounts for only a small number of hypoglycemia cases. Abdominal surgery may initiate a temporary hyperinsulinism-like condition. Such a condition is aggravated by the necessity to provide cellular fuel to these persons in the form of intravenous feedings of a 5% glucose solution. This constant supply of glucose then stimulates more insulin, which because of gluca-gon and stress is unable to promote the passage of glucose into the cells when the stress response is acti-vated. When the insulin is still active, the adrenalin can-not cause an increase in the blood sugar, and the hypo-glycemia persists.

A long list of other causes of hypoglycemia is known. In most cases there is no recognized anatomical growth, no structural deficiency or distinct physiological prob-lem. Some of these "functional" hypoglycemias have now been traced to specific enzyme defects which are known to be hereditary. At least a dozen varieties of hereditary enzymatic deficiencies are able to cause hypo-glycemia as the primary or secondary characteristic of the gene. Most cases of hypoglycemia, however, seem to be induced by the presence of carbohydrates in the diet, which cause the release of insulin. The majority of such hypoglycemias are either misdiagnosed as some other ailment or go undiagnosed entirely. Since the symptoms are so varied and are consistent with a large variety of other illnesses, the hypoglycemia is frequently not recognized.

. The actual diagnosis of hypoglycemia from the in-formation obtained from repeated measurements of the concentration of sugar in the blood is currently the most reliable quantitative measure. If the low glucose episodes are quite transient or sporadic, a diagnosis of hypoglycemia from blood sample information alone is unreliable. It is necessary to remember that the stress response to the apprehension of obtaining a blood sample can raise the blood sugar level and thus gives a higher reading than was present just moments before. Other tests and evidences are required.

The glucose tolerance test has frequently been used to indicate the extent of hypoglycemic responses. Sometimes this test is of distinct benefit, particularly so in detecting hyperinsulinism. For other varieties of hypoglycemia the test may be of less value. It does not measure the effectiveness of the conversion of glycogen to glucose, nor does it test the amount of adrenalin necessary for this regulation. In many people the hypoglycemia is just the trigger which initiates the stress response, and the symptoms which cause the most distress are affiliated with the high adrenalin level.

The usual glucose tolerance test consists of giving the subject an oral load of 100 grams of pure glucose in a syrupy drink. He is given this dose of glucose in the morning without any other food for breakfast. Blood samples are then collected every half hour for at least three, and preferably for five, hours. The glucose present in each blood sample is plotted on a graph to display the changes in the blood sugar concentration as it is used by cells or stored by the liberated insulin. A test of this nature for a hypoglycemic who is able to keep the blood glucose concentration up by secreting massive amounts of adrenalin does not have a record that is easily distinguished from that of a normal person. Nevertheless, he has a variety of other symptoms which develop as a consequence of this high adrenalin secretion. For most persons the most reliable diagnosis is based on a reduction of the hypoglycemic symptoms when effective dietary control is established.

A diet which contains rather large amounts of proteins (100–140 grams per day) and severely reduced amounts of carbohydrate (75–100 grams per day) was introduced for hypoglycemics by Conn in 1936. Until now this diet has been the best treatment available for functional hypoglycemia, although most people found it difficult to contend with the fatigue, depression, and irritability that accompanied it.

Until Dr. Conn's diet is analyzed, it seems to defy common sense. It would seem reasonable to give someone who is low in blood glucose additional amounts of the sugar. Dr. Conn's diet suggests a decrease in the carbohydrates since functional hypoglycemia frequently results when the body overresponds in the homeostatic regulation of the blood glucose level.

Ironically, it is the diet—both the kinds of foods and the eating habits—of people in the most affluent nations that is responsible for most cases of hypoglycemic responses. Only there does the diet contain a sufficient amount of slowly digested protein that three meals a day are customary. In less affluent countries such elegant food is not generally available. With a scarcity of protein in the diet, the primary foods are high in bulky carbohydrates. In these countries people eat smaller meals more often. As soon as their usable carbohydrates are digested and stored, another batch of carbohydrates is provided by the next meal. Of distinct value is the presence of the usable carbohydrates within a mass of undigestible bulk and the absence of sugars in the diet.

This is not to say that proteins are not good foods. Exactly the opposite. They are excellent foods. The problem develops when we rely on the amino acids from the digestive tract to provide needed energy but also provide the carbohydrates as sugars and easily digested starch. The carbohydrates are rapidly transferred into the blood and cause insulin release. This glucose is stored long before the amino acids from the digestion of protein are available. Between the time the carbohydrates are stored as glycogen and the amino acids are made available the stress of hypoglycemia develops.

The prime offender in our diets is sucrose, our refined table sugar. Sucrose is a very good energy-providing food. In many ways it is a bit too good. Sucrose is converted into glucose and fructose by an enzyme called sucrase. This enzyme is attached to the exposed ends of the cells which line the digestive tract. When sucrose is included in the diet, the sucrase splits the glucose from the fructose, but the glucose is then rapidly transported into the cell, from which it passes into the blood. The sucrase seems to hold the glucose and the fructose in such a manner that it promotes the movement into the cells of these monosaccharides obtained from sucrose. Other carbohydrates, such as maltose and starches, must be digested before they are absorbed as glucose, but the enzymes which accomplish this digestion are part of the digestive fluids. Glucose derived from these sources is not held in position for transfer, as is the case for sucrose. As indicated in the Appendices, the rate of transfer of glucose from sucrose is almost identical to that of pure glucose, which requires no enzymatic action at all.

The more rapid the accumulation of glucose in the blood, the more likely it is that some of it will accumulate in the pancreatic cells and thus initiate insulin release.

When fats are provided with the carbohydrates and proteins, the stress response can be depressed, and the fats used to provide energy for most of the activities of most cells. The brain, however, cannot use fats for energy. It requires sugars not only for energy but also as material from which some of the nervous system regulator compounds can be synthesized. If fats are eaten without carbohydrates their complete utilization is disrupted, as the stress response causes more fats to be mobilized than can be used effectively.

We are indeed fortunate that nature provided us with the simple sugar fructose, which can be used as a source of energy and as a substrate for the nervous system synthesis but which does not cause the release of insulin itself. Fructose is a natural food, but until recently has not been available in pure form for dietary use. Now its known advantages can be used for the regulation of hypoglycemia.

CHAPTER EIGHT

The Dietary Use of Fructose

Fructose is an ideal food for a hypoglycemic person. It has all the desirable characteristics a food should have to prevent the onset of low blood sugar and the development of the associated stress response. Fructose is not a magic potion, something exotic, mysterious, and unknown. Fructose is well known. It is unfortunate that the information available about it has not included the fact that it is distinctly advantageous in the prevention of hypoglycemia, and it is worth while to repeat some of the facts about fructose so that they can be analyzed simultaneously. Only in this way can a diet based on the inclusion of fructose be seen in its proper perspective.

The molecular arrangement of the atoms of fructose is different from that of glucose. Glucose is called an aldehyde sugar (aldose) because of its structure, while fructose, which has exactly the same atoms in a slightly different arrangement, is a ketone sugar (ketose). These differences affect the metabolism of these simple sugars.

In contrast to glucose, fructose is slowly absorbed from the digestive tract and never accumulates to a high concentration in the blood. While glucose in high concentration in the blood leads to the secretion of insulin from the beta cells of the pancreas, fructose does not stimulate insulin secretion. Fructose can be converted into glucose by the process of gluconeogenesis. These characteristics lead to the understanding that fructose has a stabilizing effect on the blood sugar level, which avoids the possibility of hyperglycemic reaction to rapid blood glucose increase and subsequent insulin release. Fructose, but not glucose, can also be assimilated directly into muscle and adipose cells, thus providing energy directly without dependence on insulin.

Fructose is not a new or recently discovered food. It has been a part of our diet for eons. Honey has always been a delectable food. It contains as much fructose as glucose. The sugars in honey are simple sugars, not disaccharides. It is only in the recent history of man that sucrose, the disaccharide, has been available in pure form, either from sugar cane or from sugar beets. As previously mentioned, it is the *sucrase* enzyme on the membranes of the cells of the digestive tract lining that splits sucrose to glucose and fructose. It is the effectiveness of this enzyme and the availability of the glucose transfer system which promote the rapid accumulation of glucose in the blood and the subsequent secretion of insulin when sucrose is included in the diet. Before sucrose became generally available the only sweet carbohydrates were those of honey and the various fruits.

The name fructose or fruit sugar means that it is found in some ripe fruits. It does not mean that it is the most prevalent sugar in all fruits. Most fruits contain more glucose than fructose and only a few, such as dates and some grapes, have as much fructose as glucose. Pure fructose (some writers call it levulose, and refer to glucose as dextrose or grape sugar) is obtained by chemical separation from other sugars. Pure fructose and pure glucose are both expensive sugars. The costs result from the chemical processing necessary to obtain these sugars in usable form. Previously, fructose was obtained from the Jerusalem artichoke, chicory, or the ti plant. Some fructose was formed by the enzymatic conversion of glucose. The new technology of fructose manufacture is based on the separation of the glucose and fructose halves of the sucrose molecule or an enzymatic conversion of glucose obtained from corn starch. Industrial-scale production in Europe has already reduced the price of fructose there to less than half of what it was only a few years ago. It is assumed that widespread knowledge and increasing use of fructose will soon bring these economies to this country as well. Even at the present time, however, the value of fructose to those who use it is greater than its price.

Fructose is the sweetest of all of the sugars, but its sweetness does change with the temperature of the food. In hot beverages it does not seem to be sweeter than sucrose. In cold drinks it is usually perceived to be considerably sweeter than either glucose or sucrose. Equivalent sweetness of cold drinks requires nearly twice as much glucose or half again as much sucrose than if fructose is used. These measures must be by weight since crystalline fructose is usually a combination of powder and crystal, so that a rounded teaspoon of fructose weighs the same as a level teaspoon of sucrose. Since less fructose is needed to obtain the same sweetness there is, of course, a marginal saving in calories. The real advantage of fructose, however, is its effectiveness in maintaining a stable and sufficient level of blood sugar and thus eliminating the necessity of the stress response to correct the condition of hypoglycemia. It is in this regard that the slower transfer of fructose from the digestive tract into the blood is of highest significance.

Fructose is available as a syrup containing 77% pure sugar solids in a water solution in Europe and in some areas of the United States. The costs of production of this syrup are less than for the crystal product, but packaging and shipping costs reduce much of the price advantage. Since fructose will not easily crystallize from water solutions, it cannot be used to make fudge-like candies. Tabletized fructose, made by compressing crystalline sugar, is for sale throughout Europe and in some places in the United States. Some tablets contain a binder substance or a small amount of magnesium stearate to help in getting the tablet out of the mold into which it is pressed. These substances do not affect the metabolism of the fructose. The fructose tablets can be flavored and colored without modifying their use.

Fructose, like all other carbohydrates, provides four

calories per gram of weight. A teaspoon of sucrose weighs 4 grams. A rounded teaspoon of crystallized fructose weighs 4 grams. A teaspoon of sucrose thus provides 16 calories of energy. An apple, orange, or banana each contains approximately 16 grams of carbohydrate and thus provides 64 calories each. A slice of unbuttered toast, or just bread, provides 12 grams of carbohydrate. Each slice of bread therefore contains the equivalent caloric content of three heaping teaspoons of fructose. (Appendix 4 lists the carbohydrate, fat, and protein content of a large variety of foods.) Fruits and flour products, such as bread, cookies, and cake, provide rather large amounts of readily available glucose. Whole grains, nuts, and cooked fibrous vegetables provide starch which we digest to glucose. They may be slightly better for a person with hypoglycemic symptoms than pure glucose or sucrose would be, but fructose is still preferable: it eliminates the primary problem of the high-protein, low-carbohydrate diet for hypoglycemia. Such a diet without fructose is not unpalatable but it lacks the repression of the symptoms initiated by the adrenalin that is released to readjust the blood sugar concentration after insulin has stored the sugars.

It should be apparent that the value of fructose in the diet is dependent on the concurrent reduction in the intake of glucose-providing carbohydrates for best effectiveness. Usually it is sufficient to just eliminate the sucrose and some of the more easily digested starchy carbohydrates. Unfortunately, the majority of our fresh fruits are very high in glucose. If it is necessary to trade off one benefit for another, the vitamins of fresh fruits can be provided from synthetic sources. Small amounts of fruits can usually be accommodated without problem so long as they are spread out through the day. There is hardly a better way to initiate a hypoglycemic episode than having a fruit salad and non-nutritious celery and lettuce as a meal. The celery and lettuce are fine bulky foods which aid the actions of the lower digestive tract, but they provide no energy and only slight amounts of vitamins while the fruits are very high in glucose.

One of the problems with all diets is that many people consider sweet things as gustatory rewards. They seem to think that people like to eat sweet things just because of their taste. They have conned themselves into believing that saccharine and cyclamates are as satisfying to the body as they are to the tongue. They keep trying, in other words, to fool nature, and that is impossible. We like things that are sweet because we have learned that sweet foods provide us with energy and promote a feeling of well-being. Since the synthetic sweeteners do not provide this benefit, they just do not satisfy the way that natural sugars do.

There are a few persons whose systems cannot tolerate fructose because they lack the gene which regulates the formation of an enzyme necessary for metabolizing fructose. These unfortunate persons develop a very strong dislike for sweets, even though they could use glucose without any difficulty. The diet suggested here is not appropriate for them; they must provide proteins or glucose from fruits to adjust their blood sugar requirements if their starch intake is restricted.

A satisfying diet for the hypoglycemic would include a small amount, perhaps a teaspoon or two, of fructose each hour in addition to small amounts of other carbohydrates which do not trigger a massive release of insulin. The total amount of carbohydrates each day should be at least 75 grams. A diet containing 100 grams of carbohydrate may be safer to insure the complete oxidation of fats. One author has illustrated this requirement with the metaphor that fats are burned in a flame of carbohydrate. Actually, carbohydrates are not directly involved in the metabolism of fats. The carbohydrates prevent the hypoglycemia and thus eliminate the necessity for the secretion of steroid hormones, which would mobilize more fat than the enzymes can effectively oxidize. If less than 75 grams of carbohydrate is available, the metabolism of fats may be incomplete and lead to the formation of ketone bodies.

This is generally believed to be biochemically dangerous because ketosis is associated with acidosis, and this complication makes physiologists and nutritionists very skeptical about the safety of the high-fat, low-carbohydrate fat diet which advertises that you don't need to count calories. Everyone with a background in basic biochemistry would agree that you don't have to count calories if you force the body to continuously excrete partially oxidized fats as ketones. The inclusion of fructose in the diet given here is intended to provide for the complete metabolism of fats, both in the diet and the stored fats of the body, while at the same time to prevent the onset of the symptoms associated with hypoglycemia. (Chapter Fourteen, on diabetes, presents a more detailed description of the interrelationships between carbohydrate metabolism and the complete metabolism of fats.)

The hourly intake of fructose, whether as a sweetener in beverages, gelatin, tablets, or in candies, will suppress the onset of hypoglycemia if the protein and fat metabolism provides the remainder of the energy requirements. Since hypoglycemia-initiated symptoms usually begin with fatigue, even before the vague feeling of uneasiness, many persons can adjust their intake of fructose to such times. This means that many can rely on their own perceptive mechanisms to time the fructose rather than relying on the clock. The fructose will provide some relief for such early symptoms within just a few minutes. Additional fructose at this time will insure the repression of the most drastic symptoms accompanying a stress response to readjust the hypoglycemia.

Fructose is commonly available in Europe in almost every grocery and candy store, either in crystalline form or as the sole carbohydrate in chocolates, candy bars, and some quite hard but jelly-like candies. (For its sources in this country, see Appendix 3.) A variety of marmalades and jams made with fructose are also for sale. In Europe it is used not only as a long-lasting

energy supply for athletes and sports car drivers but
also as an energy source for many diabetics. It is
possible that the designation of diabetes in Europe may
include the pre-diabetes condition of hypoglycemia but
extensive studies on diabetes using fructose there have
been reported in a large number of very reputable
journals. There are some data that suggest that hyper-
insulin hypoglycemia leads to the later development
of late-onset diabetes. In other conditions frequently
associated with hypoglycemia there is also a much
higher than normal incidence of diabetes. There have
been no long-term studies providing data to support
directly the proposition that those who are hypoglycemic at one time will become diabetic later on.

Hypoglycemia in association with a variety of other
disorders makes it especially important to prevent this
condition. Hypoglycemia is a commonly recognized
problem among alcoholics, schizophrenics, depressed
persons, hyperkinetic children, the obese, and people
with migraine headaches. Previously these disorders
have been considered wholly separate and unrelated.
Hypoglycemia in their victims has been thought to be
a complicating factor. There has been no previous suggestion that hypoglycemia is a prime contributing factor
in the onset of most of these disorders.

The remainder of this book is intended to provide
the logic that these conditions may develop directly
from hypoglycemia and from the stress responses (that
is, the homeostatic mechanism to regulate the blood
sugar concentration). The key to all of these disorders
is generally recognized to be a stress. The persistence
of the hypoglycemia is dramatic evidence that the homeostatic adjustment systems are not functioning adequately. The stress relationship to peptic ulcer, impotence,
and all of the other stress-related problems of the
circulatory system can also be included. It is generally
assumed that if you can reduce the stress these associated maladies will be eliminated. We have previously
virtually ignored the implications of internal stress, as

opposed to stress arising from the external environment or of emotional origin.

Whether the stress is initially internal or external, the way to manage a continuing hypoglycemia is with a rational diet. That diet which will best provide relief for these conditions is the same for all of them: a high-protein, low-carbohydrate diet with the majority of the carbohydrate being fructose taken as a food in a rather regular sequence throughout the day. Fructose is not just added to the diet, it should be exchanged for the other carbohydrates. We don't lose anything. We provide fructose. We gain an external control of the blood sugar concentration.

Some hypoglycemics suffer only from extreme continuous fatigue. Apparently they are unable to mobilize the adrenalin which is the complicating factor in most of the other hypoglycemia-related disorders. The diet works here too. It is very important to remember that fructose is a food. It is not a drug. It only provides energy and substrate for synthesis to the cells, and by so doing it prevents the necessity of the stress response. It does not inhibit any of the normal cellular functions. Its two advantages over glucose are that it passes more slowly from the digestive tract into the blood so the digestive tract serves as a reservoir to provide sugar over a long period of time and that it does not stimulate insulin release.

Although fructose has long been available on the shelves of the chemist and pharmacist, its use until now has not been fully appreciated. Many research papers have been published about the metabolism of fructose, information often interpreted from a point of view different from that presented here. Some investigators who recognized that pure fructose will not cause the release of insulin but who know that it would be converted to fat if consumed in excess of immediate use have viewed this as disadvantageous. Certainly it would be if the subject were provided with a challenge dose of excess fructose. But if a minor conversion of fructose to glucose phosphate is seen as an unfortunate rearrangement of an expensive food into a much cheaper product, the lack of insulin release or requirement is not appreciated.

The facts remain the same: (1) In the absence of insulin, excess fructose (that beyond immediate cellular needs) is usually converted to triglycerides and stored as fat. (2)) Fructose is not actively transported into the blood from the digestive tract. (3) If only fructose is present, it will not normally be stored as glycogen in the liver. (4) If insulin is present but the glucose concentration is low, fructose phosphate can be rearranged to glucose phosphate and stored as glycogen.

The interpretations are different: (1) Triglycerides, which temporarily accumulate in the blood, are common products of both glucose and fructose if the glycogen-holding capacity is full or if no insulin is secreted by the pancreas. (2) The decreased rate of transfer of dietary fructose provides more time for the direct cellular use of fructose. This decreases the likelihood of the onset of the hypoglycemia stress response. (3) Dietary fructose does not lead to insulin release. It would not stimulate a condition of hyperinsulinism. (4) Except for the stimulus for insulin secretion, the metabolic pathways of fructose and glucose are essentially the same. Both glucose and fructose are metabolic substrates which can provide energy directly to cells or be stored as glycogen or fat. The major differences are that only glucose stimulates insulin release and is dependent upon insulin both for entry into muscle and adipose cells and for phosphorylation in the liver.

Fructose is not a miracle drug. It is a natural food. Its value in helping to avoid the various symptoms associated with the stress response to hypoglycemia has now been recognized. Until now the technological difficulties in producing fructose have unfortunately prevented it from being generally available to the consuming public at a reasonable cost. New technological developments, however, should soon make fructose increasingly available in all parts of the country.

CHAPTER NINE

The Problems of Alcoholism and Overweight

The hypothalamus is the crave control center of the nervous system. It is the hypothalamus portion of the brain which recognizes the need to adjust the systems of the body. If the cells of the hypothalamus are physiologically satiated, they do not stimulate the formation of the trophic hormones in the pituitary which initiate the stress response. On the other hand, if the hypothalamus is not satisfied with the physiological conditions which it monitors, it stimulates the pituitary to secrete its hormones. As previously noted, the stress of hypoglycemia—an insufficiency of sugar in the blood supplied to the hypothalamus—results in the mobilization of noradrenalin and adrenalin. This adrenalin from the adrenal medulla is intended to cause the conversion of glycogen to glucose and thus return the blood to the optimal cell fuel concentration, but if some problem prevents that, more and more adrenalin is secreted. This portion of the stress response is added to the mobilization of additional steroid hormones which produce other changes.

Adrenalin has other effects in addition to the conversion of liver glycogen to glucose, one being the cessation of peristaltic activity of the digestive tract. Many people are familiar with the cramping of the abdomen when they have had excessive coffee on an empty stomach. Adrenalin has this same effect in a more generalized way. It blocks digestive motility, allows gas accumulation, and increases the tonus of the abdominal musculature so we feel hungry. More importantly, when the digestive tract motion has ceased, the digestive juices and enzymes can erode the protective mucous covering of the cells lining the digestive tract. When the nerve endings are exposed the muscle cells go into spasm while ulcers develop.

Hunger is a stimulus for us to eat. It will not develop if adrenalin is not released from the adrenal gland. If the blood sugar is kept at a sufficient level there will not be any hypoglycemic stress or the response to this stress of cellular fuel deficiency. Persons given sugars by intravenous feeding, for example, seldom if ever experience hunger although they have no dietary intake of food.

Hunger, essentially, is a craving for food. We have learned to respond to this stimulus. We eat when we are hungry. If we consume more calories than we use for the continuation of cellular activities, we store the excess as glycogen and fat. When we continuously eat more than the body can use at the time, we gain weight. Sometimes this weight gain continues until severe obesity develops.

Adrenalin also increases the tonus of voluntary (skeletal) muscles. Many people call this "tension." An awareness or recognition that this increased muscle contraction has occurred is also often called "anxiety" or "stress." By following our instincts, we learn that eating represses these manifestations if the actual stress condition is a deficiency of blood sugar. By eating, to prevent the secretion of adrenalin, we can raise the blood sugar. The overweight person may have been able to accommodate the stress of hypoglycemia by a continuous intake of food; he thereby eliminates the hypoglycemia temporarily, but he gains weight.

The initiating stress may not always be actual hypoglycemia, but since hypoglycemia is the most frequent stress we have all experienced, we have become accustomed to eating as a means of eliminating stress. The current stress may be either emotional or physiological, but the adrenalin-related reactions and the recognition that they stem from stress prompt continued eating. We have all learned that eating, particularly sweet foods that are just "loaded with available calories," stops the reactions which are regulated by adrenalin when the blood sugar level is low. The increased food thus satiates the appetite control function of the hypothalamus. The concessionaires at football and baseball parks may not understand the psychological-physiological inter-relationships of our eating habits but they are aware that their sales of candy bars, peanuts, popcorn, hot dogs, soft drinks, and beer are much better if the game is exciting and the adrenalin flow in the spectator is high, yet eating does not reduce the psychic or emotional stress of an athletic event. We have acquired an eating behavior association with stress.

Alcoholism is also an acquired condition, as is every drug and food dependency. The alcoholic has learned about the rewarding effects of alcohol. In times of stress response, when adrenalin has been released from the adrenal gland and has initiated what we identify as "tension," "anxiety," or "stress," the alcoholic knows that relief is available in the bottle. Although alcohol is a cellular fuel which supplies 7 calories per gram (in comparison to carbohydrates=4, fats=8), it is not the provision of the calories which is satisfying but the fact that alcohol is a depressant drug. It does not stop the actual stress. It blocks the hypothalamus from responding to the sugar deficiency and from stimulating the release of adrenalin through its action on the pituitary gland. Some of the intermediate products of alcohol metabolism stimulate the parasympathetic system instead. This causes some drinkers to hiccup but it also influences the blood flow to the skin to promote that feeling of warmth and well-being. Nothing else that the alcoholic has tried, other than other addictive drugs, gives him the initial calm and satisfaction that alcohol does. Alcoholism is a disorder of health that is misunderstood by both the alcoholic and many of the professionals who treat it. Until now rehabilitation has been focused on identifying the dependency, and on programs dealing with its psychological, economic, social, marital, and physical aspects, the latter including liver damage, vitamin deficiencies, neurological problems, and other overt deteriorative processes. Instead of discovering and eliminating the cause of alcoholism, programs have fostered guilt and shame in alcoholics. Yet an effective program for breaking the cycle of alcohol addiction requires understanding the biochemical background of dependency itself. This includes the biological changes induced by heavy drinking, those undertaken by the alcoholic to depress the necessity of the stress response, and the most persistent, continuous, repetitive, and obscured stress, that of a deficiency of sugar supplied in the blood to the brain.

Alcohol is a drug. Alcohol addiction and other forms of drug dependency cannot be separated. They are different aspects of the same problem. Alcoholics and other drug-dependent people can switch from alcohol to barbiturates or other tranquilizers or even stimulants very easily. The tranquilizing drugs turn off the brain's ability to recognize the stress so that no adrenalin is released or absorbed, while other drugs actually block adrenalin secretion. The stimulant drugs increase the activity of the sympathetic nervous system or may actually mimic adrenalin. These stimulants thus create the contentment and composure that accompany a homeostatic or adjusted state. The availability and social acceptance of alcohol allow the drug user to shift to alcohol and thus escape the stigma applied to the drug culture. Dependency remains, but the drug is alcohol.

Although alcohol is metabolized (oxidized or burned) to obtain energy, it cannot be converted to sugar. It enters the metabolic cycle at the same level as fats. Alcohol that is not oxidized immediately is converted to fat and stored in the fatty tissues of the body. (The drugs used by some members of the drug culture do not, by the way, provide any food value whatever.) Alcohol is not, of course, a balanced food: it does not contain any protein, vitamins, or minerals. A person who is drinking, but not eating other food, soon depletes his reserves of these necessary food materials. Even if some food is consumed with the alcohol the alcohol promotes an increase in the motility of the digestive tract which prevents the absorption of some essential food elements. People who join rehabilitation programs are usually given vitamins to correct any deficiency which may have developed when the diet was alcohol. A good diet containing all of the amino acids and minerals can then begin to make other repairs.

Alcohol does not need to be digested to pass from the digestive tract into the blood stream. It is completely soluble in water; because of this, it passes through the membranes of the cells of the digestive tract with ease. Whereas fats are unable to pass into cells of the nervous system, alcohol moves in rapidly. Deactivating alcohol, either by using it as a cellular fuel to provide seven calories of energy per gram, or by storing it as fat, requires enyzmes. The availability of these enzymes, and therefore the rate at which they make these conversions, is directly related to the cells' demand for them. If the alcohol concentration in the cells increases, the cells initially compensate by making more deactivating enzymes, and the body thus becomes more tolerant to the ingested alcohol. A high tolerance to alcohol is one of the distinguishing characteristics of most persons who drink large amounts of ethyl alcohol. The ability of the cells, particularly in the liver, to deactivate or modify alcohol is a built-in protective mechanism—one of the homeostatic systems, in fact. This system of adaptation eventually prevents the drinker from achieving the same state of euphoria that initially came with drinking, and the absence of this depression of the nervous system removes the suppression of the hypothalamus. The hypothalamus therefore reinstates the stress response, which stimulates more alcohol consumption, which again blots out the response to the stress.

The enzymes of the body rapidly convert alcohol into a molecule called acetate. This is one of the same intermediate compounds in the decomposition of sugar and from the initial steps in the metabolism of fat. If the alcohol consumption maintains a depression of the hypothalamus so that no stress response is initiated by the hypoglycemia, no glycogen will be converted to glucose. The absence of the glucose prevents the brain from forming an essential regulatory compound. The nervous system does not then function properly. Physiological restrictors cannot be made if no sugar is provided to the nerve cells, and neural impulses are less regulated and controlled.

If the alcohol is consumed faster than it can be burned as a fuel or stored as fat, it will temporarily accumulate as acetaldehyde. Acetaldehyde is known to precipitate nausea, cause profuse sweating, decrease the heart rate and blood pressure, and result in severe headaches. Acetaldehyde is converted into various organic acids or ketones which are excreted in the urine and exhaled in the breath, since they are volatile substances. The effects of acetaldehyde and the ketones produce the typical signs of a hangover.

To sober up a drunken friend, it is helpful to increase the metabolic rate and to raise the blood sugar level. Coffee, strong and black, is the best and most easily available means of doing so. At this stage it would be best not to provide sucrose. It would require insulin release to the extent that hypoglycemia would again act as a stress or promote a diabeteslike state. You should not include cream in the coffee because the fat would compete with alcohol for the same enzymes and so could contribute to the accumulation of acetaldehyde and ketones. Cream provides calories, but so does the alcohol that is present. If fructose is provided the brain cell demand for sugar can be satisfied without triggering the insulin release.

If alcohol is consumed in a high-carbohydrate drink which triggers insulin release, hypoglycemia will be alleviated only temporarily and then be repeated as soon as the sugars are stored by insulin. The hangover will probably be worse the following day because the brain will remain starved for sugar as the alcohol is metabolized to the acetaldehyde which the brain cannot use.

If the consumption of alcohol was initiated by the "anxiety" and "tension" or "stress" brought about by hypoglycemia, the alcohol may not depress the hypothalamus so much as it anesthetizes the higher centers of the brain. If the hypothalamus responds by causing adrenalin and steroid hormone release, the blood sugar may be increased to eliminate the original stress condition, but the fats that were mobilized by the hormones of the adrenal cortex now will compete with the alcohol for the enzymes while the action of the adrenalin may interfere with the conversion of the alcohol into fat storage. Hypoglycemia can serve both as the stimulus to drink and as the cause of the nausea and the hangover that are consequences of it. The consumption of alcohol is only a very temporary relief from the stress response initiated by hypoglycemia.

The "stress eaters" try to eliminate their craving, their recognition of hypothalamic demand, by eating. They prefer high-carbohydrate foods. The alcoholic attempts to readjust his body by drinking. He craves alcohol. He has learned that for him alcohol is temporarily satisfying. The "glucaholics" are easy to identify. Their bulk gives them away. The alcoholic is harder to spot, but there are some telltale characteristics.

The alcoholic has a drinking pattern different from that of a non-alcoholic social drinker. The former is frequently preoccupied with thoughts about the next drink. He will squirrel away bottles of alcoholic beverages at the office, in the car, and in various places at home. He needs the reassurance that alcohol is available. He uses it as a medicine to cure his ills of the stress response. He does not need an excuse to drink. He will drink alone. He does not bother savoring the bouquet or the flavor of the beverage, he merely gulps his drinks. He is after the calming effect produced by the alcohol. Alcohol provides him with the ability to manage one part of his life. It causes the deterioration of the rest of it.

The alcoholic becomes completely conditioned to seek this one reward and to obliterate other concerns. He is unable to control his drinking. One drink in a social setting will trigger a bout of continued drinking until he is intoxicated or broke. (Frequently the two occur simultaneously.) He knows that his drinking will soon make him sick and that a hangover will develop when he stops but these physical punishments do not deter his drinking.

Pavlov, the Russian experimentalist, conditioned his animals with rewards and punishments. He found that if the rewards were great enough the punishments did not prevent the seeking for the reward. Alcoholism is a conditioned response, both biological and psychological, which must be understood in the terms of the reward for drinking. If a hypoglycemic person drank an alcoholic beverage, he would inadvertently learn the metabolic lesson that ethyl alcohol is a cellular fuel which depresses the hypothalamus. He does not learn at the same time that alcohol consumption might become the dominant influence of his life.

The obese, and other obsessive eaters, also reinforce their hypoglycemia. They have learned that they feel better if they are eating continuously and are therefore able to keep their blood sugar level high. The side effects of the increased weight are tolerated to gain the composure which comes from a sufficiency of blood sugar. The additional glucose and the other carbohydrates which are converted to glucose stimulate the release of large amounts of insulin. Since the insulin causes the storage of glucose as glycogen, the excess food intake is converted to fat stored in the adipose (fatty) tissues of the body. The rapid storage of glucose as glycogen reinitiates the hypoglycemia, and that, in turn, reinitiates the noradrenalin and adrenalin release and the resulting hunger pangs. The cycle then starts all over again.

Alcohol differs in many ways from the carbohydrates

consumed by overweight individuals. Notably, it cannot be converted to sugar, which is required by the brain, and it does not induce insulin release. It temporarily satisfies the hypothalamus. It provides a cellular fuel for some cells of the body and depresses the central nervous system. The other unfortunate side effects —the depression of the thinking processes of the brain, the anti-social behavior, the eventual damage to the liver and to the nervous system—prevent alcohol from being considered an adequate and acceptable substitute for the insulin-inducing carbohydrates eaten by overweight persons. Yet excess alcohol, like excess sugar, accumulates as fat.

Since we know that alcoholics and overweight persons are often found by laboratory tests to be hypoglycemic, it seems that this condition of low cellular fuel and substrate for the nervous system initiated the drinking and eating rather than developing as a consequence of them. The biological need for adequate and appropriate cellular provisions would be sufficient stimulus to seek relief. Overweight persons, even if they are not actually obese, are prime examples of the inadequacy of additional glucose to relieve their problems of regulation, and alcohol is not an acceptable alternative. We must learn to break this cycle.

The alcoholic cannot "unlearn" his lesson that alcohol is immediately satisfying, the overweight person cannot "unlearn" that eating relieves his feelings of anxiety, but both of them can be taught a new lesson. They can learn that if they manage their biological need for sugar for the brain without triggering the storage of this sugar by causing insulin release they can gain a measure of tranquillity. The alcoholic will not need his alcohol if his stress is effectively reduced. The overweight person will not demand food beyond his immediate biological need. Both needs can be met by pure fructose in an adequate diet.

Each pound of fat provides 3500 calories of energy when it is oxidized either by burning or by the enzymatic processes of living organisms. Whether this fat is accumulated by an excess intake of fat in the diet or from excessive carbohydrate intake, the energy content of fat is the same. On the other side of the coin, the accumulation of each and every pound of fat indicates an excess of intake of 3500 calories over the amount necessary to maintain the activities of the body. To lose weight the diet must be deficient in calories so that the body is forced to mobilize and oxidize the stored fuels.

The metabolic requirements differ for each person. A large man who is doing heavy physical labor will require a higher intake of food than a small man whose work is less strenuous. The metabolic rate depends on age to some degree. Young people who are still growing require more energy than they will need when they complete the maturation processes. A nursing mother will require considerably more calories than one who is not nursing her baby. The metabolic rate is controlled by the thyroid gland in the throat. This gland, like the adrenal gland, is also regulated by the pituitary, which in turn is controlled by the hypothalamus of the brain. When thyroid secretions are low, the metabolic rate is decreased and energy requirements of the body are low. If the intake of food is maintained when the thyroid activity is low, more of the calories will be stored as fat. When the thyroid secretions are high, the excess intake will also be stored. A high thyroid activity just decreases the amount of calories that are excess. A satisfactory weight loss will still require a decrease in intake of calories regardless of the thyroid function.

If a person's activities require 2400 calories each day, any diet that provides less than this will result in a weight loss. If such a person reduces his intake to 1800 calories each day, he will lose one pound each week or a few more than fifty pounds in a year. This diet of 1800 calories is deficient by 600 calories each day, so that every week the body has used up the equivalent of a pound of accumulated fat. If a person's metabolic demand is satisfied by a daily intake of 2000 calories, a 200-calorie deficiency each day will cause a two-pound-per-month weight loss. After all, a twenty-five-pound weight loss in a year may be sufficient for most persons who are only slightly overweight. That kind of weight loss would account for a three-to-five inch decrease in the waistline. Good dietary habits which then provide only the amount of energy required will allow this lower weight to be maintained.

Good exercise is beneficial in maintaining the breathing apparatus, muscle tonus, the heart and circulation. Just increasing one's exercise usually does not result in a satisfactory weight loss. A strenuous game of handball for an hour will require an expenditure of only 400 calories. At that rate it would take a game every day for a week to lose a pound of fat if the intake of food is exactly matched to the metabolic demand without the exercise. A two-mile hike hardly shows up as a deficiency in the caloric accounting sheet. It may be of more importance because it keeps the person from eating during the time of the exercise. Even a reasonable amount of exercise will raise the adrenalin level somewhat. This results in an increase in hunger sensation which develops without a cellular fuel deficiency. Because of this sensation of hunger many persons eat again and thus gain more weight.

Many of the overweight members in our society know that they must decrease their caloric intake below that amount required to maintain their activities if they wish to lose weight. There is no magic formula here unless a person follows the questionable practice of eating excess fats together with a carbohydrate-deficient diet. This type of diet produces a condition in which partially oxidized fats known as ketones are excreted in the urine. Such a diet will certainly cause a person to lose weight. A mechanical analogy to this situation would be to decrease the efficiency of an automobile by blocking a couple of the exhaust valves of the engine so that the unoxidized fuel will produce a cloud of bluish smoke out of the exhaust pipe. Any mechanic can assure you that such a disruption of the engine will probably cause a variety of other malfunctions. The same can be expected if we make our own bodies inefficient.

The problem of diet for most people who wish to lose weight is their persistent hunger for food, their irritability and nervousness, and their belief that their metabolic rate is adjusted in such a manner that they require a constant intake of food. By following the diet suggested here, all of these problems can be resolved. The diet is designed to provide all of the daily necessary vitamins and minerals for good nutrition. It provides a sufficiency of protein to supply the necessary amino acids. Some protein will be oxidized to provide energy. It also provides a small amount of fat. Although this fat will provide 8 calories of energy per gram, the inclusion of dietary fat is necessary to insure that some fat-soluble vitamins which are synthesized by the bacteria in our digestive tracts can be absorbed into the cells of the lower digestive tract and finally be transferred into the circulatory system fluids. Without some fats there will be no bile salt secretion and thus no way to absorb these essential bacterial-synthesized chemicals. The diet is different from all other diets in that, although there is a general reduction in the inclusion of the usual digestible carbohydrates which appear in the blood stream as glucose, there is a specific provision of fructose. The fructose can be used to sweeten coffee, tea, or Kool-Aid. It can be used in salad dressings or desserts or eaten as candy. The diet works to cause weight loss because it provides only 1200 calories of energy each day, including the fructose. The fructose is provided to maintain a sufficiency of sugar for the cells of the nervous system so that the hunger, nervousness, and fatigue which accompany most other weight-loss diets can be prevented. The fructose is not a reward for following the diet. It is not a placebo or false medication to fool the psyche. It is included as a specific cellular fuel.

The most satisfactory weight loss depends on the regular use of fructose. The diet specifies between 75 and 100 grams of fructose each day. The amount of variation will depend on the amount of protein as well as on the other variables in the physiology of the dieter. The trick is to eat the fructose in small amounts at regular intervals throughout the day so that the digestive tract will serve as a reservoir. If you start feeling fatigued, if you yawn in the middle of the day or feel sleepy, you should eat some fructose then. If you start to feel edgy or tense you probably have already initiated the beginnings of the stress response. Some fructose will relieve this condition of sugar insufficiency in a few minutes.

If the fructose is eaten regularly in adequate amounts it should entirely prevent any feelings of hunger. It is a good idea to eat some fructose fifteen minutes before each meal so that, when you do sit down to eat, you eat not because you are hungry but because you know that good health requires the proteins, fats, vitamins, and minerals in the food.

It may be easier to stay on the diet if you eat at home but it is possible to eat in commercial establishments and still lose weight if you order rationally and avoid the fried potatoes, chips, and bread that accompany your meal.

As noted in Chapter Three, fish and meats should be broiled, baked, or boiled. Fried food should be avoided unless you use only the amount of fat you are allowed in your meal. Uncooked green and yellow vegetables are almost indigestible. They provide no calories although they are a good source of vitamins, minerals, and bulk, so they can be eaten at any time in any amount. By themselves they are not able to stop hunger or depress the other attributes of the stress response. That effect is achieved by the fructose. It is a very good idea to eat a sizable portion of these foods at each meal to insure an adequate amount of bulk in the diet for good digestive tract regularity and as a mass to slow the digestive tract motility so that the fructose is absorbed in the upper regions. If the fructose is not absorbed it can serve as an elegant food for some gas-producing microorganisms or may, by its osmotic effect, promote loose bowel movements. If either gas or loose bowel problems develop during the first few days on the diet, it is only necessary to decrease the amount of fructose consumed at any one time. Eat the same amount but spread it out a little more.

The general rule is to avoid starchy foods and those that contain sucrose or glucose (dextrose). This would then exclude pancakes, cakes, cookies, noodles, spaghetti, macaroni, potatoes, bread, candies, and ice cream and would severely limit milk (not because of the fat but because of the lactose sugar). Since weight loss depends on a reduction in total calories, the amount of fat in the diet should be restricted. For a person who follows the diet because of alcoholism and does not need to lose weight, the fat of fried foods, butter, and oil dressings can provide additional energy.

The very heart of this diet is the exchange of fructose for the majority of the normal "insulin inducing" carbohydrates of the common foods. The diet was particularly designed for persons who suffer from functional hypoglycemia and who also need to lose weight. In addition to the foods listed in the sample meals it is expected that the dieter will consume 75 to 100 grams of fructose each day. The sugar is a ready source of energy for the body but it is also adequate food for the bacteria of the mouth. Adults should not need a reminder that they should brush their teeth after every meal and snack but it is surprising how many neglect this common-sense practice.

The diet provides more protein than is necessary for amino acid replacement. The remainder of the protein will be used by the body as fuel. Since proteins are slowly digested and their components provided to the blood over an extended period of time, the additional protein provided in this diet will also help to avoid the onset of hunger.

Sample Menu Pattern*	Sample Meal

Breakfast

1 tomato juice or citrus fruit	½ cup tomato juice
2 meat group: egg, cheese, bacon, breakfast sausage, milk	Egg omelet with 1 ounce Cheddar cheese
1 bread or cereal group	1 slice whole wheat toast, with ½ pat butter or margarine
Coffee or tea if desired	Coffee or tea with fructose

Lunch

3 meat group: egg, cheese, fish, beef, pork, poultry	Chef's salad made with 1½ cups lettuce, 2 slices
2 vegetable or fruit group	tomato, 1 ounce Cheddar
1 bread group	cheese, and 1 ounce
1 fat group	diced summer sausage with Sweet-Sour Dressing (Chapter Three)
Coffee or tea if desired	Coffee, tea, or Kool-Aid made with fructose

Dinner

2 meat group: egg, cheese, fish, beef, pork, poultry	1 cup clear onion soup
	6-ounce lean broiled steak
2 vegetable or fruit group	1 cup Stay-Crisp Cole Slaw (Chapter Three)
	6 spears asparagus
1 dessert	1 serving Swedish Cheesecake (Chapter Three)
Coffee or tea if deired	Coffee or tea or Kool-Aid

* Table 1 lists foods in groups of exchanges to maintain total nutritional adequacy. See pages 22–25.

The sample meals of this minimal diet provide 850 calories and 75 grams of protein. With the inclusion of 75 to 100 grams of fructose this diet can be considered a 1200-calorie diet.

CHAPTER TEN

Migraine Headaches and Hypoglycemia

The unfortunate people who suffer from migraine headaches are frequently doubly abused. First, they suffer the most excruciating pains and discomforts for many hours without the possibility of medicinal relief. Second, many are unjustifiably accused by their physicians, their associates, and even by their families of malingering or at least succumbing to a psychosomatic illness, that is, one originating in the mind rather than in some physiological dysfunction. By using well-established information about migraines, and by looking at the conditions which initiate the development of the symptoms from a new perspective, we can instead see that migraine headaches may be related to hypoglycemia.

Despite a confusing array of differing opinions and hypotheses about migraine headaches found in both professional journals and laymen's magazines, there are some points of general agreement. The headaches develop at times set aside for relaxation, on weekends or at the beginning of vacations, and therefore appear to follow rather than accompany stress situations. Virtually all investigators report evidence that they are much more frequent among females than among males. Very often a retention of extra fluids during the day before the onset of the headache causes a noticeable swelling (edema) of the soft tissues. That additional water in the tissues results in a weight gain of two to three pounds just before the onset of the headache. In some persons migraine headaches can be precipitated by specific foods. In most cases there is a family history of severe headaches or neuropsychiatric problems. At the time of the headache an array of related physiological conditions usually occur: low blood pressure; profuse sweating; relaxation of the sphincter muscle at the junction of the esophagus and stomach, causing a flow of gastric juices upward to the mouth; and a highly active digestive tract peristalsis (wavelike contractions with attendant cramping so that regurgitation of gastric contents is common). If all of this information is regarded as pieces of a symptomatic jigsaw puzzle, other relationships can be expected.

The times which people set aside for relaxation are expected to be either free of stress or at least lower in stress than the usual work week. At such times there is a diminution of steroid hormone release and a decrease in the amount of adrenalin secreted into the blood. Changes in steroid hormone levels are known to accompany other physiological events. In the human female a parallel series of changes develops when gonadal hormone concentrations are reduced. Steroid hormones produced in the ovary maintain the tissues of the uterine lining for a lunar month. When the concentrations of these hormones are not maintained in a continued synthesis by the ovarian cells, the lining of the uterus is sloughed off. Steroid hormones thus prevent the onset of menstruation. Menses ensues when the ovarian hormones are at their lowest concentration. The steroid hormones of the adrenal cortex and those of the ovary are biochemically similar. Since migraine headaches develop after stress situations, they also occur after the steroid hormones of the stress response disappear from the circulating blood. The migraine headaches differ principally from those headaches which accompany the onset of menses only in the place of origin of the responsible steroid hormones. Both varieties of hormones control cell activities when they are present. When the hormones disappear, these activities cease.

In many women the onset of migraine-like headaches accompanies the beginning of menstruation almost every month. These headaches are not otherwise symptomatically different from headaches which occur at other times. They, of course, increase the total number of headaches among females. If the number of menstrual cycle headaches is subtracted from the total number of headaches that females have, the frequency of migraines among females and males is virtually the same.

Associated with the headaches of menses, the mood and emotional interactions are frequently disturbed. A decrease in circulating steroid hormones decreases the amount of adrenalin that is delivered into the blood. The woman goes into a physiological and psychological depression. When the ovarian steroids are depleted, the primary steroids are those from the adrenal cortex. Some of these adrenal cortical hormones are androgenic; that is, they induce male-like characteristics. When these hormones are not balanced by the gonadal hormones of the female, they cause the development of an oily skin and skin eruptions similar to teen-age acne. High muscle tonus leads to backache and "tension." These are the same general symptoms associated with hypoglycemic episodes.

The changes in steroid production in pregnancy tend to keep steroid concentration high during this time by virtue of constant placental hormone secretion. Migraine-prone females frequently are completely free of headaches during pregnancy. Similarly, arthritic symptoms which have been evident in some females before they become pregnant disappear when placental hormone concentration rises.

All steroid hormones are synthesized from cholesterol. They differ only slightly from each other in the arrangements of only a few atoms but they produce specific physiological changes. Unfortunately some women metabolically modify some of the hormones so that they produce effects which were not expected from the original hormone. Most of the birth control pills contain progesterone to maintain the uterine lining and to inhibit the secretion of trophic hormones by the pituitary to initiate the maturation of ova. Progesterone can be converted by some into androgenic hormones and thus promote the development of male-like characteristics: male hair-growth patterns, oily skin, aggressive behavior, and distinct changes in the sex drive. Retention of additional extracellular body fluids and the onset of migraine headaches are also too common to be ignored. These are prices too high for some to pay to prevent unwanted pregnancies.

The drastic shifts of steroid production at the beginning of menopause are also correlated with increased migraine headaches. Women in this age group have other indications of steroid changes, including emotional outbursts, depression, insomnia, and, in some, delusional episodes. Certain physical changes can also be noted in the skin, hair-growth patterns, and the distributions of body fat. Again, in these disorders, as in the migraine headache, it is not necessarily the previous presence of the steroid hormones which initiates the symptoms but the drastic and rapid decrease in the concentration of the steroid hormones on which these women have relied for stability.

It is commonly known that a retention of water, caused by an increased reabsorption of sodium salts, precedes menses by a day or two in many if not most females. Usually a reabsorption of sodium salts by the kidney is the result of the action of the antidiuretic hormone (ADH) produced in the adrenal cortex. This is also a steroid hormone. ADH promotes the retention of water by increasing the absorption of sodium salts, which then bind water molecules. The body compensates for the reabsorption of sodium by allowing an increased loss of potassium in the urine. Potassium is normally accumulated in cells, whereas sodium is usually excluded from cells. Sodium is in high concentration in the fluids which bathe the cells and in the blood. Recently it was discovered that potassium salts were excreted at a high rate the day before the onset of migraine headaches in males as well as in females. This was what one would expect, since the water retention problem was well known, but it did indicate that the physiological conditions which would lead to a migraine were occurring at least twenty-four hours before the onset of the symptoms. Since the effects occur simultaneously, it is not evident whether the loss of potassium from the cells or the edema which accompanies the retention of the sodium salts or some other associated metabolic problem is the prime contributor to the precipitation of the headache.

The retention of the sodium salts and the resulting retention of water are not capricious or disadvantageous side effects of the stress response. Adrenalin increases the flow of blood to the head but it also increases the flow of blood to, and the blood pressure in, the other major organs of the body, including the kidney. If the sodium salts were not reabsorbed by the kidney cells, the water portion of the blood would spill over into the urine and lower the blood volume. The blood pressure would then fall. To maintain the blood flow and pressure it is necessary that some system be used to prevent this loss of a desirable stress-response effect.

When the stress situation is abated, the cells must then readjust the potassium-sodium concentrations under conditions of reduced blood flow and decreased cellular fuel supply. These are detrimental conditions for required cell activity. It is not known whether the loss of potassium into the urine seriously depletes the body store of this mineral if the stress response is prolonged. It is not known whether the requirement for the sodium pump activity under these detrimental conditions contributes to the development of the migraine headache. Yet a deficiency of intracellular potassium would drastically interfere with many body processes.

In some people migraine headaches are specifically related to allergic sensitivities. Allergic reactions can usually be controlled or eliminated by providing steroid or sympathetic system hormones. The steroids may act on the sensitized tissues directly, or they may cause the release of sympathetic system hormones from the adrenal medulla. The exposure of sensitized cells to allergin-containing foods causes a massive release of histamine from some affected cells. (The allergins are substances to which some people are sensitive; they are, therefore, the materials which cause the onset of allergic reactions.) Histamine produces tissue reactions that are nearly opposite those of adrenalin. For example, it increases the blood flow to the skin whereas adrenalin decreases this flow. The release of histamine into the fluids which surround the cells produces a localized stress situation. The onset of migraine headaches following allergic reactions is also thus related to a stress condition. If the body responds to the histamine by secreting additional steroid hormones and additional adrenalin, the direct effect of the histamine may be masked. An itching of abused epithelial tissue (eczema) or swelling of mucous membranes (as in hay fever or a severe head cold) may not be evident if sufficient stress-response hormones are released.

An illustration of the relationship of adrenalin to the allergic reaction may clarify this point. When one is given a skin test for allergies, the skin is lightly scratched and a potential allergin is applied. If one is allergic (sensitive) to this material, a reddened, raised weal will form like a mosquito bite. The degree of sensitivity to the allergins tested will be indicated by the size and persistence of the weal. If one is tested a few days later for the same allergins, and if a small amount of adrenalin is injected under the skin at the beginning of the test so that the hormone can be distributed by the blood to the entire body, no weal will develop. The adrenalin does not change the sensitivity of the tissues. Instead it compensates for the histamine released by the traumatized cells. This second skin test would be of no value in determining which substances were allergins. As long as the adrenalin concentration remains high, no allergic responses can be detected. This adrenalin may be provided by the stress response as well as in this experiment with the injected adrenalin.

There may also be an additional component of the stress response involved in the initiation of edema and the onset of migraine headaches. It has long been recognized that some persons with migraine headaches have high levels of histamine in the blood, even though there is no known allergic reaction. One of the well-documented cellular changes initiated by the stress response is the liberation of a variety of blood cells into the circulation. This is of distinct advantage if the stress results from the presence of toxins or bacteria, since some of these white cells can engulf and destroy both types of disease-causing materials. Some of the blood cells are called mast cells; they contain large amounts of histamine, which is liberated into the blood stream when they interact with disease-causing toxins or microorganisms. The histamine of these mast cells is also released when the cells are ruptured because of some bruise, cut, puncture, chemical disruption, or even a severe restriction of a capillary which could squeeze the fragile mast cells. Inside the mast cells the histamine is associated with an anti-coagulant called heparin. The action of heparin is to prevent blood clotting. Histamine causes the constriction of the veins and the dilation of arteries. Therefore more blood is brought to the tissue and less is allowed to leave. As a consequence the blood in the tissue pools in the capillaries. The increased pressure within the capillary promotes the release of histamine, which locally causes little gaps to develop in the inner lining of the blood vessels. This increases the flow of fluids into the surrounding tissues, causing the edema. At the same time the squeezing of the mast cells to cause the histamine release could be expected to initiate the clotting of some of the other blood components. Clotting is normally caused by small blood elements called platelets. It would be very dangerous if the clot developed in the brain, heart, kidney, or other vital organ.

Clotting is desirable when a blood vessel ruptures but would be disastrous if it occured inside the circulatory system under most circumstances. It is here that the advantageous action of heparin and histamine is noticed. The heparin would be released with the histamine if mast cells were among those ruptured. The heparin would decrease the likelihood of a clot, and the histamine would promote a local lowering of the blood pressure by moving blood fluids through the walls into the surrounding tissues. This action, coupled with restriction of the veins, could prevent a blood clot (embolism) from being carried into the heart or to other tissues.

The logic story doesn't stop here. There is evidence that histamine from the nervous system can trigger the pituitary to release its ACTH, which would then re-initiate a stress response. If the stress is so great that histamine is released in high concentration, the stress response will be automatic and will not even require the interaction of the hypothalamus of the brain.

Other aspects of the stress response can also be involved in initiating migraine headaches. It is known that the presence of many if not all steroid hormones results in the conversion of stored fat into free fatty acids and triglycerides and the release of these molecules into the circulation as cellular fuels. A new piece of information which correlates with our understanding of the inefficiency of triglyceride oxidation has come from some of the treatment programs for alcoholics. In some institutions alcoholics are given the drug Antabuse, which interferes with the normal metabolism of ethyl alcohol. Any person who is taking this drug and then has some alcoholic beverage becomes very sick. The drug is given for this reason. It is not a medicine. It serves to inhibit the person from taking a drink when he knows he will get very ill because of it.

It is known that Antabuse causes an accumulation of acetaldehyde, an intermediate product in the metabolism of ethyl alcohol. Antabuse interferes with the normal conversion of acetaldehyde to acetate, which normally is either oxidized or combined with other molecules to form fat. The symptoms of high acetaldehyde concentration are virtually identical to the symptoms of a migraine headache: profuse sweating, low blood pressure, nausea, cramping, and a severe headache. Such symptoms can be obtained without Antabuse and alcohol if someone is given acetaldehyde beyond his ability to metabolize it. If the normal pathway is blocked, the acetaldehyde will be converted into a group of compounds called ketones and some organic acids. A condition of acidosis develops in the body. This, in turn, interferes with a variety of metabolic processes. Since ketones are volatile at body temperatures, they are exhaled with the breath, where they can be detected as the sweet but undesirable odor of acetone. If a stress response causes more fat mobilization as fatty acids and triglycerides so that some of the molecules are converted to acetaldehyde, a physiological basis for the onset of migraine headache is available.

Other chemicals are also known to initiate migraine headaches. In some persons, eating certain varieties of cheese which contain high concentrations of the chemical called tyramine can trigger the onset of a severe headache. This is particularly true if one has been using drugs of the "psychic energizer" variety which block the action of MAO (monoamine oxidase, the enzyme which removes the nitrogen portion of amino acids and such compounds as adrenalin). Tyramine and the amphetamine drugs can interfere with the regulation of the sympathetic system hormones directly. Normally it is noradrenalin, the compound from which adrenalin is made, which regulates the hour-to-hour dilation of the blood vessels of the body.

This control is particularly important in the regulation of the vessels which supply the brain. If the blood pressure is increased, the force of the blood will cause the ballooning of the capillaries and an increased passage of blood fluids into the spaces of the surrounding tissues, causing an edema. The edema causes pressure and irritation to the nerve cells associated with the blood vessels. The expansion of the capillaries in areas which accumulate fluids is probably directly involved in the development of headaches in many people. Both tyramine and the amphetamines are believed to induce severe headaches by mimicking the noradrenalin control of vessels to the brain.

Cluster headaches—headaches of a defined area of the head rather than the more generalized migraine headaches—usually develop very early in the morning hours. They begin most frequently between four and five-thirty in the morning, the time of night which coincides with the lowest blood sugar concentration. Most people have a rather cyclical rising and falling of the steroid hormones throughout a twenty-four-hour cycle. The lowest concentration occurs between near midnight and 2:00 A.M., after which time the concentration rises. The increased steroid hormone concentration then is related to the release of adrenalin and fat molecules into the blood as cellular fuels. If the blood glucose concentration does not rise, the additional adrenalin secretion is a continuation of the normal stress response to hypoglycemia. It is adrenalin which serves as our normal wake-up stimulus. In people with cluster headaches the increase in blood glucose seems to be insufficient to provide the control for the nerve cells and for the regulation of the circulatory control to specific areas. Anatomically the cluster headaches differ from migraine headaches, but the physiological relationships to the stress control seem to be the same. Those other people who require a cup of coffee in the morning before they function normally are using the coffee to mimic adrenalin action and to thus raise the blood sugar level.

Many treatment regimens have been based on what has been known about migraine and cluster headaches. Drugs which either mimic the action of adrenalin or increase the effectiveness of adrenalin have been prescribed with some advantageous results in some people. These drugs include benzedrine, caffeine, and ephedrine. Intravenous injections of the steroid dexamethasone have been advocated, as well as injections of pituitrin, a drug which causes the eventual release of adrenal steroids. Certain chemical derivatives of ergotamine have often been used. Such drugs increase the vasoconstrictive (decrease the diameter of blood vessels) effect of noradrenalin and adrenalin, particularly in the vessels which serve the head. Tranquilizers and sedatives have been prescribed to reduce anxiety and tension which precede the migraine episodes in some patients. None of these treatment programs has been more than partially successful in most people. The majority of migraine sufferers have not been helped by medication nor has psychiatric treatment for either migraine or cluster headaches been any more effective.

The primary questions about migraine headache should therefore not deal with the psychosomatic induction but with the elimination of the stress and the stress responses which can be involved in the initiation of the headache. Many questions that demand further investigation have to do with the proportion of migraine headaches which are induced or maintained by a deficiency of blood sugar. This stress can effectively be eliminated by following the high-protein, low-carbohydrate, fructose-substitution diet suggested in this book. People who have headaches only on the weekends may need to follow the diet only from Thursday until Sunday. A considerable amount of individual variation should be expected. If the diet is closely followed for a few periods during which severe headaches are common and expected and if these periods pass without a headache, it may be possible to modify the diet to some extent and still be free of headaches. Fructose should not be expected to have any beneficial effect after the headache has begun. It is only a food which will prevent the onset of hypoglycemia, which may be a component of the initiation of the headache.

A one-and-a-half-day eating plan is provided as a pre-weekend diet for those who are prone to develop migraine headaches and as a diet to precede the onset of menstruation. The diet is not primarily designed to promote any weight loss. Instead it is designed to insure an adequate intake of energy-providing foods while severely reducing the consumption of carbohydrates, which promote glucose accumulation and thus may lead to the release of insulin. In order to decrease the possibility that egg or cheese allergies may be involved in the precipitation of headaches, this food plan decreases the normal amounts of these staples. If there is no evidence of allergies to these foods, they can be substituted for other foods in the meat group.

This eating plan requires the consumption of 75 to 100 grams of fructose in one form or another each day of the diet. For those who are subject to migraine headaches which occur early in the morning it is especially important that they eat at least 20 grams of fructose between dinnertime and when they retire to act as insurance that they have enough sugar available to the cells during the night. The diet also supplies a major portion of the protein in the evening meal to make available more fuel at this time of the day.

The diet as given in the sample meals provides 1600 calories without including the fructose, which is used to sweeten various of the foods. When the fructose is included in the total caloric computation, the diet provides between 2100 and 2400 calories. If a late evening or between-meal snack is desired, try celery filled with a peanut butter and fructose mixture.

The various meals can be modified in various ways. If eggs can be included in the diet they can be boiled, scrambled, coddled, fried, or served as omelets with mushrooms, anchovies, onions, or even diced sweet pickles. The meat servings can alternate between beef, pork, lamb, fish, or poultry without any loss of protein content. Fresh raw tomatoes, onions, radishes, carrots, lettuce, endive, cabbage, and cauliflower can be eaten in unrestricted amounts. If these green and yellow vegetables are cooked, they should be limited to a total of one cup of cooked vegetable per meal. The desserts and snacks made with fructose for which recipes are given in Chapter Three can top off any meal, or they may be eaten between meals to provide needed carbohydrates which will not initiate the secretion of insulin.

THURSDAY EVENING

*Sample Menu Pattern**   *Sample Meal*

Dinner

Unrestricted foods (provide   Onion soup or bouillon
  a negligible amount of
  insulin-inducing carbo-
  hydrates)   Cabbage-Hamburger
Meat, fish, poultry, cheese   Casserole (Chapter
                                       Three), large serving

Vegetable   Boiled broccoli with melted
                                       cheese or butter

Salad   Celery sticks filled with
                                       cottage cheese (sprinkled
                                       with paprika or pickle
                                       relish)

Dessert (fructose-sweetened)   Swedish Cheesecake with
                                       Lemon Custard Topping
                                       (Chapter Three)

Coffee or tea if desired   Coffee or tea with fructose

FRIDAY

Breakfast

1 fruit   4 ounces tomato juice or ½
                                       broiled grapefruit with
                                       fructose

1 bread group   2 slices melba toast, or
                                       Swedish rye crisp

1 fat group   1 pat butter
1 meat group   Small breakfast steak, or 3
                                       ounces fried breakfast
                                       sausage

Coffee or tea if desired   Coffee or tea with fructose

---

* Table 1 lists foods in groups of exchanges to maintain total
nutritional adequacy. See pages 22–25.

Lunch

Green vegetables
1 fat group

Lettuce and tomato salad
    with French, mayonnaise,
    or Thousand Island
    dressing

2 meat group

Beef-Cabbage Rolls or
    Stuffed Peppers (Chapter
    Three), 2 servings

Coffee or tea or lemonade
    made with fructose

Coffee, tea, or lemonade

Dinner

Appetizer

1 bowl vegetable soup (no
    noodles or rice)

Salad

Cottage cheese and tomato
    salad on lettuce leaf

Meat

1 steak (6 ounces) broiled,
    dry pan-fried, or
    barbecued, or

1 serving seafood (4 to 6
    ounces)

Dessert

Homemade Coconut
    Macaroon

Haystacks with Lemon
    Custard Sauce (Chapter
    Three), or

Fructose gelatine dessert

Coffee, tea, or fructose-
    sweetened Kool-Aid

Coffee

Evening Snack

Dan's Special Eggnog with
    chocolate, rum or other
    favorite flavoring (see
    page 150)

This special attention to extra food before bedtime is to insure that the blood sugar, amino acids, and fats are available throughout the night. The sample meals suggested above provide between 1800 and 2000 calories (depending on combinations) while the addition of the 75 to 100 grams of fructose (at least 4 to 6 grams every hour except just after meals) brings this diet program to 2100 to 2400 calories. Such a diet should be sufficient for most women, but if it is continued over an extended period of time by a man who is moderately active, it could be expected to cause some weight loss.

CHAPTER ELEVEN

Schizophrenia, a Stress-Response Disorder

The ancient Greeks attributed mental illness to improper balances of body fluids. Some of our words for certain personality characteristics are inherited from them, terms like "melancholy," "bilious" and "choleric" (although we now know, for example, that an accumulation of bile in the body fluids is not a primary cause of personality differences). The Greeks had no science to support their expectation of biochemical involvement in behavioral disorders, but they also believed that the only alternative to some internal health problem was to continue to ascribe mental illness to the caprice of the gods. They thought that if psychiatric disorders were in fact due to the actions of gods, as many other civilizations had taught, then nothing could be done to aid the affected persons. Yet because they favored some kind of therapy, they preferred to believe that the problem must come from within the sufferer.

No one now believes that schizophrenia is inflicted by gods or devils or demons. Nevertheless, although some psychotic disorders are known to be associated with specific physiological malfunction, others have been as baffling to us as they were to the early Greeks.

When the psychiatrist Eugen Bleuler established the criteria for the diagnosis of schizophrenia, he excluded all the known causes of psychiatric disorders. We are thus left without a circumscribed diagnostic limitation for this disease, and without an understanding of the basis or cause of the abnormal behavior characteristic

132

of it. The behavior of the schizophrenic appears irrational to others because it often seems to serve no other purpose than to isolate him from society. And this may be the clue.

Common sense tells us that schizophrenia develops when the fears, worries, apprehensions, and the strain of living in a structured society become so great that one cannot adjust himself to them in a fashion acceptable to society. The schizophrenic then "turns off" his responses to the real world. He seems to build a new world of his own imagining, and he responds only to the rules and regulations of that imagination. He mentally isolates himself and ceases to be receptive to the stimuli that regulate most of us.

Psychotherapy and counseling are both intended to ferret out and expose the cause of the abnormal responses and irrational behavioral changes which characterize schizophrenia. Psychoanalysts believe that if the cause of the anxiety and fear can be identified and recognized, the conscientious patient can learn to refrain from exaggerated and irrational responses to stress-producing situations. Current psychotherapy and psychology hold that the cause of schizophrenia is an improper perception of the stress because of some previous psychological trauma, and that the problem is essentially mental, not biological. A lower level of anxiety in the patient by any psychotherapy is acknowledged to be distinctly advantageous, even if the reason for the treatment is not universally accepted.

Medicinal, physical, and surgical therapies are not intended to eliminate the actual cause of psychotic behavior but instead to reduce the magnitude of the exaggerated responses to stress and thereby to depress the symptoms. These treatment programs are frequently used to reinforce psychotherapeutics. A decrease in the symptoms allows the schizophrenic to continue to live in society.

All well-controlled investigations of the genetics of schizophrenia provide conclusive evidence of hereditary influences in its development. Despite this agreement there is no conclusive evidence of the distinct mode of inheritance. The specific action of the genes which seem to promote the development of schizophrenia is not understood.

The substantiated findings of the genetic research programs can be summarized in a few sentences. The frequency of schizophrenia is much higher in some family groups than in others. If one member of a pair of identical twins develops schizophrenia, the likelihood of the other twin also developing schizophrenia is several times higher than for other members of the family. (On the other hand, if one member of a pair of like-sex fraternal twins develops schizophrenia, the probability of the other twin also developing it is no greater than for other brothers and sisters in the family.) The natural children of a schizophrenic mother have a higher risk of schizophrenia than adopted children who are brought up by schizophrenic foster mothers. Children of schizophrenic mothers reared by non-schizophrenic foster mothers have the same probability of developing schizophrenia as if they had been reared by their schizophrenic mothers. Children who have schizophrenic fathers have the same risk of developing schizophrenia as those who have schizophrenic mothers.

No single type of genetic transmission has been consistently reported by the scientists studying it. Different modes of inheritance have been proposed, and adequately supported, by different authors. The identification that genetic factors are involved in schizophrenia, however, even without an agreement about the type of inheritance, has provided clues for new biochemical investigations.

The biologically oriented research programs are directed to investigate what kinds of metabolic flaw keep the schizophrenic from being able to continue a normal existence and, necessarily, to cope with the problems of daily life. They investigate why some people can tolerate rather fantastic amounts of stress and trauma but seem to remain free of psychosis while others, exposed to fewer apparent strains and stresses, develop schizophrenia. The biologist thus investigates schizophrenia from a perspective different from that of the psychiatrist. He attempts to determine which biochemical reactions can contribute the biological component of schizophrenia inferred from the genetic studies.

It is generally known that the gene, the hereditary unit, is responsible for directing the synthesis of proteins, many of which are enzymes. Enzymes are unusual proteins which can influence the rates of chemical reactions. In short, enzymes are organic molecules which function as catalysts. Most of the reactions of synthesis (manufacture) of compounds by living organisms as well as the destruction of these compounds require enzymes. If the enzymes are changed or are inadequate in their actions, new or unusual compounds can be formed or other products can accumulate.

The enzymes do not become incorporated into the products formed. They influence the physical state of the reacting materials in such a manner that chemical and physical changes in the molecules are possible even though such changes would otherwise be unlikely at body temperatures and at the low concentrations of reactants in most biological systems.

Enzymes are specific in the kinds of chemical reactions they influence. Many enzymes are so specific that they react with only particular kinds of molecules. We can picture them as having particular "active sites" which, like locks, only specific keys can fit. The "key" portion of this analogy is the substrates or substances which can combine with and be affected by the enzyme. Abnormal genes would cause the production of abnormal enzymes, which in turn would lead to the formation of unusual products, the accumulation of specific intermediate products, a deficiency of normal enzymatic products, or any combination of these complex characteristics. Since specific enzymes, formed under the control of the genes, are known to be necessary to maintain normal existence, pathological changes are to be expected if some of these genes are not providing their influences.

The involvement of enzymes in the chemicals of behavioral control can be studied in various ways. They can, for instance, be extracted and isolated from the tissues and can then be studied with the utmost precision. To do that, it is necessary to know exactly which enzymes to study and their characteristics. Another kind of enzyme analysis involves the isolation and identification of the products of enzyme activities. These chemical products of enzyme action can be found in the body fluids. Some of them can be isolated from the blood; others accumulate in the urine.

Some researchers have reported that in their samples there is less serotonin, a compound known to be associated with the activities of some cells of the nervous system, in the brains of schizophrenics than in brain tissue removed from non-psychotic persons. Other investigators have reported finding unusual protein substances in the blood and spinal fluid of schizophrenics. These compounds seem to precipitate behavioral changes in test animals. Several scientists have investigated a compound in the urine of schizophrenics on the basis of which they have developed the "pink spot" test. Still others have reported a high activity of copper-containing enzymes in the blood of schizophrenics. Studies have been reported in which massive doses of nicotinamide are apparently beneficial in the treatment of some schizophrenics.

Most of these research programs were designed to identify some common denominator among all schizophrenics which could then be used to diagnose schizophrenia and to distinguish it from other psychoses. This has not been accomplished. Despite the many research projects there is still no specific laboratory test able to identify a basic metabolic problem specific and common to all schizophrenics. If, as has been suggested by several investigators, schizophrenia can result from different biochemical anomalies, the search for detecting metabolic problems must continue but must not require that all schizophrenics share the same genetic flaw.

A layman's description of schizophrenia as "a disorder (of behavior, perception, and intellectual acuity) caused by stress beyond one's ability to cope" cannot define this tragic disorder, for no one has yet been able to do so to the satisfaction of all concerned. We have not yet gotten so far as general agreement on the diagnostic criteria for the disease. No good evidence is available to support the view that schizophrenia is a discrete disorder, or even that the name "schizophrenia" (which implies a split mind or split personality) is in any way appropriate. Different groups of psychiatrists, psychologists, and physiologists disagree with each other on its probable causes and on its treatment. They even disagree among themselves.

Unfortunately, disagreements about the name, the symptoms, the treatments, the diagnosis, and the causes do not make the problem go away. The symptoms of paranoia, catatonia, bizarre behavior, hallucinations, illusions, delusions, depersonalization, and the many other manifestations which together are usually diagnosed as "schizophrenia" cannot be ignored. It is impossible to dismiss these symptoms as if they did not exist. But treating the symptoms with drugs and without eliminating the cause of the problem is insufficient.

A diagnosis of schizophrenia by one clinician or even by a clinical group does not mean that naming the problem removes the ambiguities. In the medical history of virtually every patient a variety of prior, and even possibly conflicting, diagnostic terms have been applied. Such diagnoses may be "manic," "affective," or "schizoid." These are all descriptive terms. They describe behavior. Different kinds of behavior are not good criteria for distinguishing specific diseases.

It is not necessary to assume that all previous diagnoses were in error. The patient probably manifested different symptoms at some prior time. A thorough reading of the literature bears out the conclusion that names have been given to each kind of behavior which was not understood. Patients have been accorded different semantic diagnoses without clear-cut differentiation of their problems. For scientists as much as for laymen, it seems that euphemisms, like "mental disease" are often used to cover up ignorance. Phrases like "traumatic damage to the psyche" have been substituted for the "demons" of the medieval philosophers as the cause of unusual behavior and irrational thought. Furthermore, the behavior of schizophrenics cannot be said to be biologically abnormal or even biologically disadvantageous. Biologically inadequate adjustments lead to cellular deterioration and cell death. The behavior of the patients can be socially disruptive but still be biologically acceptable. Nevertheless, if there is some inheritable (genetic) "biological component" of schizophrenia that has been maintained in the human gene pool through prior generations, socially detrimental behavior could be tolerated only if it is physiologically beneficial.

Perhaps the behavior of the schizophrenic is the result of his best attempt to adjust himself to his individual physiological condition. Chronic schizophrenics seem to be shielded from the environment so that they do not respond to stresses. Perhaps some patients are better adjusted biochemically when they have developed symptoms which isolate them from part of their stress-inducing environment, the society in which they live.

Such considerations have led to other interpretations of what is generally called schizophrenia. If the behavior of a schizophrenic is evidence of his best accommodation to a physiological condition, the nervous system is not functioning the way it should. Since there is no characteristic anatomical identity which distinguishes the brain of a schizophrenic from that of a non-schizophrenic, the cells must be physiologically damaged. It is axiomatic in biology that damaged cells cannot function properly. In fact, physiologically damaged cells usually do not function at all. If damaged cells are not functioning, but the behavior is modified and the mental activities are disturbed, the behavior of the schizophrenic may result from a lack of some cellular regulation. Some cells are just not doing their job.

Traditionally, the control of the nervous system has been thought to be activated by various stimuli. The stimuli are believed to initiate the propagation of an impulse down the nerve pathway, and this impulse is thought to cause a release of a chemical "transmitter" from the end of the nerve cell axon to serve as the means of initiating a change in the next nerve in the path or changes in a muscle or a gland tissue. The transmitter (adrenalin is one of the well-known transmitter substances) then stimulates the nerve, or gland, or muscle to respond in its characteristic manner. This reasoning is the basis for all of the models of the nervous system in contemporary books and literature. In turn, the implications about nervous system regulation inherent in them have been incorporated into current interpretations of abnormal behavior disorders.

Recently it was discovered that some of the cells associated with the nerve cells throughout the nervous system secrete a chemical known as GABA (gamma amino butryic acid). This substance has been shown to depress or inhibit the transmission of impulses across synapses (spaces between nerve cells into which the impulse-inducing transmitters are secreted) to the next nerve cell. Such GABA-producing cells could be used to regulate the transmission and the pathways of the impulse. If nerve cells are held in check by the inhibitory action of GABA and controlled by hormones of the sympathetic nervous system, a new interpretation of the control of the nervous system and a new model of nervous system action and control can be proposed.

Perhaps the nerve cells are continuously discharging impulses at near-maximal rate but GABA inhibits the propagation of the impulse by inactivating the transmitter or the receptor cell in some manner. This is analogous to the design of an electronic organ. In an organ the tone generators are continuously forming the characteristic electronic signal for each and every note. Unless a key is depressed to break the circuit, this signal is kept grounded out. In the nervous system some changes in the environment of the cell may act to depress the formation of GABA. The GABA-producing cells could be deactivated so that they do not release this inhibitor (the term "disinhibited" can be applied to the nerve cells which are normally under GABA suppression) by a variety of conditions: the presence of transmitters from other regulatory cells of the brain; a deficiency of cellular fuel or an insufficiency of substrate (glutamic acid) from which GABA is synthesized; a deficiency of oxygen which could interfere with the availability of energy-containing compounds needed by the cells; or the presence of toxic products either from the improper conversion of cellular products or from drugs which affect the metabolism of the cells. A lack of GABA production and regulated release would promote erratic transmission of impulses. An "unloading" of impulses could be expected if GABA regulation is missing. This lack of nervous system control could be expected to result in bizarre mental processing of information and abnormal motor activity.

An example of this GABA control system may be helpful. Everyone is somewhat familiar with the physiology of drowning. When a person is under water and runs out of available oxygen, he inhales even though he knows that this will fill his lungs with water and cause his death. The higher centers of the brain which control thought patterns and voluntary actions can inhibit the lower, automatic reactions only just so long. When carbon dioxide accumulates and oxygen is depleted, involuntary breathing occurs. It may not be the presence of the CO_2 which stimulates the cells and reinitiates the breathing; it may instead be a lack of a necessary cellular commodity, oxygen, which influences the cellular regulation and results in the contraction of the diaphragm and the chest muscles involved in breathing. The oxygen depletion of the GABA cells may prevent these regulator cells from doing their normal job, and it is possible that when the GABA cells in part of the brain are inactivated, the impulses cascade, usually but not necessarily following normal pathways.

The suggestion that GABA inhibition of the brain may account for some kinds of schizophrenic behavior was recently made by Dr. Eugene Roberts of the City of Hope National Medical Center. He further postulated that the sympathetic nervous system is also specifically involved in the regulation of impulse transmission in the brain. It is known that a barrier between the blood stream and the brain cells prevents adrenalin from affecting the brain. Yet the brain has been shown to be highly sensitive to any adrenalin injected into its ventricles. Noradrenalin and dopamine, the precursors of adrenalin, are found in high concentrations in certain areas of the brain and seem to be the normal transmitters of many brain cells. The cells which synthesize noradrenalin could act like in-circuit inhibitors which would require the stimulation of these cells and the secretion of the noradrenalin into the synaptic space before certain normal pathways could be activated. A system of this nature would provide for facilitated action within the nervous system at times of stress. A stress condition which both inactivates the GABA cells and activates the noradrenalin-and dopamine-secreting cells could therefore be expected to promote bizarre behavior and erratic thought patterns.

GABA, noradrenalin, dopamine, serotonin, and other transmitters of the brain are discretely located in distinct areas of the brain. One region may have a high concentration of one of the transmitters but usually lacks some other transmitter whose function is similar but not identical. Some of the transmitters, such as noradrenalin and dopamine, are stimulatory. They cause the initiation of a nerve cell reaction by making the cell membrane permeable so that ions (charged molecules) can pass in or out of the cells. Other transmitters, such as GABA, are inhibitory. They prevent the stimulation of the cells. Many questions, however, remain unanswered.

All of the four transmitters listed above are synthesized by cells in the brain from amino acids. These amino acids must be supplied to the cells. In the case of GABA the amino acid called glutamic acid is the required substrate. It may be supplied to the cells as the acid or as glutamine, a molecule which is convertible to glutamic acid, or it can be made from sugar after the nitrogenous portion of the molecule is added. It is this conversion, the formation of GABA from sugar, that concerns us here. The body does not have a large store of free amino acids. Most of the amino acids are combined into proteins as structural parts of cells, enzymes, and some labile proteins which are mobilized, like the fats, as a part of the stress response. If no glycogen is available, the GABA can be formed only from glutamic acid. To get sufficient glutamic acid for GABA synthesis delivered to the brain takes time and a massive stress-response steroid release. If sugar is provided, the GABA will be made without the necessity of the steroid mobilization and their conversion of proteins to amino acids. If GABA is not formed, the nerve impulses can "cascade" through the brain.

The idea that nerve impulses can under certain conditions virtually pour through the brain is not completely unfamiliar to most people although they may be unaware of it. But if, upon awakening, one remembers a dream, he must usually make a very conscious and immediate effort to recall the details so that he will go on remembering it for a while. Otherwise he will forget the dream completely. During sleep he has not transferred any particular or consequential perceptions to his memory; therefore in the morning he has no difficulty in distinguishing the dream from reality. One can recognize that during sleep, somehow or other, he activated a portion of his subconscious and transferred his information to the recent-recall area of the brain. This constituted the memory of the dream in the morning. The retention of the dream requires reinforcement, since the brain is unable to store the information without some clue as to its origin. It is likely that we store visual imagery in a location different from the spot where we stock information obtained from the ear or from our tactile senses. If new information does not come by one of these routes but instead just arrives in the brain by some awakening of the subconscious, the brain will be unable to store it unless the dream content was of such impact that it became incorporated into the thinking and was stored as a conscious thought pattern.

Many schizophrenics encounter something analogous to a dreamlike state during their waking hours. Sometimes they experience a delusion when nothing in the environment initiates the event. Other times they perceive something. A bona fide stimulus is present, but they interpret it erroneously. This is called an illusion. Some schizophrenics mentally encounter a kaleidoscope of hallucinogenic manifestations while they simultaneously are aware of and partly conscious of some reality. In all of these cases, the inputs of information, both those of reality and those without reality, combine to form a hodgepodge of information in the recent recall portion of the brain. Information from the subconscious and the conscious are superimposed. It is difficult for these persons to distinguish what is true and what is false in their memory of either the moment immediately past or the completed event.

A memory that is untrustworthy, that cannot clearly distinguish what was real and what was irrationally and unpredictably transferred from the subconscious as a cascade of neural impulses, would certainly be stressful. We're back on the same bandwagon. In this situation the symptoms become part of a system which reinforces certain original physiological problems. If the illusions, delusions, and hallucinations originate from toxemia, intoxication, the effect of other drugs, or a deficiency of blood sugar to maintain the cells, they all act like a stress which would in turn act like an amplifier. More adrenalin would be secreted. More anxiety and tension would develop. The only stresses that most people have previously considered have been those from the en-

vironment, the society in which they live. Most of the
environmental stresses can be identified. Those that
cannot have been thought to come from those psychic
traumas which have been inferred but never truly quan-
tified. The behavior of the schizophrenic may be an
attempt to exclude all of these stresses.

Schizophrenia develops as a consequence of stress.
Despite the many differing orientations of the psychiatrists, psychologists, and physiologists who have
conducted research on affective disorders, of which
schizophrenia is one, there is unanimity of opinion on
that one conclusion alone. The various investigators
have reached this conclusion by different routes. They
have postulated different initiating stresses and different
stress-control problems as the cause of the stress. Stress
is a challenge. The stress response is a physiological
readjustment which is known to depend on the brain,
the pituitary gland, the adrenal gland, and the other
cells of the sympathetic system. It is also known that
stresses are additive. The emotional stresses are added
to the physiological stresses of infection, trauma, toxemia, and low blood sugar. It is not rational to focus
all of our attention on just one of these stresses. But
neither can we focus on just one portion of the stress
response. The stresses are not separable. One stress
can reinforce another stress. It is generally acknowledged that the stress of a low blood sugar is the most
frequent, consistent, and in some persons the most prolonged of the stresses. Hypoglycemia can initiate the
stress response which terminates as schizophrenia.

Perhaps it should be stated that all of the available
data suggests that hypoglycemia appears to be a sufficient, but not necessary, condition to initiate the physiological and behavioral changes which lead to a
diagnosis of schizophrenia. The skin disease pellagra
and other vitamin deficiencies can also induce behavioral changes. In such a case, when the vitamin is
properly supplied, the abnormal behavior subsides with
the healing of the skin lesions. In like manner, tumors
of the adrenal gland can lead to hypersecretion of

adrenal cortical steroid hormones. The presence of the excessive steroids in the blood induces the adrenal gland to secrete enormous amounts of adrenalin. Simultaneously the excess steroid hormones affect various cells throughout the body and cause both the conversion of stored fats to triglycerides and fatty acids, which leads to an oily skin, acne, ketosis and thus to a disturbing set of changes in the acidity of the body fluids, and the conversion of some cellular proteins into free amino acids for the repair of tissues and for further conversion into sugars. This changing of proteins into sugars, called gluconeogenesis by the physiologist, provides a buffer to prevent such a depletion of blood sugar that shock is imminent. It is the overmobilization of adrenalin by the steroid hormones that initiates the onset of classical schizophrenic behavior. All of the symptoms disappear when the adrenal tumor is surgically removed. The elimination of the schizophrenia symptoms when the vitamins are supplied to the pellagra victims and when the tumors of the adrenal gland are corrected gives hope to the proposal that correction of the stress condition for other varieties of schizophrenia will result in the complete remission of the symptoms of the psychosis. If physiological regulation can result in the abolition of symptoms in the varieties of schizophrenic behavior which are known to develop as a consequence of physiological function, the same can be expected for the schizophrenias that are initiated by the stress response to hypoglycemia.

Such drastic environmental stresses as war and natural catastrophes do not necessarily result in a direct increase in the number of diagnosed schizophrenia cases, but abnormal behavior called schizoid (schizophrenia-like but less pronounced than typical schizophrenia) and various neuroses are more common at such times. If the schizoid behavior is a direct result of the actions of the hormones of the sympathetic system, including the adrenalin from the adrenal medulla, superimposed on a deficiency of GABA, that some temporary behavioral disruptions as well as persistent abnormal behavior and symptoms could be expected.

Dietary limitations are common at times of war and following natural catastrophes. When food is scarce, the deficiency of protein in the diet, which could serve to provide for the synthesis of GABA if the blood sugar concentration is low, adds additional problems to the regulation of the nervous system. The foods available at such times are primarily carbohydrates. These carbohydrates are digested to glucose and cause the release of insulin. If adrenalin and insulin are present simultaneously, they are unable to regulate the storage and mobilization of blood sugars. Shortly after a meal some of the sugars spill over into the urine while others are stored as fat, but no liver glycogen is formed if the adrenalin level is high. This will lead to hypoglycemia as soon as the demand for sugar for the formation of GABA exceeds the ability of the liver to supply it.

A somewhat comparable situation exists in most hospitals and institutions charged with the care of schizophrenics and other psychotic persons. Budget restrictions prevent the administrators from providing nutritious high-protein, low-carbohydrate meals for the patients. The diet is primarily carbohydrate. It is hard to imagine a worse diet for a person who has a problem regulating the stress responses. The presence of a high glucose concentration in the blood following a high-carbohydrate meal will initiate a temporary diabetes-like condition if adrenalin is present. A later demand for glucose for the synthesis of GABA cannot be met if no glycogen has been stored. If depressants which interfere with adrenalin mobilization are used to suppress abnormal behavior, the lack of adrenalin action will result in a continuation of hypoglycemia, even if the insulin has caused the accumulation of glycogen, since adrenalin action is needed to reconvert this glycogen to glucose. In both cases the hypoglycemia is intimately involved in continuing behavioral problems.

These are not hypotheses which are subject to verification. They are well-known consequences of the homeostatic regulators of blood sugar concentrations. The only questions deal with the extent of the effect of these deleterious situations on the initiation and perpetuation of abnormal behavior.

Stress conditions and normal stress responses cannot be avoided. Interference with those normal responses prevents the development of some obvious behavioral difficulties but invariably introduces other unwanted, and frequently unrecognized, problems which cannot easily be eliminated. Many medications have such undesirable consequences. Both physicians and patients should be aware that treating and eliminating the symptoms can be expected to introduce problems which may be of a much more disastrous nature.

The logic presented in this book, which ties alcoholism, obesity, drug dependency, schizophrenia, and other disorders to the regulation of blood sugar, carries with it other implications. If the alcoholic can prevent the stress response by suppressing detection of the stress with the depressant drug alcohol, he may avoid schizophrenic symptoms as long as he is drinking. If overweight and obese people can keep their blood sugar level high by a constant intake of food, they may be able to prevent the onset of schizophrenic symptoms. It would follow, then, that fat people are not schizophrenic as often as those who are slender and who have not learned that they can eat their way from the stress of hypoglycemia if they pay the penalty of overweight. To put it another way, schizophrenic persons should tend to be skinny or slender and the number of fat schizophrenics should be very small. A visit to any schizophrenic ward will verify that.

Since the regulation of blood sugar concentration is so vital to the continuation of normal activities, the stress of low blood sugar should certainly be given priority in our treatment of psychotic illnesses. The first requirement is a complete diet which includes the proteins, fats, vitamins, and minerals necessary for good cellular metabolism. Although some glucose-producing carbohydrates can be judiciously included in the diet, the most reasonable dietary suggestion would be to substitute pure fructose for most of the carbohydrates and to meter this excellent hypoglycemia-preventing food in small amounts of regularly timed intake.

The mere provision of fructose and the elimination of the stress response to hypoglycemia cannot be expected to result immediately in the abolition of all schizophrenic symptoms. The schizophrenic learned the behavior he exhibits. He has practiced it well. Fructose will not carry with it an automatic trust and a resolve to interact openly with others. It will only provide an opportunity to relearn acceptable kinds of behavior. These cannot be imposed from the outside. Schizophrenic habits cannot be unlearned, but they can be replaced in time with good guidance.

Since the serious budgetary restrictions of most hospitals and institutions dictate a diet that contains a predominant proportion of easily digested carbohydrates, the major portions of protein are also obtained from vegetable sources. Although these are excellent proteins, they are available only in combination with large amounts of starch, which is also present in the food. It is highly unlikely that any institution could increase its provision of animal proteins (eggs, meat, fish, and cheese) sufficiently to afford a significant abolition of vegetable protein sources, which contain those undesirable insulin-inducing carbohydrates. The body can, and does, convert proteins into glucose by the process known as gluconeogenesis when proteins are present in large amounts. However, it does this only when the glucose concentration is low. If the glucose concentration is high, the excess proteins are stored as fat. A reduction in dietary carbohydrates must accompany an increase in protein intake to provide sugar for the brain from protein sources.

The mere addition of fructose to the diet without exchanging this slowly absorbed carbohydrate for the normal starches and sucrose may be of some benefit if it is provided between meals rather than with the meals. The psychological state of most institutionalized schizophrenics prevents them from recognizing that they should eat the meals that are provided even if they are not hungry because of the appetite-suppression effect of the fructose. This adds another complication since the primary advantage of fructose is the suppression of the stress of low cellular sugar which then leads to hunger. If the schizophrenic then bypasses the regular meals he is deprived of the proteins and other nutrients which cannot be provided by the fructose.

Because of the stress-response and stress-induction cycle problems which culminate in the expression of the anti-social behavior of the schizophrenic, a modification in diet can be expected to produce less dramatic results initially than those seen in the overweight, in alcoholics, or in those who are subject to migraine headaches. Schizophrenia certainly does not develop solely as a behavioral change to compensate for a deficiency of sugar for the brain cells. Many other stresses are also involved. Fructose can be expected only to regulate the one stress of an insufficiency of sugar for the cells of the nervous system. If the hallucinations, illusions, delusions, and abnormal thought patterns result from a sugar deficiency, the provision of fructose between meals, and particularly in the evening, may be of a real benefit. Unfortunately, fructose does not directly result in the abolition of abnormal behavior. It can be used to provide a constant source of fuel for the brain cells, but behavior has been learned and the provision of fructose will not automatically change that behavior. The provision of fructose may allow a person to modify behavior patterns, but the impetus to make these changes must come from rational processes unless we rely only on the suppressive effects of medication.

A convenient, nutritionally excellent, and relatively low-cost liquid lunch supplement can easily be made at home. This special eggnog is an excellent bedtime snack. All of the components are slowly absorbed. Although the drink is presented here particularly for schizophrenics, it is equally good for persons with migraine headaches or other problems of blood sugar management.

DAN'S SPECIAL EGGNOG

1 egg
2 ounces creamed or small-curd cottage cheese
1 tablespoon salad or cooking oil

1 tablespoon liquid fructose syrup (70% solids) or 4 teaspoons crystalline fructose
¼ cup cold water

Mix all ingredients in a blender at moderate speed. Add one of the flavorings listed below.

Flavorings to Taste

1. The traditional flavorings for eggnog of ¼ teaspoon vanilla and a pinch of nutmeg
2. 2 drops rum flavoring
3. 3 drops butterscotch flavoring
4. 3 drops artificial fruit flavoring or 1 tablespoon fresh strawberries, raspberries, or blueberries
5. 1 tablespoon cocoa or 3 drops chocolate flavoring
6. 1 tablespoon peanut butter with a drop or two of butter flavoring. The peanut butter will add another 4 grams of protein and 8 grams of fat without increasing the glucose carbohydrates appreciably.

The basic recipe provides 16 grams of protein, 20 grams of fat, and 16 grams of fructose as the carbohydrate. This provides 285 to 300 calories.

CHAPTER TWELVE

Sex and the Stress Response

Dramatic changes in patterns of sexual activities, extending from obvious increases in sexual demand to a rejection of sexual interaction, are intimately intertwined with the effects of the stress response. These changes in sexuality serve as a bridge between regarding psychoses as resulting from stress situations and inclining instead to various psychoanalytic theories of etiology of abnormal human behavior. In some situations these relationships are quite simple, under other conditions complex.

The most recurrent theme of all the theories of etiology of psychoses is the involvement of sex in most psychotic disorders. Certainly the most influential single contributor to our attitudes about normal interpersonal behavior and sexual responses was Sigmund Freud. Despite continuing controversy over the validity of his generalizations, he continues to color our thinking. Freud believed that "the factors arising in sexual life represent the nearest and practically the most momentous cause of every single case of nervous illness." His observations on sexual life and on psychosis encompassed both near-normal neuroses and the degenerative diseases of the brain. They are part of the common ground of psychiatry.

Many contemporary psychoanalysts take a more liberal attitude. The regard sexuality as one facet of the personality, as a single component of one's view of oneself and of others in which certain basic compulsions or drives are manifested. If it is true that the emotional energy connected with those basic drives fosters some kind of accommodation or discharge, then sexual activity, like other behavior, can be generated by excessive tension, anxiety, and other overt symptoms of pathology.

The depth and severity of psychopathology are suggested by defects in interpersonal relations. At first glance these may appear normal but their real nature is revealed by the compulsive, often obsessive, anxiety-ridden, and at times hysterical overtones that color each human encounter. Sexuality becomes a bridge to others. It serves as a mode of introduction. It may be a means of injecting oneself into a new societal framework. Sexuality is primarily physical. It may be partially or wholly devoid of its human, warm, and empathy-providing qualities. To some it can be a non-emotional vehicle to "burn off" tension. It seems to be a way of reaching out physically while remaining emotionally detached.

Many people have an intense need for an experience capable of dissipating this huge emotional charge. Sex, with its strong potential for defusing tensions, becomes a safety valve, a convenient method of externalizing conflict, of allaying anxiety, and of providing the individual with temporary relief from his problems. It has become a "do it yourself" psychotherapy, used to release emotional energy built up by the unremitting sequence of tension-producing events undergone day after day. While tranquilizers can do the same thing temporarily, sex produces a short-term profound anesthesia. It solves no problems, but—even though it consumes cellular energy—it represses the release of sympathetic system hormones until climax or ejaculation. When the circulatory system is swamped with noradrenalin and adrenalin, the blood sugar concentration rises rapidly but the enzymatic products of the hormones may act as depressants. They may repress additional adrenalin release. The initial sympathetic response is massive but of short duration. Homeostasis is re-established. Only then is there internal calm and repose. Most adults have learned that the more intense the stress problem the more frenetic is the sexual activity and the greater is the relief from tension.

It is almost fruitless to debate whether sexuality is the primary or secondary reaction in the development of emotional and mental disorders. Responses to one stress condition can establish the basis for other stresses and additional physiological changes and reactions. However, since sexuality is one aspect of life and may reflect other physiological and emotional malfunctions, new interpretations of its role in emotional disorder should always be considered. Sexual life is quite an accurate barometer of physiological-emotional adjustment. Its level may rise and fall depending on the current set of conflicts, turmoil, or physiological-homeostatic problems.

A sudden increase in sexual desire may be wholly physiological. It might be caused, for instance, in older women by an infection of the genital membranes (senile pruritus) or in men by an irritation of the urethra. It is common in disorders of the temporal lobe of the brain which develop from a nervous system malfunction initiated by tumor, degeneration, or infection of the brain coverings (encephalitis), general paresis, or other changes in the brain. Such instances of hyperlibido are almost exclusively restricted to people beyond middle age who are generally less active sexually than younger people.

Heightened sexual responsiveness has been reported following the use of such stimulants as amphetamine and its related compounds and cocaine. Certain of the metabolic actions of these drugs allow their classification as sympathomimetics, which mimic the action of noradrenalin and adrenalin. Other drugs seem actually to increase adrenalin secretion. Some experimental data also indicate a strong link between anger and sexual motivation: aggression seems to be an attribute of the particular stress response which raises both sexual appeal and appetite in both sexes under experimental conditions. Thus, increased aggressive tendencies may directly lead to increased sexual motivation. A general rise in stress factors, and hence an increased stress response in an entire population, would be expected to be accompanied by an increased amount of sexual activity. It is difficult to garner statistics, but an increase in sexual activities at time of war can be inferred from increased birth rate. The sexual appetite of soldiers following a battle has been documented throughout all of history; it certainly seems to be a result of the stress factors they have just endured. It is, of course, also true that they have been away from their wives and homes for some time. The apparent increase in sex drive may be a normal demand which cannot be satisfied in the normal manner.

A continued increase in the stress response can eventually produce the exact opposite effect, the rejection of sexual activity. It can be expected when a heightened release of noradrenalin and adrenalin prevents the blood flow to the sex organs in the quantity required to continue the sex act. Diminution of blood flow to the peripheral tissues can prevent the erection of the penis of the male and of the clitoris of the female, inhibiting consummation by reducing the stimulation necessary for orgasm.

The most common cause of a real increase in sexual desire and activity is mania or the subacute disorder which we can call hypomania. (This term, implying a low-level mania, is used to extend the idea of hyperactivity up to the pathological behavior which would be classified as mania.) The changes which occur during a hypomanic episode may be barely perceptible. Indeed, an increase in sexual desire and activity may be the very first sign of the onset of some manic illness which, when the sexual desire is only mildly intensified, is accompanied by very desirable changes in the behavior of the affected person. There usually is an increased sociability, an increase in productivity, and extended economic drive. While such persons may first have only a resurgence of sexual interest in his or her normal partner, there may also be an elevation in the level of instinctual energies accompanied by an appetite for new relationships. When a new partner is found in such circumstances, the social and sexual life mirror the progression of the manic state. When mild hypomanic episodes occur in middle-aged individuals, this is usually interpreted psychologically as panic of aging, and is interpreted so partly because the sex hormones decrease with age in many (though not all) persons. However, interest in new and younger partners, particularly when paralleled by increased energy and assertiveness in other areas, usually means that an elevated mood state is the driving force behind the behavior. Sometimes, of course, these manic episodes are mild, subside within a reasonably short period of time, and are not followed or preceded by depressive episodes. As a result, all that is apparent to the external observer is the shedding of an old partner and the acquisition of a new one.

When changes in sexual behavior and desire for a new partner are observed in persons with pathologically altered mood states, it should be emphasized that such behavior is not always the result of manic-depressive illness. Indeed, in the absence of past history of mood swings or a family history of manic-depressive illness, the identification of hypomania may be difficult to make. This is particularly true in young persons for whom such elevations of mood are almost all physiological expressions which follow directly the discovery of a new partner.

Exactly the opposite is true of a drastic decrease in sexual drive. Diminution of sexual activity in a young person may be the earliest sign of depression. This is of far less significance in middle-aged or older persons, who commonly experience a temporary decrease in sex drive in response to a wide variety of physical and physiological changes.

A heightening of the sexual drive in both sexes as the result of mania does not necessarily lead to an increase in sexual satisfaction. In some cases the increased aggressiveness may, in the male, only mean that novel experiences are necessary to him to reinforce the physiological regulation which can compensate for an impotence that occurs after adrenalin triggered by the stress response has swamped the nervous system. Impotence is a common problem of men who are drinking heavily even if they are not classified as alcoholics. In this circumstance it is impossible to separate the stress response from the depressive effect of the alcohol.

In the female an increased sex drive initiated in a hypomanic episode is frequently called nymphomania. It isn't all fun and games. The behavior is usually misunderstood. Nymphomania is not the final and top grade of desirable female sexuality. The list of sex responses does not proceed from cold, balanced and warm, sensual, hypersexual, to nymphomania. Nymphomania is a disorder. It is an insatiable drive for sex. Yet the most common or frequent characteristic of nymphomania is frigidity. Orgasm incapacity is the medical term for this condition. It is a lack of sex satisfaction. Nymphomaniacs need sexual gratification, but many admit an inability to achieve orgasm during intercourse although they desperately demand sex. The nymphomaniac's drive is to all men in a hope that one will satisfy her. Some recognize their sex drive to be associated with their inability to gain relief. Others delude themselves into thinking they possess an insatiable erotic drive. Life for them becomes a frenzied effort to act out a false sex-starved image.

No more than the kleptomaniac steals for love of stealing or the dipsomaniac drinks for the love of the taste of liquor does the nymphomaniac go to bed with almost any male because she loves sex. It may be an escape into sex to attempt or to get relief from deeper troubles. Sex is no real pleasure for her. She isn't satisfied. Because she recognizes that sexual intercourse should give her some relief from her drive, she appears to demand constant admiration from others. Although it is commonly thought that she gives herself to men for the narcissistic, childish reason of wishing men to admire her in bed, and that she is therefore emotionally immature, her behavior, like the behavior of a schizophrenic, is more accurately viewed as an inadequate or inappropriate accommodation to a physiological problem.

Depending on their prior experiences and on their awareness of their current lack of satiation, the hypomanic drive in some women may lead away from nymphomania to a complete rejection of sex activity. An initial sexual stimulus followed by a lack of satisfaction can add just one more stress. In this situation, instead of sex being a safety valve for the stress response, it becomes an added stress. Frigidity can be more than a manipulation of a sex partner for personal emotional gain. It can be an ineffective response of an emotionally detached but compliant woman as well as an attribute of those who are hostile, vindictive, and aggressive. It can be a response learned to hide a strong desire to be needed and loved. Yet this response is modified by the frustrations which follow a physiological lack of satisfaction in sexual acts.

The possibility that sexual responsiveness can be a direct outgrowth of the stress response is a new proposition. Psychiatrists, who initially may be unwilling to accept the premise that a hereditary predisposition or specific genetic problem of blood sugar regulation is involved in the development of schizophrenia, will frequently accept the idea that at least two genetic types of depressive illnesses exist. Although the genetic mechanism is not specified, undoubtedly it involves the regulation of the sympathetic nervous system. In the first type, called unipolar (recurrent depressive illness), there is no associated mania. In this disorder the depressive episodes are characterized by anxiety, agitation, a lack of ability to sleep, and a profound decrease in sex drive. In the second type of affective disorder, called bipolar (sometimes called manic-depressive illness), there is usually a personal or family history of periodic mania. The depressive periods are characterized by an obvious lack of energy, an excessive demand for sleep, and a loss of sexual interest. The periods of mania are associated with restlessness, irritability, hyperactivity, and a distinct increase in sex demand. With the exception of the references about sexual responsiveness, the symptoms of these disorders are wholly reminiscent of those associated with classic hypoglycemia, which is followed by the adrenalin-mediated stress response to the deficiency of blood sugar.

A third variety of depressive illness is known which fits midway between the diagnostic characteristics of the monopolar and bipolar varieties. This third type of disorder manifests itself as recurrent depressive episodes of fatigue accompanied by outbursts of crying, feelings of worthlessness, self-recrimination, isolation, and occasional suicidal thoughts. The only emotional stability these persons really know is a constancy of the unacceptable depressed state. They have discovered that they temporarily feel better when they are constantly stimulated. Like some juveniles, they require repetitive praise and reinforcement. Many of the stimuli they experience are stressful. These persons actually seem to seek out stress situations instead of seeking to escape from stress. They go looking for trouble. If their social environment is not sufficiently stimulating they create their own stress. They may become inveterate and incessant gamblers because the excitement fulfills their need for stress. They get as much from losing as from winning. Students with this variety of depressive disorder sometimes enroll in college courses that do not conform to their native abilities just to. get the added support of the stress of such situations. These students want others to know that they are taking the hardest courses in the college and are stimulated by the awe which these courses inspire in others. Some set unrealistic goals for themselves and some of those do strive to perform beyond their capabilities. Others will pick fights or tease to promote aggressive responses, both sexual and non-sexual. Such persons reject any comfort and sympathy when they are depressed although they wish others to know of their depression.

They don't suffer in silence. They become cantankerous, irritable, and spiteful. They get picky. They complain about inconsequential circumstances or they invent problems. They distort and warp what others say and thus isolate themselves. They are argumentative and intractable. They seem unwilling to accept a cogent logic that opposes their current feelings about social situations, but they may seem to be extremely hard-working and dedicated to their jobs.

The personalities of such people are like yoyos, up and down, again and again. To those with whom they have casual contact they may seem to be ebullient, effusive, and vivacious. To members of their families, supervisors, and close associates they can be sarcastic, insensitive to the feelings of others, and almost vindictive and paranoiac.

Within hours of an emotional manic outburst they can be on the verge of the physical and emotional collapse of the depressed state. It seems as if they have no emotional balance point. They vacillate erratically between deep depression and hyperactivity. They reject sex at both emotional extremes although they may foster sexual activity during the transition from the depressed state to the anxious, somewhat irrational, mean, loud, and obnoxious behavior which characterizes the manic phase. They may use their sexuality not as an emotional release but as a stress promoter. This sex drive may be directed to others outside of their normal relationships to insure the continuation of the stress stimuli. They are attention grabbers and thus revel in the attention given some sexual activities.

The period of time from depression to hypomania may extend over several to many days. Following each manic phase a depressive state develops rapidly, usually within a day. The length and magnitude of each phase are not consistent. These parameters depend on emotional and physical characteristics because of the physiological components of the stress response.

Many of these persons go on eating binges when they

are in the depressed state. They usually prefer ice cream, candy, or cake although they seem to be aware that such foods will precipitate a return of depression. On the other hand, possibly to compensate for the feeling of well-being they temporarily experience after the intake of carbohydrates, they may subject themselves to virtual starvation diets when they are in the manic phase. As expected, this promotes a re-establishment of the stress response. It is this characteristic which suggests a relationship between the disorder and hypoglycemia.

The management of this disorder is more difficult than the other varieties of depressive illness because constancy is not desirable to those who have it. They try to avoid extreme stress since they recognize that this leads to the recurrence of the depressed state, but they are unsatisfied without some hyperactivity which then, because of the stress-response cycle, keeps them off balance.

Fortunately the severity of most cases of emotional and psychic disorders does not justify a diagnosis of schizophrenia or manic-depressive psychosis. These names have such a stigma attached to them that most diagnosticians hesitate to apply them except in the most compelling situations. The abnormalities of the sexual activities are only components of the symptomatology of these disorders.

If the stress-response secretion of adrenal cortical hormones results in a change or overbalancing of androgenic hormones over the estrogenic hormones, some changes occur in the female sexual organs. It is the ratio of the androgenic hormones to the female hormones, estrogen and progesterone, rather than their absolute concentrations, which affects behavior. Excessive androgens in the female can lead to fibrosis of the clitoris and labia, together with a decrease in the secretions of the vagina. This would normally only be associated with a prolonged disruption of menses, acne, and skin pustules accompanied by an oily skin and a general increase in body hair. High androgen concentrations in the female would be expected to increase aggressiveness and thus increase the sexual drive. At the same time they would disrupt the normal satisfaction from sexual intercourse. Whereas the manic or hypomanic disorders are associated with an increased sex appetite, the schizophrenic, in his or her rejection of society, usually does not respond to sexual stimuli.

A high frequency of psychotic disorders, which individually are somewhat less onerous than schizophrenia or classic manic-depressive illness, may collectively cause society more problems. If the burden to society is calculated by the number of work hours lost, the less dramatic psychoses may be more detrimental to society than the severe disorders. Psychotic episodes which are lightly passed off as depression, anxiety, hypochondriasis, involutional melancholia, or hypomania affect a substantial portion of the population at one time or another. The criteria for distinguishing one of these behavioral or psychotic conditions from another are arbitrary. They grade almost imperceptibly from one to another as well as changing intensity, and they constitute a large bulk of the work load of psychiatrists and counselors.

The symptoms of many of these disorders can be relieved with drugs. In turn, psychiatrists expect the best prognoses when treating these problems. Psychotherapy and various medicines are combined in their treatment. Some of the drugs used for treatment of depression inhibit the enzymatic destruction of noradrenalin and adrenalin. For other diseases the prescribed drugs mimic the sympathetic nervous system hormones, noradrenalin and adrenalin. Steroid therapy is often used for some varieties of depression. These steroids, like the natural adrenal cortex steroids, cause adrenalin release as one of their actions. Many drugs which are used to depress or decrease anxiety deplete the body of much of its adrenalin store so their is no hormone available when demanded as a part of the stress response. Certain others suppress the responsiveness of the cells to the noradrenalin and adrenalin when these hormones are secreted. In every such case the drugs may be expected to cause changes in sexual responsiveness. Depressive drugs are expected to decrease sex drive, while stimulants normally increase it.

If persons for whom these medications are prescribed were not having problems in regulating blood sugar concentration before they began taking them, many of the drugs may be expected to precipitate difficulties. Drugs which mimic the sympathetic system hormones may interfere with insulin action. This would prevent the storage of glucose as liver glycogen, which can be reconverted to sugar when the blood glucose concentration is low. Drugs which deplete the body of adrenalin actually can suppress, if not eliminate, the body's normal ability to raise the blood sugar level by decreasing the conversion of glycogen to glucose. In any case of drug therapy the intention is to abolish or decrease the undesirable behavior. Drugs are not intended to eliminate the causes of the mood and behavior shifts.

As in all of the other disorders considered in this book, there is no previous specific evidence which requires the conclusion that a deficiency in the blood sugar is any more than a complicating stress which is added to all of the other stresses encountered in the physical environment and from the emotions. But it is possible that the stress response to a deficiency of blood sugar for the cells of the brain is an initiating condition which precipitates the changes in mood and behavior that disrupt the lives of many persons. The ability to reduce this problem, to eliminate the stress and therefore to depress the stress responses which are regulated by the steroid and sympathetic hormones, by a simple dietary regimen is exciting to anticipate. It is almost mandatory to eliminate the stress of blood sugar regulation as a contributing factor in psychotic disorders of all descriptions. No one should expect that a dietary program which merely substitutes fructose for most of the other carbohydrates of the diet will automatically make for a satisfactory sex life. Similarly, no one can expect a satisfactory sexual life if the stress responses to any stress condition disrupt the necessary homeostatic adjustments.

Advantageous changes in the sex drive, abolition of excess facial and body hair in females with high androgen ratios, resolution of all the problems of impotence and frigidity, and the disappearance of oily skin and acne eruptions cannot be expected as immediate consequences of a dietary change which prevents a deficiency of sugar supply to cells of the nervous system. Since it is acknowledged that these physical and psychological problems are distinctly stress-related and that the only known way to eliminate the stress of functional hypoglycemia or a deficiency of sugar absorption ability among unregulated diabetics is a provision of additional protein and fructose, dietary changes are indicated for persons with these problems. If one is overweight the dietary suggestions given at the end of Chapter Nine should do double duty. If a person follows a calorie-deficient diet with adequate proteins and fructose as the primary carbohydrate, he should relieve the stress of an insufficiency of sugar for the brain, lose weight, and reduce the stresses which contribute to these other problems. Indications of abnormal fat metabolism (oily skin, bad breath caused by exhaling ketones associated with some of these conditions) lead to the suggestion that some people may benefit from a decrease in fat in their diet. Certainly all fat should not be eliminated. A good rule of thumb may be to limit fat intake to the amount provided in the diet for weight loss. Additional protein can be included to prevent weight loss, or these persons may be able to tolerate a very normal and average amount of mealtime carbohydrates such as milk, grain products, and starchy vegetables; nevertheless, they should shy away from starchy and sucrose-laden between-meal snacks and substitute fructose instead.

Sample Menu Pattern*   *Sample Meal*

Breakfast

1 bread or cereal group	1 cup high-protein granola
1 milk group	½ cup whole milk
1 fruit	½ cup fresh strawberries
1 meat group	1 cup yogurt (Mash the strawberries and mix with the yogurt. Add sucrose to sweeten to taste.)
Coffee or tea if desired	Coffee or tea (sweeten with fructose)

Lunch

3 meat group: fish, beef, pork, poultry	1 cup clam chowder (commercial ready-to-serve)
1 vegetable	4 ounces tuna canned in oil, drained, in salad with lettuce and celery
1 fat or oil	1 tablespoon salad dressing or mayonnaise
Coffee or tea if desired	Coffee or tea (sweeten with fructose)

Dinner

2 vegetable-fruit group	½ cup tomato-vegetable cocktail
3 meat group: fish, beef, pork, poultry	2 large slices roast beef (6 ounces)
1 fat or oil	1 cup cooked cauliflower with 1 tablespoon melted butter

---

* Table 1 lists foods in groups of exchanges to maintain total nutritional adequacy. See pages 22–25.

Unrestricted foods (those
    which provide no insulin-
    inducing carbohydrates)

Carrot sticks
Gelatine salad flavored
    with lemon juice and a
    bit of grated lemon peel
    mixed with fructose. Firm
    gelatine can be cut into
    ½-inch cubes and glazed
    with sour cream and
    crystal fructose.

Dessert (fructose-sweetened
    but low content of
    insulin-inducing carbo-
    hydrates)

1 serving Lemon Sponge
    (Chapter Three)

Between meals eat additional fructose as candies or in beverages to provide approximately 20 grams of additional carbohydrate each day beyond the amount included in the diet listed here.

CHAPTER THIRTEEN

Other Stress-Related Disorders

There is no published list of all the disorders which are stress-related. This is not because few persons are aware of the stress-response component of many health problems. The list is not available because stress is so all-pervasive that it is a component of all disease states. Included in such a list would be disorders in which the symptoms, both physiological and behavioral, are exaggerated under conditions of stress. The symptoms may come from the stress condition itself, from the steroids and adrenalin which are secreted, or from an insufficiency of steroid and adrenalin secretion. Thus this list should include all of the disorders which are treated with adrenalin or with drugs which mimic its action. It would also include all disorders treated by inhibiting the enzymatic destruction of adrenalin as well as those in which the action of the drug is intended to decrease the adrenalin secretion (as is the case with many tranquilizers). The list would include all disorders that are medically treated by steroid therapy, primarily the steroids of the adrenal cortical variety but also those whose actions closely parallel the gonadal hormones.

The management of all such disorders, regardless of their initial cause, requires an effective decrease of the stress conditions. Since all stresses, including the stress of low blood sugar, rely on the sequential action of the hypothalamus, pituitary, adrenal cortex, and adrenal medulla, the abolition of any stressful condition would be beneficial.

Many persons who suffer from a stress-related disorder have normal blood sugar concentration. This cannot be cited as evidence that there is no defect in the management of the blood sugar. It may instead be evidence that these persons are naturally and effectively adjusting. Yet, by responding to this necessity of blood sugar regulation, they may be secreting large amounts of steroids and adrenalin, which then provide the conditions for the onset of other disorders. As an example, if adrenalin secretion is required for management of the blood sugar concentration of a person with hardening of the arteries, the effect of the adrenalin on the blood pressure and heart rate is just as detrimental as if the stress came from some physical exercise or severe emotional trauma. Although the blood sugar may be kept within the optional range, the other effects of the adrenalin are potentially disastrous. The end result of any stress to some persons may involve tissue damage or modification that is quite remote from the actual stress response. Under certain conditions the homeostatic regulation of one system may produce dire consequences in some other organ or body system.

An accumulation of cholesterol together with some mineral salts in the linings of the blood vessels leads to the condition of atherosclerosis or hardening of the arteries. We have no specific system within our bodies to detect the cholesterol concentration in the blood so that it can be regulated by a separate homeostatic system. Instead, we synthesize cholesterol whenever fat fragments accumulate in the blood sera, the fluid portion of the blood. Cholesterol is the substrate from which we synthesize steroid hormones and bile salts. When steroid hormones are mobilized, they cause fat cells to release triglycerides into the blood. These fat fragments are good energy sources for most of the cells of the body. Bile salts are needed to absorb dietary fats. Some steroid hormones are lost across the kidney tubules into the urine, and bile is lost in the feces. These molecules must be replaced. Since they are synthesized from cholesterol, the body uses the presence of the high concentration of fats as the signal to synthesize cholesterol from these materials. The stress response therefore initiates cholesterol synthesis. An accumulation of excess cholesterol provides for the eventual hardening of the arteries. If the stress responses are depressed, and food intake regulated, cholesterol synthesis can be decreased. Both of these effects can be accomplished with fructose.

Hyperkinesis is a diagnostic term applied to highly active, aggressive young children who have a very short attention span, who have difficulty in concentrating, who, because they seem "like time bombs that are ready to go off," frequently get into trouble at school and at home. Very young hyperactive children shake their cribs and playpens until the furniture breaks. When they are older, they may rock themselves back and forth as they pound their heads against the wall. For several years it was common to give these children tranquilizers to reduce these symptoms. The drugs were intended to decrease the secretion of adrenalin. In most cases no specific improvement in the child's behavior was noted. They still threw tantrums. They still flitted from one activity to another. They still had difficulty with reading and seemed to "tune out" even when given oral instructions. It was then discovered that when these children were given amphetamines, the "speed" drug which has also been used for dieting, their attention span and behavior actually improved. In other words, a drug which is normally expected to increase activity acted in these children as if it were a depressant or a tranquilizer. The amphetamines are drugs which mimic the action of adrenalin. They are adrenalin-like. They produce most of the same effects as pure adrenalin. It is unlikely that the beneficial effect of the amphetamines in the hyperactive children is due to the associated increase of blood pressure and heart rate. The decreased motility of the digestive tract would not seem to be of any specific benefit. The sole advantage of the amphetamines seems to be their action in promoting the conversion of glycogen to glucose.

Nearly everyone now knows that amphetamines are

rather dangerous drugs. Excessive use or overdose of amphetamines is known to have caused damage to the nervous system and may cause death. In the vernacular of the street people, "Speed fries brains." This drug therapy for the hyperactive-hyperkinetic child is not to be taken lightly.

If the primary or exclusive beneficial effect of the amphetamines for the hyperkinetic child is the adjustment of the blood sugar level, this effect can be better accomplished by providing a good diet in which fructose is substituted for most of the other carbohydrates. A number of children have learned that they are much better socially adjusted when they have chewed a few fructose tablets occasionally throughout the day. The primary benefit is that fructose is slowly absorbed from the digestive tract and does not induce insulin release. This provides the sugar requirement over a long period of time. The metabolic rate of hyperkinetic children is high. They burn off a lot of energy in their incessant activity. To provide this amount of energy in an initial treatment program requires over 100 grams per day, perhaps much more than this.

The mere provision of fructose does not solve all the problems of hyperkinesis. Even with fructose it is necessary for these children to form new habits and to repair the deficiencies in their learning habits which developed when their behavior was so erratic. Fructose cannot be expected to turn every rambunctious child into an angel. At the same time, no one should punish a child for being hyperactive if the child has learned that he is physiologically better adjusted if he maintains a near-constant physical activity which then promotes an increase in available adrenalin and an increase in blood glucose from the conversion of glycogen. (These children seem to have learned a variation of the lesson of the alcoholic and the overweight who develop behavior to regulate their stress response to hypoglycemia even if the side effects are detrimental.) Some of their rather bizarre behavior can also be the result of their being ostracized by their parents, schoolteachers, and even playmates because of their continuous disruptive activity. Psychotherapy will be needed to correct such problems. But if the original problem came from the stress response to a low blood sugar, psychological therapy without dietary management will have little chance for success. Not only must there be control of the blood sugar but, as with hypomania and manic disorders, more information is needed about the effect of the adrenal cortical hormones in promoting aggression.

A variation on this same theme can be found among adults. Some compulsive gamblers apparently need high emotional stimulation. If they drink or overeat continuously, they can reduce their otherwise insatiable demand for stress. It would seem as if these persons require external stresses to accomplish the necessary adjustment in blood sugar level. People who feel better if they take a long brisk walk when they are nervous are not burning off excess energy. They are, in effect, increasing available energy by causing the conversion of glycogen to glucose and the mobilization of fats and amino acids as a part of the stress response to their physical activity. A measure of the blood sugar, triglycerides, and amino acids after the walk shows that these are higher than before. It seems that everyone has learned how to help himself to some extent but most people have no idea why their devices do help. At best they generally offer only an inaccurate piece of armchair psychology.

Peptic ulcers are products of stress. Whenever stress causes adrenalin release sufficient to inhibit the motility of the digestive tract, the possibility of ulceration is increased. Unless there are sufficient foods and bulk in the digestive tract to "tie up" the active digestive enzymes and juices, these secretions begin to work on the cells lining the digestive cavities. In this instance it is impossible to indict hypoglycemia for ulceration of the digestive tract. It is also impossible to eliminate this possibility. All stresses are additive. They all result in the secretion of the adrenal cortical steroids and adrenalin secretion. Steroids are known to inhibit the healing of both internal and external ulcerations. Decreasing hypoglycemia-inducing carbohydrates in the diet of an ulcer patient would have the advantage of decreasing the steroid secretion and thus decreasing the adrenalin release. Even if other stress conditions appear to have initiated the ulcer, the patient should be particularly careful to avoid the stress-response hormones which would accompany any low blood sugar condition.

Impotence is believed to be a stress-response syndrome. Usually it has been treated by psychiatry, not drugs, in an attempt to reduce the stress which led to this problem. Since adrenalin is known to decrease the blood flow to the exterior of the body and since the external genital organs are supplied blood from these peripheral vessels, they receive less blood under conditions of stress. A stress condition usually prevents erection of the penis of the male. In essence this would be impotence. The same is true for the female, but the erection of the clitoris is not as obvious as the erection of the penis of the male. A deficiency in erection of these organs prevents normal sex acts by the male and prevents orgasm in the female. Since impotence is a frequent complaint of alcoholics and others who have some drinking or eating problem, the actual cause of the adrenalin release must be a hidden physiological stress such as hypoglycemia.

Almost all varieties of circulatory disorders are in one way or another related to the stress response. (This has been the prime area of research for Dr. Hans Selye. His book, *The Stress of Life,* details most of what is known about the relationship between stress and the heart and blood vessels.) In addition it must be remembered that the steroid secretion portion of the stress response causes the release of triglycerides from fat storage which then results in the secretion of cholesterol. The adrenalin increases the blood pressure and thus triggers an increase in the heart rate. The steroids from the adrenal cortex cause the reabsorption of sodium and the subsequent retention of water but allow the loss of potassium into the urine. The relative changes in these ions affect the cells of the heart detrimentally. The stress response is also responsible for the regulation of some of the blood coagulants which get involved in the various circulatory system diseases.

It is almost mandatory for persons with angina pectoris, arteriosclerosis, and other problems of the heart and blood vessels to reduce their stress responses as much as possible. One of the best tests now used in our hospitals to determine the extent of heart attack damage measures the activity of enzymes which break down and build up tissues. After a heart attack, the dead cells of the affected portion of the heart wall must be removed and new cells of scar tissue put in their place. Since steroid hormones normally interfere with scar tissue formation, this repairing of the heart requires a new regulation of these hormones. In some unknown way a heart attack serves as a signal to the body both to reduce the amount of steroid hormones that are delivered from the adrenal cortex into the circulating blood and to decrease the noradrenalin secreted by the cells of the sympathetic nervous system. Whereas most persons show a fluctuation in the amount of these hormones throughout the day, this variation is almost entirely missing shortly after a heart attack.

Victims of a heart attack are in physiological depression. The decrease in the steroids and in noradrenalin and adrenalin prevents them from raising their blood sugar level when this would be advantageous. They fatigue easily. Their threshold of emotional response is lowered. They rarely get angry but exhibit the irritability of depression. Many cry easily. These are physiological responses, not just emotional control changes. Since they may soon need to raise their blood sugar level, it is safest to prevent the depletion of the blood sugar in the first place. If the blood sugar level is optimal, the rate of recovery will increase and the psychological problems associated with a heart attack will be minimized. This regulation is possible with the fructose-exchange diet.

Some physicians consider the allergies as psychosomatic problems. This is not to imply that the allergies arise as defects in the control of the nervous system but that allergic symptoms of some persons become exaggerated under conditions of stress. Such symptoms would be expected if these persons were in some way deficient in their ability to secrete sufficient adrenalin to compensate for the histamine released by cells responding to the presence of allergins. Allergies are frequently treated by providing adrenal steroid, adrenalin, or drugs which have the same action as adrenalin. It may be correct, therefore, to say that allergies are disorders of adrenalin insufficiency. A molecule of adrenalin does not do one job in one cell and then accomplish another job in some other tissue. Adrenalin is inactivated after it has entered a cell and affected the cell's metabolism. If a deficiency of adrenalin release allows the histamine to work, the symptoms will be swollen membranes of the nasal passages with a copious flow of secretions, constriction of the bronchi, hives, eczema, itching eyes, sinus headaches, sneezing, and perhaps asthma. If a stress situation demands a response, this adrenalin will not be available to counteract the histamine. Certainly, if a deficiency of adrenalin exists, it would be best to prevent hypoglycemia so that all of the available adrenalin can be used to prevent allergic reactions. Fructose is not an antihistamine or an adrenalin-release drug. It can be used to maintain the optimal blood sugar level so that adrenalin is not required for this action.

The tremor of the hands of some older persons with a disorder that is frequently called Parkinson's disease is usually increased under conditions of stress or when fatigue is evident. This tremor is not unlike the shaking hands of an alcoholic the morning after a drinking bout. The current theory is that the tremor is caused by a deficiency of some cellular substrate for cells of the brain involved in the motor control areas. In some cases of Parkinson's tremor, the condition results from a circulatory restriction. Such a defect may become evident after a cerebral hemorrhage. In other cases a hardening of the arteries without an actual stroke is suspected. The disorder may result from a deficiency of GABA in the cells of the brain's motor areas. This could result from a deficiency of either sugar or oxygen supply. The tremor could come from metabolic intermediates resulting from a deficiency of the circulation to particular parts of the brain, allowing accumulation of toxic cell products. Many patients who have the symptoms of Parkinsonism have recently been effectively treated with large doses of L-Dopa, a synthetic drug converted by nervous system cells into dopamine. Dopamine is the precursor molecule in the synthesis of noradrenalin and may itself be a transmitter of the brain. It has been suggested that a deficiency of Dopa, because of an insufficiency of enzymatic activity, prevents in these persons the normal regulatory action of dopamine and noradrenalin in the brain. If this interpretation is correct, the tremor is not the result of muscle tonus induced by adrenalin but is a more direct effect of the deficiency of a regulatory cell substrate, dopamine. If such a deficiency exists, the synthesis of adrenalin will also be inhibited. This would decrease the likelihood of effective adrenalin release for glycogen conversion to glucose. The stress of hypoglycemia in these persons would add to their problems. Adding fructose to the diet will conserve dopamine, since it will eliminate the necessity of glycogen conversion by adrenalin. The addition of fructose should not be expected to eliminate the tremor if circulatory deficiencies are initiating it.

Problems in the regulation of the stress-response steroid hormones are directly involved in disorders of mineral balance in the body. Rheumatoid arthritis is one condition that is alleviated by providing the steroid hormones. In some cases ACTH is given. This triggers the adrenal cortex to secrete steroid hormones. The relationship of these steroids to those of the gonads can be illustrated by the fact that during pregnancy many women who had arthritis previously are relatively free of symptoms. When they are pregnant, the placenta and the gonads produce large amounts of steroid hormones. The implication is that these women normally do not secrete sufficient steroids in the adrenal cortex. Without them the mineral balance of the blood and other tissues becomes disturbed. The excess minerals then accumulate in the joints as deposited salts. If there is a deficiency of steroid hormones, a deficiency of adrenalin release for glycogen conversion may also be expected. This would increase the likelihood of hypoglycemia and the onset of fatigue and physiological depression with its behavioral counterparts. This may be a basis for postpartum depression in some women who seemed to be in good emotional and physical health during pregnancy. A provision of fructose in the diet can prevent the hypoglycemia-related depression and preserve the steroids for mineral regulation requirements.

Anyone who has paced the floor at 2:00 A.M. trying to give comfort to a small baby with colic is well informed about some of the complexities of the stress response. The abdomen of the child is rigid and taut. The muscles are in spasm. Gas has accumulated because of a cessation of digestive tract motility. The child is irritable, cranky, and crying in pain whenever an attempt is made to return him to the crib. He wants to be held upright to reduce discomfort. Until now the best treatment for this condition has been to feed the children more often but with smaller amounts of milk than usual in each feeding. In other words they have been treated as if they were hypoglycemics so their dietary carbohydrates were spread throughout time rather than requiring their own regulation of the stress response. Some physicians have suggested that the mother was too anxious and therefore the child had colic. If the baby was being nursed, it is possible that the mother, trying to control her own weight, was somewhat hypoglycemic so that the milk she was providing was actually deficient in lactose, especially in the latter part of the day and evening. If the child was being bottle-fed, it is possible that his mobilization of insulin in response to the galactose and glucose was not well regulated so that the child became hypoglycemic. This is especially true if excess sugar was provided in the formula. Gastric upset or the stress of some minor infection which causes adrenalin release with the stoppage of the digestive tract can interfere with dietary sugar absorption and thus lead to a subsequent hypoglycemic state. In many cases colic has been eliminated when the baby was given a fructose solution instead of milk for the evening feedings. In other cases the nursing mothers were given supplementary fructose through the day and avoided the insulin-inducing carbohydrates in the late afternoon and evening. This diet seemed to reduce the anxiety of the mother and the child's colic ceased. The syndrome of anxious, nervous mother and colicky child is more frequent if the mother is dieting to lose weight; nursing requires nearly one third more calories than normal to provide an adequate diet for both child and mother.

Acne and other complexion problems have been previously mentioned as stress-related disorders, but they are such common occurrences that this connection should be reinforced. Acne and skin blemishes are most common in teenagers. This is the time when the gonadal steroids are being added to the adrenal cortical steroids which have been secreted throughout their growing years. When the level of androgen hormones is high, the skin gets oily. The oils of the skin pores (sebaceous glands) promote the growth of bacteria, which actually cause the pustules. The androgen steroids also interfere with the healing processes and scar tissue formation. This keeps the skin in a very susceptible condition. There is a common belief that among American teenagers the consumption of chocolate candy causes acne. A group of research programs have tested chocolate and have not verified that conclusion. But if acne is a component of the stress-response steroid release, the candy ingestion may be not a cause of the acne but an attempt to relieve hypoglycemia. The fat content of the chocolate bars would then be added to the triglycerides mobilized by the steroids of the stress response or excess gonadal steroids. This excess of fats coupled with the insulin-inducing carbohydrates of the candy seems to explain its connection to acne. The sugar-insulin reaction reinitiates the hypoglycemia, which then results in more steroid release. The steroids cause fat and amino acid mobilization. The adrenalin released by the steroids decreases the flow of the blood to the skin and the pustules develop.

Acne is not a problem for sexually mature males but continues to be a problem for many females at the time of menstruation. It is only at this time that the female has a ratio of male/female hormones that could initiate the skin problems. At the time of menses both estrogen and progesterone are at their lowest concentration. The androgenic hormones of the adrenal cortex are thus able to exert their effect. Since the female hormones normally cause the deposition of a fatty tissue layer just below the skin it is these fats that are particularly vulnerable for androgen steroid mobilization.

The substitution of fructose for most of the insulin-inducing carbohydrates a few days before the onset of menses seems to decrease the problem for many adult women. The dietary regulation of the teenager must be continued for a longer time. The healing of the pustules and the prevention of additional infections requires a drastic reduction in steroid mobilization. Only the stress-response steroids can be controlled externally.

An interesting piece of logic can demonstrate the relationship of the stress response to the disorder of gout. This disease involves the accumulation of chalky mineral deposits in the joints. It was so common among the nobility and landowners in England in past centuries that it was first believed to be a disease exclusively of the rich. It has since been found among the poor as well. A century ago a distinguished London physician, Sir Archibald Garrod, discovered that if a thread were suspended in the blood serum of a person with gout symptoms a layer of uric acid crystals would accumu-

late on it. It is well known that uric acid is a primary
excretion product for some nitrogenous molecules associated with high-protein diets. In old England, glut-
tony was quite usual among the wealthy. Many of the
meals included several varieties of meats, all high in
protein. If one's kidneys inadequately excrete the uric
acid accumulation, gout develops. There is a limit in
all of us for the excretion of uric acid. If the consumption of animal proteins, which are high in purine content, exceeds this limit, the onset of gout is inevitable.
Some people just ate too much meat for their normal
kidneys to handle. Others had a defect in the kidney
so that they retained the uric acid even if their consumption of meat was quite moderate.

Consumption of alcohol can also be involved in
gout. The stress-response mobilization of fat can lead
to the accumulation of ketones, or they can accumulate
because of an incomplete oxidation of alcohol. Ketones
interfere with the excretion of uric acid, which then
promotes the salt deposits which cause the discomfort
of gout. The stress-response mobilization of cellular
proteins and disruption of ion exchanges by the steroid
hormones would be a further complicating factor. If
the stress response is prevented by fructose, and if
alcohol and high-purine meats are provided in reasonable amounts, gout may become a disease of the past.

Stress-related problems are not limited to one age
group. They extend from colic in babies, to hyperactivity
of children, to acne and behavior problems in teenagers,
to alcoholism in adults, to tremor in senior citizens, and
to overweight and anxiety or psychiatric problems in
every age group. The listing of stress-related disorders
could go on and on. In all cases the management of
the diet to decrease the high carbohydrate intake which
might precipitate hypoglycemia is suggested. The best
way to provide the necessary carbohydrates is by exchanging fructose for the insulin-inducing and -requir-
ing carbohydrates in an adequate diet which also supplies bulk, amino acids, fats, vitamins and minerals
necessary for good health.

CHAPTER FOURTEEN

Diabetes,
the Other Sugar Metabolism Disorder

Diabetes, because of its devastating effect on the lives of a large number of people, is the best known and most conspicuous disorder of sugar metabolism. Whereas hypoglycemia often severely limits effective social interaction, diabetes kills. In the United States it ranks as the eighth most common cause of death. It would be presumptuous to attempt a simplified account of the disease unless the discussion is strictly limited to the possible relationships between diabetes and hypoglycemia and to the use of fructose by diabetics.

Diabetes has been recognized as a major medical problem since antiquity. The name "diabetes" actually is applied to two distinct and unrelated disorders. When the disorder is due to a problem of the pituitary gland secretions which act through the adrenal cortex to regulate the reabsorption of water from the kidney tubules, the name is diabetes insipidus. This is a rare condition which can be treated effectively by providing a pituitary hormone. The most common variety of diabetes involves the regulation of sugar metabolism and is called diabetes mellitus. It results from a relative or complete lack of action of insulin, a hormore produced in the beta cell of the Islets of Langerhans of the pancreas. Throughout this book the name "diabetes" refers to this disease of insulin insufficiency. There are two major types of this variety of diabetes. In one, distinguished as the juvenile type, there is a demonstrable deficiency of insulin secretion because of a lack of secretory cells of the pancreas. The other type of diabetes is known as the adult or maturity-onset form. In this disease the pancreatic cells seem nearly normal, but the patient suffers from an insufficiency of insulin-promoted action while glucagon is normally present in excess. This is also the case in the juvenile type.

The characteristic involvement of an overabundance of glucagon in diabetes mellitus demonstrates that this disease involves more than just a defect in the beta cells of the pancreas. It is generally accepted that the primary site of glucagon synthesis and release is the alpha cells of the pancreas. Both varieties of cells of the islets of Langerhans of the pancreas are therefore involved in the regulation of the blood sugar concentration. The major role of insulin is its activation of the enzymatic phosphorylation of glucose to promote transfer of the sugar from the blood to storage in insulin-responsive tissues such as liver, adipose, and muscle. In contrast, the role of glucagon, like adrenalin, is the homeostatic regulation of the liver-mediated mobilization of glycogen to raise the blood glucose concentration to supply such vital tissues as the brain. Glucagon and insulin normally balance their actions. While high concentrations of insulin suppress glucagon release, low concentrations stimulate glucagon availability. Yet the control of glucagon depends on the hypothalamic control of the growth hormone secretion by the pituitary gland. A suppression of the growth hormone prevents the synthesis and release of both insulin and glucagon. It is the interaction of each of these regulatory systems, only recently understood by many scientists and physicians, that unquestionably relates hyperglycemia (high blood sugar) to the pathological condition of diabetes mellitus and to the overall stress responses.

Some studies have shown a hereditary link in juvenile diabetes although the actual cellular cause of this disorder is unknown. The onset of the adult form is thought to be related to stress. Included in the stress component are emotional stress, toxemia, infection, and endocrine control problems which originate in the hypothalamus or pituitary gland. Although most published commentary on the stress factors as causative agents of diabetes has focused on emotional or psychic stress, the stress of hypoglycemia must also be considered. Diabetes usually refers to a disorder characterized by an accumulation of sugar in the body fluids and in the urine. It has features of hypoglycemia since the body is unable to store glucose as glycogen. The blood sugar concentration of an unregulated diabetic is like a pendulum which swings from one extreme to another. After a meal the blood sugar concentration remains high. Some of the sugar is lost in the urine, but no liver glycogen is synthesized and no fat is added to the adipose cells. When the body has lost sugar in the urine and used up the remainder, the deficiency of glycogen prevents the stress response from re-establishing the required blood sugar level. This is hypoglycemia.

The distinguishing features which causes the victims to seek help from their physicians are related to both the hyperglycemia problems and the hypoglycemic difficulties. Diabetics frequently exhibit excessive thirst, excessive hunger, and excessive urination. These difficulties are the combined result of hypoglycemia complicated by the loss of sugar into the urine. The presence of sugar in the urine prevents the effective reabsorption of the water from the kidney tubules. The loss of this water also causes a loss of both sodium and potassium salts. Depression and fatigue may accompany the hypoglycemic periods.

Among juvenile diabetics the symptoms which cause the parents to seek help are bed wetting, excessive fatigue, a distinct change in appetite, and irritability. Some parents do not recognize some of these early symptoms and do not bring the problems to the attention of their physicians until the child goes into a diabetic coma. Of the initial features of juvenile diabetes, the symptoms are more distinctly related to the lack of insulin action and subsequent inability of glucose to enter the body cells with the accompanying ketoacidosis than to the sluggishness, loss of appetite, and excessive urination which are distinctly related to the excessive accumulation of sugar in the blood. Among adults who seek advice the common complaint is a drastic drop in weight and frequent urination. However, more are found during routine examinations or massive public test programs than present themselves because of symptoms of diabetes. Whereas juvenile diabetics are almost never overweight, a preponderance of persons who develop the adult-onset diabetes are considerably overweight—frequently, in fact, obese.

It can be postulated that some cases of adult diabetes result from a fatigue of some cells of the Islets of Langerhans. In some, the cells may actually deteriorate from overuse. Prior to the deficiency of insulin action, many persons who develop distinct diabetes had problems of hypoglycemia when the demands on the pancreatic cells were extensive. A diet which provides a high carbohydrate intake requires the synthesis and release of large amounts of insulin to provide for the synthesis of glycogen in the liver and muscles to reduce the blood sugar level so that it will not spill over the kidney tubules into the urine. At such times these prediabetics do not produce more insulin than is required, but their diet demands a high insulin secretion rate. In other diabetics the cells may have become desensitized to the glucose or to the action of insulin so that the insulin which is produced is not sufficient to facilitate the effective use or storage of the sugars. The persons in this category are those who benefit from the oral medications which promote insulin release. These drugs do not have the action of insulin themselves. They are of no value to persons who are deficient in secretory cells of the pancreas. Another variety of adult diabetes seems to be related to the synthesis in the pancreas of an inappropriate "insulin-like" molecule prematurely released before the synthesis of the active insulin molecule is completed. Such abnormal molecules are inefficient in promoting the storage of glucose as glycogen.

For many years it was hoped and even anticipated

that the problems of diabetics would be solved when the structure of the insulin molecule was known. Insulin is a protein molecule made of two chains of amino acids. When Margaret Sanger determined the exact sequence of the twenty-one amino acids in the short chain and the thirty amino acids of the longer chain, the molecule could be completely described. Although this was a monumental work which enhanced the knowledge of protein chemistry, it did not solve any problems about the disease of diabetes. Certainly the defect which leads to diabetes and the precise mode of action of insulin are intimately related, but answers about the physiological action of insulin seem to be coming from the new understandings about certain adrenalin actions. When Dr. Earl Sutherland discovered cyclic AMP (3'5'AMP) and demonstrated that this molecule was synthesized inside of cells and maintained when adrenalin was provided to the liver, he provided some new ideas about insulin as well. When insulin is present, no cyclic AMP is formed and the cyclic AMP that is present is not maintained. As yet it is not known exactly how insulin prevents the synthesis of new cyclic AMP or how it promotes the synthesis of the enzymes which destroy cyclic AMP but these actions are now well recognized. This also brings diabetes into the list of disorders initiated by or directly related to stress. The stress can be hypoglycemia as well as any of the other stress conditions. It is interesting to note that long before Sutherland elucidated the action of cyclic AMP in converting the liver glycogen to glucose it had been recognized that high stress conditions such as emotional or physical trauma, infections, and toxemias frequently preceded the onset of overt diabetes. If adrenalin is released while insulin is present, the regulation of the blood sugar concentration is disrupted. As fast as one molecule of adrenalin causes the formation of cyclic AMP to influence the conversion of glycogen of the liver to glucose, the insulin promotes the destruction of the cyclic AMP and the storage of the glucose as glycogen. Under such conditions nothing works right. As long as the adrenalin remains, the pancreatic cells will continue to respond to the high glucose level and will secrete insulin. The presence of adrenalin will require much higher than normal amounts of insulin to store the blood sugar. This is almost a self-destruct system. Either the stress-response system wears out or the insulin secretion cells of the pancreas deteriorate. Depending on which system breaks down first, the victims of this internal physiological battle will develop either diabetes or hypoglycemic depression.

Diabetes is not just a disorder of sugar storage. When insulin action is deficient, the primary concern is an improper and incomplete use of fat. When a non-diabetic person eats a normal diet, the body uses about half of the carbohydrates for immediate energy, stores about 5% as glycogen, uses 5 to 10% as substrates for the synthesis of new compounds, particularly in the nervous system, and converts the remaining 30 to 40% of the carbohydrates to fat stored in the adipose tissues.

Fat is a more efficient way to store energy than putting it all as glycogen into the liver and muscles. The liver only stores 100 grams of glycogen at any one time. The remaining excess sugar of the diet is made into fat. The fat molecules that are synthesized from the excess dietary sugars do not accumulate as droplets in the blood. They are actually synthesized in adipose cells of the body. When the steroid hormones of the adrenal cortex affect these cells, they cause the stored fat to be released into the blood as small fragments, the triglycerides and various lipoproteins. These fat metabolites are used as energy sources by most of the cells of the body, but fat cannot be reconverted to sugar. We just do not have the enzymes to make that transformation. In that absence of sugar, however, fat usage by the cells is abnormal. The complete oxidation of fat fragments requires a set of reactions which involve molecules normally made from carbohydrates.

Dietary carbohydrates are digested to single sugar molecules, the monosaccharides, by enzymes in the digestive fluids and on the membranes of the cells which line the digestive cavities. Most of our sugars are six carbon compounds which are used in either of two pathways. The terminal product of both of these paths is a molecule called pyruvate. This pyruvate is involved in cell functions in many ways. It can be combined with nitrogen-containing amino groups and so converted into the amino acid alanine. Oxaloacetate is formed in liver cells by combining pyruvate with carbon dioxide. This molecule is an important intermediate in the primary-energy-providing metabolic cycle, the Krebs or citric acid cycle, which is the common pathway for energy production from carbohydrates, fats, and proteins. The most important reaction of pyruvate is its reaction with a molecule called coenzyme A. The product of this reaction is acetyl coenzyme A, frequently called acetyl co-A, which provides the route for the metabolism of fats into the citric acid cycle as well as being a building block for a variety of other molecules.

When acetyl co-A is oxidized to provide the energy for the cells, the bond energy is trapped in a series of intermediate compounds instead of being dissipated as useless heat. The coenzyme portion of the molecule contains the vitamin pantothenic acid. The molecules which trap the energy when acetyl co-A is oxidized also include a variety of vitamins. A deficiency of vitamins will therefore seriously disrupt this most important of the energy-providing systems of the body.

Acetyl co-A can be oxidized to carbon dioxide and water plus energy, or it can be modified into another molecule called acetoacetate. This molecule does not accumulate. It is converted to cholesterol or into a group of compounds called ketones. Usually ketones are used as fuels, but they may accumulate to harmful levels in disorders such as diabetes.

When a deficiency of blood sugar occurs, the metabolic demands of the body are met by using the fatty acids from the triglycerides as fuel. The steroids of the stress response are required to mobilize the triglycerides from the adipose cells where they were stored as fat. The fatty acids are converted to acetyl co-A, but the remainder of the path through the citric acid cycle is blocked unless some oxaloacetate is provided. This molecule is normally regenerated in the citric acid cycle unless one of the molecules in this chain of reactions is used for some other synthesis. Then new oxaloacetate must be provided. Since this molecule is formed from pyruvic acid, which is usually derived from carbohydrates, the ketone production increases and these molecules accumulate unless sugar is provided. The ketones are excreted in the urine and even in the air we exhale. One of the ketones, acetone, smells somewhat sweet while other ketones produce bad breath and a foul taste in the mouth. The presence of ketones in the urine and in the breath is evidence of incomplete oxidation of fats.

The excessive production and excretion of ketones results in diabetic coma. The accumulation of ketones and the acetoacetate from which they are formed produces a state of intoxication. To excrete the ketones the body must expend base (alkali). To obtain these ions the potassium, sodium, calcium, and magnesium of the cells are drawn out of the tissues. This disrupts the buffering capacity of the blood and body fluids, and the acidity of the fluids increases. The body tries to compensate for this acid. The high acid concentration stimulates the breathing center to increase the breathing rate, but try as it may it cannot readjust the system. In a diabetic this acidity, which accompanies the loss of ions with the loss of sugar into the urine, leads to disruption of the nervous system, dehydration, circulatory collapse, kidney failure, stupor, coma, and finally death. It is far easier to prevent ketoacidosis than to correct it after it develops. Irreversible damage to tissues throughout the body occurs each time ketoacidosis leads to coma, so the management of the ions (salts) is as important as the control of the sugar metabolism in the unregulated diabetic.

If the amount of insulin provided to a diabetic is not matched by a sufficiency of carbohydrate intake, the blood sugar may fall to the level of severe hypoglycemia. In diabetics, as in others, the first symptoms are those of the sympathetic nervous system, stress-response hormonal actions. If the hypoglycemia continues, the higher levels of the brain are affected and uncoordination and disorientation develop. Other symptoms associated with hypoglycemia—hunger, weakness, fatigue, headache, nervous instability, mild confusion, detachment, anxiety, delirium, profuse sweating, hands and face cold and clammy, and finally loss of consciousness and deep coma—lead to death unless sugar is provided. This form of hypoglycemia is called insulin shock.

Diabetic coma, the end result of severe ketoacidosis, and insulin shock, the severe hypoglycemia induced by an insufficiency of balance between the amount of injected insulin and the carbohydrate intake, have in common the problem of the availability of sugar to maintain the normal functions of the nervous system or the complications of the stress response. They differ in their symptoms and the rate at which these symptoms are manifested. Insulin shock is more rapid in its onset and can be corrected by getting sugar into the blood stream. The sugar may be provided by intravenous injection or by dietary means. Sometimes the patient is given injections of glucagon, the pancreatic hormone which acts to convert the liver glycogen to glucose without having the other effects of adrenalin. This is of particular value if some previous stress has initiated adrenalin release which stopped digestive tract motility and thus interfered with absorption of sugars. Diabetic coma usually follows a severe stress condition. The stress may be emotional or physical but frequently involves some bacterial infection which triggers the stress response of adrenal steroids with their additional fat-mobilizing power as well as release of adrenalin with all of its actions on the circulatory system. Diabetic coma requires the readjustment of the mineral ion balance of the body in addition to providing sugar to the cells.

In this condition it is the simultaneous presence of insulin which was injected too late to move the glucose into the cells and the stress-response hormones which prevent the action of either the insulin or adrenalin in regulating the blood sugar in addition to the swamping of the fat metabolism system that is at the root of the problem.

Fructose has some characteristics which can make it of value in the dietary management of some diabetics. Its slow absorption from the digestive tract means that it will have a damping effect on blood sugar fluctuations. If the diabetic patient's disease is balanced and under control, the fact that some fructose can enter the muscle and adipose tissue cells without requiring the facilitating action of insulin may be beneficial. The same may also be said of its metabolism to energy-supplying substrates in the liver independent of insulin. And using fructose as a sweetening agent is distinctly advantageous in families where there is a single diabetic member. Fructose-sweetened food is quite acceptable to the entire family. This can reduce the psychological problem imposed upon the diabetic of having to eat "different" and often less palatable foods, making the diet easier to keep.

It must be remembered, however, in considering the use of fructose in diabetic diets, that fructose contains calories. Its inclusion in the diet should be made only along with a commensurate reduction in the intake of other carbohydrates. Fructose is definitely not a "free food" and should be used only in carefully controlled amounts and only as a part of the over-all diet prescribed by the diabetic's physician.

Individual differences in the extent and form of diabetes are the most frustrating problems for the physician. Managing the diet, convincing the patient of the importance of frequent urinalysis for sugar and ketones, preventing infections or other physical stresses must all be accomplished. When an insufficiency of insulin action interferes with the accumulation of glycogen, the hypoglycemic events which develop subsequently can precipitate the food binges of some diabetics which then prepare the way for more serious diabetic conditions. Fructose will not prevent all the problems the diabetic faces.

CHAPTER FIFTEEN

The Advantageous Use of Fructose by Healthy People

It is not necessary to become grossly overweight, psychotic, or alcoholic to discover for yourself the benefits of a dietary exchange of fructose for other carbohydrates. Healthy people must also maintain enough blood sugar to function adequately. If the blood sugar is not regulated by the diet, it will automatically be accomplished by the release of adrenalin. It is the other effects of adrenalin which one may wish to avoid, for many reasons.

Most people, even those who normally follow a good dietary regimen, experience a midmorning and a midafternoon slump. Their nerve cells are just not being supplied with sufficient sugar. Others seem to fade out toward the end of the day, particularly if they have been physically active earlier. A test of the blood will show an insufficiency of blood sugar and a very low amount of adrenalin. The irritability of children when they return home from school can frequently be relieved by giving them some rapidly usable carbohydrates, not as a reward for behaving but as a cellular food. Mothers who are short-tempered for an hour or two before dinner are probably responding to the stress of a blood glucose deficiency compounded by the problems of being the cook, housekeeper, mother, taxi driver, and wife. An increase in sugar intake will not remove all of these stresses but it can alleviate the stress of hypoglycemia which contributes to the other stresses. The early morning grouch who is unable to function until at least one cup of coffee has done its metabolic job has become a cartoon character. Coffee is a stimulant which promotes an increase in his heart rate, his blood pressure, and his blood glucose level.

It certainly is not necessary for people with these disorders to exchange all of their dietary carbohydrates for fructose to get relief from their problems. Unless there is a demonstrable need to cut the caloric intake to lose weight or to prevent the secretion of insulin and the storage of the sugars, the sugar of choice may be sucrose. Sucrose is less expensive and is more readily available. It provides energy to the cells more rapidly than fructose. But it is for this last reason that fructose may be the sugar of choice to relieve fatigue followed by anxiety and the stress response. Since the fructose passes slowly from the digestive tract to the blood and does not cause the release of insulin, it may take less fructose to maintain an adequate regulation of blood sugar than is possible with sucrose or pure glucose. Only 6 to 10 grams of fructose one and a half to two hours after a meal normally will prevent excessive fatigue caused by hypoglycemia. Repeating this amount (1½ to 2½ teaspoons) each hour or so later will maintain enough blood sugar to prevent the stress response that many experience before the evening meal. Some people will discover that they do not need this much; few, if any, will need more. Since fructose does provide 4 calories per gram as does every other sugar, it should be exchanged for the other carbohydrates if one is conscientiously regulating his weight by restricting his intake of calories. If the fructose is exchanged for a sweet role or a doughnut, a candy bar or an ice cream cone, or for an alcoholic beverage, the caloric intake from the fructose will be much less than from these other high-calorie products. The advantage of fructose does not lie in its relatively greater sweetness than the other sugars but in its slower transfer into the blood and the lack of insulin release.

Persons who normally are quite active physically maintain enough blood sugar for neural regulation by the release of adrenalin initiated by the homeostatic demands of the circulatory system and muscle regulation. For them the adrenalin release, although involuntary, also acts to keep the blood sugar level high. As long as they remain active they continue to be adjusted. If, however, they are required to sit quietly at sales meetings, or in a classroom, or at Sunday church service, or at a theatrical production, or a concert that begins two or three hours after their last meal, they will be drowsy and may actually fall asleep. If they get up and walk around, the level of adrenalin in the blood will be increased. If physical activity is impossible or inconvenient, most of them will discover that 6 to 8 grams of fructose taken ten or fifteen minutes before they settle into their seats too comfortably will prevent sleepiness. The same is true for the truck driver or commuter who gets drowsy at the steering wheel. Fructose is the ideal sugar to prevent this fatigue, which develops as the consequence of a deficiency of blood sugar.

Fructose is, of course, valuable to athletes and sportsmen and its value has been recognized by the overseers of the Olympics. They have provided fructose tablets for energy to the contestants at many events in the past few Games. Again, fructose is of distinct benefit if it is desirable to provide a carbohydrate which does not rapidly swamp the blood stream or cause the release of insulin. It is especially desirable because the digestive tract rather than the blood serves as the reservoir of the available sugar. How much to take depends on the sport being played since some require more energy and a greater adrenalin release than others.

The problems of blood sugar management for the business or professional man who plays an occasional game of handball or tennis are different from those of the athlete who keeps in constant training with daily physical activity. Certainly no reasonable person would eat a large meal and then run right out to tennis or handball. When the blood sugar is high immediately after a meal, you feel sluggish. Therefore most people eat after exercise. This has merit. Yet one does run the risk of an insufficiency of glycogen to maintain the necessary level of blood sugar to prevent fatigue related to hypoglycemia. If you intend to postpone a meal but at the same time to increase your metabolic demands by some kind of athletic endeavor, 6 to 10 grams of fructose can then be eaten to maintain the required blood sugar level. It is not a good idea to eat double the amount at the beginning. Since fructose is slowly absorbed into the blood, excess sugar can remain in the digestive tract and be lost in the feces four to six hours later. Good fructose should not be wasted that way. The actual amount of fructose required will certainly vary from one person to the next depending on his physical state, age, weight, previous eating habits, and other factors, so the amounts given above are only a guide, not hard and fast rules.

Competitive swimming and wrestling are remarkably different sports, yet both require fantastic energy expenditures in short periods of time. There is an old adage that one should not go swimming for at least an hour after a meal. Certainly this does not apply to a person who swims two lengths in a backyard pool and then collapses into a lounge chair to soak up the sun. If he is a serious swimmer, the possibility of a cramp initiated by a massive release of adrenalin, like the side ache of a school child who runs home for noon lunch, must be avoided. Within the first hour after a meal, the blood glucose level continues to rise as the complex carbohydrates are digested and absorbed in the upper portion of the intestines. The amino acids from the proteins and the fat of the diet are not available as cellular fuel until some hours later. As the glucose accumulates, it triggers the pancreas to release insulin. This insulin causes the glucose to be stored as glycogen. If the metabolic demand of the swimming or wrestling exactly matches the available sugar supply in the blood there will be no hypoglycemic fatigue. Both of these sports, however, require adrenalin release to regulate the circulatory system. They are stresses.

And when adrenalin is present at the same time as insulin, neither hormone is able to do its normal job in the regulation of the blood sugar level. If the activity is delayed for two or more hours after a meal to eliminate this problem, maintaining the necessary blood sugar will require some of the adrenalin that is also needed for the heart and blood vessels. To prevent these problems for the swimmer and wrestler as well as for the athlete engaged in track and field events the most logical remedy is to eat at least two or three hours before the event and then to eat fructose just before initiating those metabolic demands. If someone wants proof, he doesn't need an expensive and difficult laboratory procedure to be convinced. All that is necessary is to follow his regular regimen of diet and then count the number of push-ups or chin-ups he can do until he tires. On another comparable day he should wait three hours after a meal and then eat 6 to 10 grams of fructose ten or fifteen minutes before trying to do push-ups until he is fatigued. Depending on his physical state, he normally can do more push-ups when he is fortified with the fructose.

The winter sports enthusiast provides a slightly different problem, but it is still a variation on the same theme. Skiing has a different requirement for sugar regulation from many other sports although the same general problems of sugar regulation apply to other cold weather activities. For many participants, skiing is an all-day activity. This usually means that a skier has a full breakfast and then takes the first chair lift to the top of the slopes. The blood sugar from the breakfast has just begun to rise when he faces the long cold ride up the mountain. Cold weather causes chill. Chill is a stress. To overcome this chill, the sympathetic system secretes noradrenalin and possibly adrenalin into the blood. Accompanying this stress response to chill are the stress responses to the anticipation of an exciting day and the exuberance of the activity. With all of this adrenalin in the blood even before the insulin is released to store the sugar, the activity of the insulin is inhibited, and little if any of the glucose is accumulated as glycogen in the liver. If the glucose concentration in the blood remains high, it is probable that some of it will spill over the kidney tubules into the urine and be lost. This is somewhat like a temporary, but not metabolically dangerous, diabetic condition. The high adrenalin can precipitate spasms of the abdominal wall which are then interpreted as hunger, so the skier eats again. This maintains the problem. If much sugar is lost into the urine, these is an accompanying loss of water into the urine with the possibility of dehydration, even though the stress response normally results in an accumulation of tissue fluids. The skier can begin at the breakfast table to prevent many of these problems. If he eats primarily protein and fat with a liberal amount of fructose in his fruit juice or beverage, he can eat additional fructose during the day: first, to prevent the fatigue of a deficiency of blood sugar and, second, to continue the effective and complete metabolism of the fats without necessitating the conversion of amino acids from the proteins into pyruvate.

Although milk is an excellent food for babies and children, the effect of the high lactose content of milk should be recognized by the athlete. Lactose is split by digestive enzymes into galactose and glucose. Both of these sugars are normally stored as glycogen. Milk is also a fine food for those adults who can digest and use it, but skiers should avoid it during the day. It is unnecessary to run the risk of insulin release while on the slopes just to get the other food values that are available in milk. If you wish to insure that you obtain the minerals, proteins, and vitamins in milk products, you can eat cheeses or yogurt without precipitating the problems of sugar regulation. In these foods most of the sugars have been converted to acids which coagulated the proteins and therefore are not present to cause the release of insulin. (No one should infer from these remarks that insulin is bad. Adrenalin isn't bad either. Both of these hormones are necessary for the normal regulation of the blood sugar level, but we should avoid situations which precipitate the simultaneous presence of the hormones so that neither is able to do its job effectively.)

For serious athletes who regularly adhere to training programs for scheduled sports like football, basketball, rugby, hockey, soccer, or other high-metabolic-demand activities, a change in dietary habits can do much to prevent early fatigue during competition. It is best to begin the day of the athletic contest with a full complement of glycogen supply in the muscles and liver. To insure this condition it is possible to use the body's regulatory system to advantage. If the cells of the liver and muscles are first depleted of glycogen and then supplied with an excess of dietary carbohydrates which causes insulin release, the cells accumulate more glycogen than is normally stored. This oversupply of glycogen can be timed to suit the athletic schedule. Take, for example, a college football player whose games occur on Saturday afternoons. On Sunday and Monday of each week the diet is a normal balanced diet of carbohydrates, fats, and proteins in addition to fresh fruits, vegetables, and dairy products. On Tuesday and Wednesday the diet should include all of the normal foods except the carbohydrates. A severe restriction or elimination of the carbohydrates on these days (during which his practice sessions are making high metabolic demands) will deplete the glycogen supply of the body, but his metabolic requirements will be met by the dietary fats, the proteins, and the glycogen stored at the beginning of the week. On Thursday and Friday the diet should be just loaded with insulin-inducing carbohydrates. A breakfast with fruit, pancakes with syrup, and a sweet roll to top it off followed by a midmorning snack of rolls or a candy bar and noon and evening meals with an oversupply of potatoes. bread, cake, and pie with ice cream will trigger an overreaction of liver and muscle cells to store more than usual amounts of glycogen. On the day of the game the diet should again be a rather normal breakfast with bran flakes, whole wheat toast, or other bulky foods which can soak up the digestive juices without causing later problems in the lower digestive tract. A late morning lunch of some eggs, cheese, and salad but no carbohydrates except fructose will insure that the total glycogen reserve will be available by the time of the game with no competition between insulin and adrenalin.

This glycogen-regulating dietary program can be adapted for high school athletes as well as for adults who participate in scheduled contests. For the track and field participant whose activities are scheduled during the morning, the breakfast that day should be free of insulin-inducing carbohydrates just like the breakfast for a skier.

This glycogen-regulating dietary program can be adapted for desirable effects, but it can only be accomplished by the depletion of glycogen followed by overstimulation. A small amount of fructose included on the low-carbohydrate days to prevent excessive fatigue and hunger may be desirable. An additional supply of 6 to 10 grams of fructose just before the athletic contest will insure the prevention of any deficiency of blood sugar until the adrenalin release mechanism initiates the conversion of the stored glycogen to glucose.

The addition of fructose to the diet of the student, housewife, businessman, or any other healthy adult can be effective in regulating the blood sugar on an irregular basis. Some people have a difficult time falling asleep because they have depleted their readily available blood sugar and have caused adrenalin release to re-establish the sufficiency of blood glucose. This adrenalin will keep them from falling asleep even though they now have enough blood sugar. If one eats an insulin-inducing carbohydrate at that time, before the adrenalin release occurs, the blood sugar level will rise but insulin will also be released. A drop in the blood sugar concentration during the night will trigger adrenalin release, and this "wake-up hormone" will do its job. A deficiency of glucose and the presence of adrenalin to re-establish the desired level can be recognized by the dryness of the mouth and a clenching of the teeth. Any sugar—fructose, glucose, or sucrose—in the middle of the night will supply the cellular needs to prevent the release of any additional adrenalin and thus decrease the possibility of insomnia then.

Certainly people who are recovering from surgery, stroke, or coronary difficulties cannot be called healthy, but at the same time they are not really sick. One of their prime problems involves the management of the blood sugar level as a consequence of their disorder. It has long been known that the stress-response mechanism is repressed in all of these persons. In normal, healthy, active adults the steroid hormones, particularly those from the adrenal cortex, rise and fall in concentration in a rather regular cyclic pattern each day. Associated with this rhythmic change in the concentration of these hormones is a change in the level of the adrenalin from the adrenal medulla while the steroid hormones cause the mobilization of the fat from fat storage cells to maintain the energy supply of most of the cells of the body. The adrenalin causes the conversion of glycogen to glucose. Together this fat and sugar supply the metabolic needs throughout the body. Steroid hormones also affect cell growth. High levels of adrenal steroids depress scar tissue growth and thus depress the repair processes of the body. Adrenalin causes an increase in heart rate, blood pressure, and the synthesis of blood-clotting substances. These attributes of the steroids and adrenalin are undesirable when body repair processes are needed to return one to good health. In some yet unknown way the body recognizes the disadvantages of these hormones and turns off their release. Although this repression of the adrenal hormones, both the steroids and the adrenalin, in those who are recovering from tissue damage serves one benefit, it also eliminates their ability to regulate the blood glucose and plasma triglycerides. The cells of the body can be deficient in fuel, but the switch mechanism is inoperative. Fructose can help here.

If small amounts of fructose (6 to 8 grams=1 to 2

teaspoons) are eaten two to three hours after meals the required energy supply of the body can be provided. If a loss of weight is desirable, the fructose can be exchanged for the other carbohydrates of the diet, and thus blood sugar regulation can be controlled externally without either the insulin release or adrenalin complicating the problem. A provision of adequate cellular energy can eliminate much of the physiological depression and thus prevent the psychological depression which normally occurs as a consequence.

There is no magic here. Fructose will not take the place of the exercise which maintains the circulatory system and the voluntary muscles of the body, but fructose can prevent the necessity of exercise to cause adrenalin release to keep the blood sugar at adequate levels. Fructose does not interfere with any drugs or medications that may be a part of the treatment regimen. It only supplies energy. The list of the uses of fructose could go on and on. Keep in mind that it is just a normal wholesome food with some distinct attributes which are well known and can be used advantageously by many persons.

The Physiology of the Stress Response

This entire book has been concerned with the psychological changes which occur in the human when he is challenged by a stressful situation. The first chapters introduced the idea that the regulation of a relatively constant internal environment requires an interaction between numerous organs and biochemical systems. Such actions involve quite complex chemical and tissue adjustments for the appropriate regulation and phasing of the interactions. The introductory chapters were intended to provide an outline of the sequences of actions of the various organs involved in the stress response. Much more detailed information is known about these organs and systems than given in those chapters. Although a complete mastery of more technical information is not necessary to understand the stress response, this Appendix is intended to provide the technically oriented reader with more specific information regarding these adjustments. The basic information of this Appendix amplifies the ideas in the first chapters.

The hypothalamus is known to be the originator of the stress-response adjustments. This section of the lower brain serves as the co-ordinator and common pathway of all stress information. It is connected to the stress sensors of the sense organs and to the emotional control centers. It detects biochemical changes and internal stresses which reflect the physiological condition of the body.

The special relationship between the hypothalamus and the remainder of the central nervous system became apparent many years ago. Like many other discoveries, the initial clues came from observations and experiments conducted on a variety of species. It was only after this mass of information became available from these different research programs that the generalities were discovered.

We have known for a long time in most species of birds ovulation timing is co-ordinated to seasonal changes in the length of day and night. Robins just don't lay eggs in autumn, only in the spring. Even though our domestic fowl are not as susceptible to changes in light as most wild species, the American farmer knows that his egg production is increased if the lights are kept on in the henhouse. This is a case of practical application of scientific information about the sex life of birds. Somehow or other the birds are able to sense the change of seasons by detecting changes in day length. This information is relayed to the cells in the ovary and testes which respond by synthesizing specific hormones. The effectiveness of this regulation can be appreciated when one stops to remember that the swallows return to specific Spanish missions in California on exactly the same day every year. This regularity depends on a kind of biological clock that is set in motion by changes in day length. The eyes are the normal organs for detecting visible light, so it is not surprising that if experimental birds are kept hooded or if their eyes are removed they do not respond to changes in light which affect their sighted companions.

A trait analagous to this perception by the birds can be found in many kinds of flowering plants. Although plants have no central nervous system, in many the initiation of flowering and the setting of seeds is directly regulated by the quantity and quality of the light provided. Many good gardeners know they can fool chrysanthemums into blooming out of season by covering them up in the afternoon to initiate chemical changes which result in bud formation. If plants can respond to such subtle changes it is no wonder that higher organisms are also influenced by changes in their environment.

The fertile periods of many mammals are also influenced by light. These environmental changes are detected by retinal cells of the eye and are communicated to the central nervous system. The hypothalamus responds to this information and regulates the body accordingly.

Human reproductive cycles are not affected by light. Yet they can be influenced by other changes in the central nervous system. As an example, the constancy of the menstrual cycle in the human female can be disrupted by emotional upsets. The effect of emotional states on the gonads is mediated by the hypothalamus. Many people maintain that their aches and pains are directly related to changes in temperature and barometric pressure. It seems like black magic until you remember that pains in the joints and headaches are directly related to the regulation of the steroid hormones. Many of these subtle effects of the environment and the hypothalamus have not as yet been elucidated.

The special relationship between the hypothalamus and the pituitary gland was discovered by observing the effects of tumors of these organs on the secretion of gonadal hormones. Additional information was obtained from transplant experiments performed on a variety of birds and mammals. When the pituitary gland was surgically implanted into the kidney or the wall of the body cavity it remained alive but it did not function. If, however, the pituitary was implanted into the hypothalamus region it resumed its normal control over the system of endocrine glands. These glands include the thyroid, gonads, adrenal, and part of the pancreas.

In other experiments electrical stimulation of the hypothalamus activated the pituitary both in its normal location and when transplanted into the hypothalamus. The activation of the pituitary can be monitored by detecting increased amounts of steroid hormones in the blood. These steroid hormones have come from certain of the endocrine glands.

The transplant experiments demonstrate that the regulation of the pituitary by the hypothalamus does not require intact nerves between the two organs. Cut nerves do not regenerate. Therefore the hypothalamus must regulate the pituitary by some chemical means, in the form of various "releasing factors" secreted by the cells of the hypothalamus. Such biochemicals could be called hypothalamic hormones, but the name that has come to be applied to them is *hypothalamic releasing factors*. This hypothalamic function is analogous to the pituitary regulation of the thyroid, gonads, and adrenal glands by the release of specific trophic hormones. The best current evidence of biochemical secretions by the cells of the hypothalamus in response to changes in their environment indicates at least five different varieties of releasing factors.

One variety causes the pituitary to secrete ACTH. Another triggers the release of FSH, a trophic hormone which stimulates the growth of the follicles of the ovary, which in turn produce the hormone estrogen. A third variety of hypothalamic releasing factor causes the pituitary to secrete LTH. This trophic hormone stimulates the formation of the corpus luteum, a mass of cells which develops in the cavity left in an ovary after ovulation. The corpus luteum cells synthesize progesterone. Whereas the female hormone estrogen promotes the development of mammary tissue and the lining of the uterine wall, the progesterone maintains the bed of tissues in the uterus which serves as the support material for the implantation of a fertilized ovum.

The fourth variety of releasing factor causes the pituitary to form a trophic hormone to control the thyroid gland. The fifth regulates the formation of growth hormone by the pituitary.

The precise chemical nature of these releasing factors is now known for some of these actions. There is considerable evidence that the hypothalamus inhibits the pituitary from secreting the trophic hormone which triggers lactation (the process of milk production by the mammary tissue). If the stalk between the hypothalamus and the pituitary is cut, lactation is stimulated, but the secretion of the other trophic hormones from the pituitary is repressed. It is therefore known that the hypothalamus can control some actions of the pituitary by inhibition while others are regulated by stimulation. Lactation, for instance, is stopped by the action of high concentrations of steroid hormones produced in the placenta of a pregnant woman. After parturition (the act of childbirth) this source of hormones is gone and the inhibition of lactation is therefore removed. Normally no lactation occurs until nearly twenty-four hours after the birth of the baby. Lactation can be continued by maintaining the mammary tissue in a productive state. Normally this is controlled by chemical and neural mechanisms which respond to the suckling stimulus in most women, although the presence of the steroid hormones of the stress response can interfere with continued milk production.

The releasing factors travel from the hypothalamus, where they are formed, to the pituitary by means of a special arrangement of blood vessels. This pattern of circulation insures that all of the blood that will reach the pituitary has already been in contact with cells of the hypothalamus. In this manner the releasing factors produced in the hypothalamus reach the pituitary in a relatively concentrated form, in contrast to the pituitary trophic hormones, which are diluted into the general circulation before they are carried to the target organs, the endocrine glands which specifically respond to these stimuli.

The influence of the releasing factors on pituitary secretion is remarkably specific. The response of the pituitary is also precise. Normally only the proper amount of the appropriate trophic hormone is released to adjust the homeostatic system. Only minute amounts of the factors are required to regulate the pituitary secretions. Although the nature of some chemicals which act like specific releasing agents is known, the manner in which they initiate the secretions of the pituitary is not. The location of the hypothalamus with its neural as well as circulatory relationships makes it the ideal organ to serve as the regulator of the pituitary. The hypothalamus can be visualized as a fantastic switchboard of the nervous system. It receives many nerve connections from other parts of the brain. In addition to direct neural stimulation and inhibition, the hypothalamus can be triggered by secretions of nerve cells which do not make actual contact with it. These transmitter substances, or neurohormones as they are called, include acetylcholine, noradrenalin, serotonin, dopamine, and GABA. The hypothalamus regulation of the pituitary is also modulated by the concentration of sugars, by some steroids, possibly by the presence of deactivated adrenal medulla hormones, and in particular by the electrically charged molecules (ions) in the blood brought to the brain.

Changes in the concentration of these non-hormonal chemicals in the blood can, by stimulation or repression, affect the release of specific releasing factors. The neurohormones also have indirect effects on the secretions of the hypothalamus by controlling the blood flow through the brain. In addition these neurohormones also have direct and specific effects on the type and quantity of the releasing factors carried by the blood vessels to the pituitary.

The balancing of regulatory mechanisms is a byword in all fields of biology. It is known that drugs which repress the stress-response hormones, noradrenalin and adrenalin, also inhibit the pituitary stimulation of the corpus luteum. When these drugs are provided, the corpus luetum becomes non-functional, so progesterone secretion ceases. In the female the progesterone's failure to maintain the uterine lining causes the onset of menses. Alternatively, high amounts of noradrenalin or adrenalin stimulate the corpus luteum by triggering the pituitary to secrete additional amounts of luteotrophic hormone (LTH). This results in additional production of progesterone. In this manner tranquilizer drugs induce menses, the psychic stimulant drugs delay menses, and a variety of stress situations can cause disturbances in the constancy of the menstrual cycle.

These drugs and the sympathetic system hormones, noradrenalin and adrenalin, affect the pituitary release of trophic hormones by acting on the cells of the hypothalamus.

This entire complex of relationships is involved in the regulation and the consequences of the stress response. Many different types of stimuli of the hypothalamus cells make them secrete the ACTH releasing factor into the blood passing to the pituitary.

All of the various stress situations—emotional, physical, or physiological—cause the onset of the same stress-response mechanism by the hypothalamus. Whether the stress situation was communicated to the hypothalamus by specific nerves, secretions of neurohormones, or physiological changes in the hypothalamic cells affected by non-hormonal chemicals in the blood, it results in the liberation of the appropriate releasing factor to influence the pituitary to secrete ACTH.

Alternatively, when certain steroids are present in high concentration in the blood reaching the hypothalamus, when sodium salts are in abundance, when the blood sugar concentration is optimal, and possibly when alcohol is present, these conditions can act to inhibit the continued release of the hypothalamic factors. In this manner the products of the action of the endocrine glands can repress the hypothalamic cells by "feedback inhibition." Although noradrenalin can stimulate the LTH releasing factor, it inhibits the ACTH releasing factor. The ACTH releasing factor is regulated by a neurohormone called serotonin, and since the effect of serotonin is thus a part of the stress-response regulating system, some investigators suggested that serotonin levels are involved in the development of schizophrenia, and further that the biochemical basis of schizophrenia might involve a defect in the regulation of serotonin. These ideas were not generally accepted, but their authors did recognize that the symptoms associated with schizophrenia were related to the regulation of stress responses. There is no doubt now that serotonin can stimulate the hypothalamus to secrete the ACTH releasing factor but the mechanism involved is not known. It may be only one of the ways by which the hypothalamus starts the stress response.

Ever since the first publications about cyclic AMP (3'5'AMP) and its relationships to cellular regulation by Nobel laureate Earl Sutherland, many physiologists have been fascinated by the simplicity and widespread biological use of this molecule. Dr. Sutherland originally demonstrated that both adrenalin and glucagon provide the initial signal to some cells to initiate synthesis of new molecules in the liver to re-establish the homeostatic state of glood sugar sufficiency. These "first messenger" molecules are carried by the blood from the endocrine glands to the cells of the target tissues where they have their effect. Dr. Sutherland recognized that these hormones cause the release of a molecule called cyclic AMP. The cyclic AMP was then interpreted as being another regulator, a "second messenger" inside the cells of the target tissue. (Other investigators have since proposed an intermediate, the prostoglandins, between the first messengers, which pass through the blood, and the second messengers, which are active inside the cell.)

The rather complex relationships between the hormones and cyclic AMP do not end here. There is evidence to support the idea that the release of trophic hormones from the pituitary—ACTH, gonadotrophins, and thyrotrophic hormones as well as the pancreatic hormone, glucagon—is also regulated by the concentration of cyclic AMP. It is also theorized that aspirin may act by influencing the cellular concentration of cyclic AMP.

In the stress response adrenalin, noradrenalin, and glucagon stimulate the production and release of cyclic AMP in the glycogen-containing cells of the liver and perhaps in some muscle cells. It is insulin released from the pancreatic cells when glucose is present which inhibits the synthesis of cyclic AMP in these cells. While insulin decreases cyclic AMP it promotes the secretion of glycogen synthetase, the enzyme which forms glycogen from glucose.

The unfamiliar words that are necessary to explain how adrenalin and insulin regulate the secretion of cyclic AMP may scare some readers. It really isn't as bad as it seems at first. Adrenalin and glucagon trigger the activation of an enzyme called adenyl cyclase. This enzyme promotes the conversion of ATP to cyclic AMP. (When sugars, fats, or proteins are oxidized, the energy of the chemical bonds is trapped in ATP molecules for use by the cells. ATP is the form of energy that is necessary for cellular actions.) AMP stands for a molecule containing one phosphate group. ATP has three phosphates and is called adenosine triphosphate. ATP is a very active molecule that is able to provide energy and phosphates to regulate cellular reactions. In these reactions, just as in the phosphorylation of sugars, ATP serves as a source of phosphate. Phosphate groups render biological molecules highly reactive. Cyclic AMP ($3'5'$) binds to an inactive enzyme called protein kinase. This combination of the enzyme and $3'5'$AMP activates or "arms" the protein kinase. The activation of this enzyme, which now serves as a catalyst to transfer other phosphates from ATP to protein molecules, provides the energy to split glycogen molecules into glucose by stimulating or activating another enzyme called phosphorylase. It actually converts an inactive phosphorylase b to an active form of the enzyme phosphorylase a.

In another action the $3'5'$AMP inactivates the enzyme glycogen synthetase (which is induced by insulin) and so blocks the conversion of glucose into glycogen. In this way the enzymes which cause the glycogen synthesis from glucose do not compete with the enzymes which cause the breakdown of glycogen to glucose. The physiological term for the conversion of glycogen to glucose is glycogenolysis. The word "lysis" means "to break down" so the word glycogenolysis=the breakdown of glycogen to its component parts, glucose molecules. The conversion of glycogen to glucose ceases when cyclic AMP is inactivated by an enzyme known as phosphodiesterase. This enzyme is induced by insulin and inhibited by adrenalin.

The recognition of the adrenalin and glucagon action in stimulating cyclic AMP and thus causing the conversion of glycogen to glucose has led to the belief that this same type of system can be used to explain other hormone actions. Cyclic AMP does not accumulate in the fluids of the body. It is present only in cells. Cyclic AMP is found in many other kinds of cells besides those that contain glycogen. In all of the cells where cyclic AMP is found it "arms" or "activates" protein kinase. In the many diverse cells it seems that the protein kinase is just the same but that it is locked into different metabolic pathways. Yet there may be different forms of protein kinase. So far the research has not provided enough information to answer all our questions about this system. Apparently in all cases the cyclic AMP binds to a group of atoms in the kinase molecule which ordinarily maintain the kinase in an inactive state. By the cyclic AMP action of "pulling this molecular firing pin," the inhibitor of the enzyme is caused to dissociate from the enzyme. The "armed grenade" of active protein kinase then can participate in regulating the metabolic processes in the cells.

Adrenalin and insulin are therefore not antagonists in the usual sense of the word. When both are present simultaneously neither is effective in doing its regular job in the liver. Since the adrenalin and insulin are not secreted in the cells where they are active in affecting the blood sugar control, neither of these hormones represses the other's formation or action in other non-competitive responses. The actions of adrenalin on the remainder of the body can be continued until the hypothalamic fuel deficiency is satisfied. The only food providing that energy directly to the brain is sugar. For many persons fructose is preferred because it can be externally regulated without initiating the release of insulin. The presence of fructose in the blood supplied to the hypothalamus eliminates the necessity of initiating the stress response which causes adrenalin to be released to convert glycogen to glucose by its initiation of cyclic AMP. Yet this same fructose does not cause insulin release. If the initial stress was hypoglycemia the fructose may have a moderating effect in that it provides food for the hypothalamus and thus reduces the level of tension-producing adrenalin secretion which would otherwise be required.

Basic Research
on Stress-Response Control

An alleviation of the demand for alcohol among alcoholics, the elimination of the craving for food among those who tend to overeat, the provision of a natural ameliorant for different varieties of psychiatric disorders, and a reduction of the frequency and magnitude of migraine headaches for persons with such problems are all logical extensions of the specific new theory which is the central theme of this book. The theory can be simply stated: When fructose is provided in a dietary regimen to supply a sufficiency of sugar to maintain the nervous system, the stress of a deficiency of intracellular sugar and the subsequent stress response which normally is initiated to correct this condition are eliminated. This theory has been developed as an extension of the data obtained in a well-controlled research program.

Questions about the effective use of fructose in a dietary regimen have been raised by previous research data reported in the scientific literature. It has been well established that, although fructose does not precipitate the release of insulin to cause the storage of the sugar as liver glycogen, excess fructose is preferentially converted into fat. At least two legitimate questions can therefore be asked: Will the provision of fructose in the diet each hour of the day lead to an accumulation in the blood of cholesterol and triglycerides (the small fragments of fat molecules)? Can the exchange of fructose for other carbohydrates actually provide for a decrease in the stress response sufficient for any practical application?

It has not been necessary to test extensively each of the specific practical implications of the theory in controlled basic research programs. Such projects will undoubtedly be conducted in the future by many persons with specific interests and facilities. Such tests can be exhaustive but they will be difficult. The difficulty must be recognized as inherent in the research because success is so hard to define and to quantify. Some alcoholics have previously been able to go on the water wagon for extended periods without eating fructose each hour. Dietary regulation has allowed many overweight persons to lose weight without using fructose. Migraine headaches are not usually predictable in frequency, nor do they follow a regular schedule. Diagnoses of schizophrenia or other psychoses are not sufficiently consistent to eliminate the criticism that the subjects should have been diagnosed differently or treated differently with drugs and counseling.

Because of these obvious practical difficulties with any research program the tests of the basic theory have been restricted to data obtained from persons with no known metabolic or psychological problems who were free of medications which might interfere with the interpretation of the results. Conducting the test programs with normal, healthy, intelligent, adult volunteers also has the added advantage of willing cooperation and an ability of the subjects to follow the prescribed directions. On the basis of the results one can go on to consider their implications for many specific disorders.

The design of the research, the data obtained, and the conclusions that were reached must be expressed in a technical language that may not be of interest to all readers of this book. They are provided here for those whose background in science research and orientation cause them to wish to have all of the information readily available.

The basic research information on this topic was first conveyed to the scientific community in a report, "Benefits of Dietary Fructose in Alleviating the Human Stress Response," by J. D. Palm. This présentation was given as a part of a Symposium on the Physiological Effects of Food Carbohydrates, sponsored by the Division of Carbohydrate Chemistry and the Division of Agriculture and Food Chemistry of the American Chemical Society. It was held as a part of the National Annual Meeting of the American Chemical Society at Atlantic City, New Jersey, September 9–13, 1974. The data and research information reported at the symposium are included here in their entirety. The form of presentation is different from the research paper presented at the symposium but the content is the same.

An initial question about the effective use of fructose in exchange for glucose was precipitated by a contention of some previous investigators that they had found that fructose was converted into glucose either in the digestive tract or in the liver and then accumulated in the blood as glucose. If such a conversion is commonplace it is not likely that fructose would be of practical significance in the prevention of the stress of hypoglycemia.

Some of the investigations which had led to this belief had involved the injection of high concentrations of fructose into laboratory animals. In other programs the investigators had given large amounts of fructose in the diet without eliminating or reducing other dietary carbohydrates. In some of these tests the blood sugar concentration had been raised beyond the levels that are normally encountered in physiological situations. Such tests may have acted as stresses because of the osmotic effect of high fructose concentrations. In the fructose exchange diet the provision of a total of 100 grams of fructose given in small portions throughout the day to maintain the sugar requirements of the cells of the central nervous system is intended to be within the normal limits of the body's ability to absorb and use the sugar. The effects of such a program may be different from those published in some of the previous research reports. It is possible to test the hypothesis that a significant amount of fructose is immediately converted into glucose, which would be expected to induce the release of insulin and cause the storage of the sugar as liver glycogen.

The volunteer subjects had not eaten for at least six hours before the test was begun at the fasting blood sugar level. In most people this level is approximately 90 mg. glucose/100 ml. of blood plasma. The subjects were made comfortable and an indwelling plastic needle-catheter was inserted into a vein of the lower arm after the venipuncture area was anesthetized by an injection of novocaine. The test subjects had no physical discomfort from the procedures after the initial insertion of the catheter. The catheter was coupled to a small sterile valve fitted with a blood-collection syringe and to a syringe containing a small amount of heparin mixed in a normal saline solution. This valve system allowed the blood samples to be collected repeatedly without complications. A small amount of the heparin solution was injected after each blood sample was drawn to prevent coagulation of the blood in the catheter. Blood samples were taken every five minutes until the blood glucose concentration had stabilized at the initial base line of 90 mg./100 ml. of plasma. This stability of the fasting blood sugar concentration was usually achieved by the time of the third or fourth sample so the test was normally begun twenty minutes after the insertion of the catheter.

Blood samples were drawn every five minutes for approximately an hour for each test. Since only 3 ml. of blood is required for each test the subjects were not stressed by a reduction in the active amount of blood required to continue normal physiological activities. The blood sugar determinations were made using a Beckman Glucose Analyzer. This instrument detects only glucose. It is not affected by other reducing sugars nor is it affected by fructose. The results of the tests are therefore given only as changes in the blood glucose concentration. Individual variability is evident in the data obtained from different subjects but no significant differences from those obtained from a typical subject were encountered. The results of these tests reported here are those of an individual typical test.

For the first test the subject was given 50 grams of sucrose (table sugar) in a syrupy drink twenty minutes after the needle was inserted into the vein. The blood glucose concentration was determined every five minutes as the concentration rose and until three successive samples showed a progressive decrease in the blood glucose level. The results of these tests were plotted on a graph given in Figure 2. The rise of the blood glucose during the first hour after the syrup was ingested can be plotted as a line with a slope of $0.983 \pm S.D. = .0555$.

On the second test day, twenty minutes after the blood-collection catheter had been inserted, the subject drank a sugar solution containing 25 grams of pure glucose instead of the 50 grams of sucrose of the first test. Since sucrose is a disaccharide (double sugar) it contains equal amounts of glucose and fructose so that the amount of glucose provided in the initial test was also 25 grams.

The test results reaffirmed that pure glucose is absorbed from the digestive tract into the blood more rapidly than glucose derived from sucrose, which must be digested before the glucose is absorbed. The slope of the plotted line of glucose-concentration change for the second test was $1.54 \pm S.D. .0656$. Although this rate of absorption of glucose from these two sources is measurably different, this change in the rate of accumulation in the blood is not of practical significance.

During both the first and second day of testing the blood glucose concentration rose to approximately 160 mg. of glucose/100 ml. of blood plasma and then decreased. The blood sampling was then discontinued. If the blood glucose concentration had gone above 160

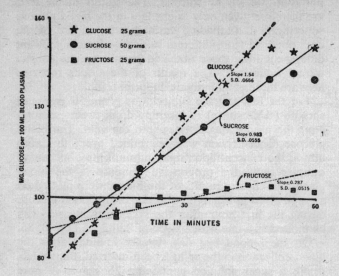

*Figure 2 Plasma Glucose Concentration Following
Ingestion of Sugars*

Typical plasma glucose concentrations following ingestion of 25 grams of glucose on day 1, 25 grams of fructose on day 2, and 50 grams of sucrose on day 3. The differences in the slopes of the glucose and glucose obtained by digestion of sucrose are inconsequential. The slope of the glucose determined after ingestion of fructose indicates that no appreciable amount of fructose is converted to glucose and returned to the blood stream.

mg./100 ml. of plasma it is possible that some sugar may have spilled into the urine. Usually the body is unable to reabsorb sugars from the kidney fluids if the blood glucose concentration exceeds 160 mg./100 ml. of blood plasma. Under such conditions the blood would be accumulating sugar from a dilute solution into a more concentrated medium. The amount of cellular work required to accomplish this makes such reabsorption metabolically inefficient.

On the day of the third test the subject was given 25 grams of fructose instead of the glucose or sucrose solutions. The blood sugar concentration was measured as glucose to determine whether the fructose was converted into glucose that was circulated in the blood. The slope of the plotted line obtained from the test data was $0.287 \pm$ S.D. .0515. This is such a slight rise in the blood glucose concentration as to be indistinguishable from a change in the blood glucose concentration which may occur as a response to the test situation. Even if some fructose is converted to glucose, the amount of this conversion, either in the digestive tract or in the liver and then back to the circulating blood, is of minor significance.

The 25 grams of fructose given at one time at the beginning of the test is two or three times the amount suggested in the fructose exchange diet for one hour. Therefore, even if the amount of fructose taken in any given hour is increased by two or three times that suggested in the diet, the blood glucose concentration does not change as a result of the dietary use of pure fructose. The likelihood of fructose being converted to glucose to cause the release of insulin is therefore negligible if 25 grams or less are ingested at a time.

Blood samples from 17 healthy adults were tested to investigate the possibility that an exchange of 100 grams of pure fructose for most of the insulin-inducing carbohydrates of a normal diet would affect the concentration of plasma triglycerides and plasma cholesterol. The persons included in this test program were not following a specific dietary regimen before the initial samples of blood were collected. These test subjects agreed to continue their normal diet practices but to exchange their sugar and starch intake for 100 grams of fructose each day for three days. The fructose was consumed as chewable tablets, candies, and beverage sweeteners. After the third day on this fructose exchange diet a second blood sample was collected. The plasma cholesterol and plasma triglycerides in the pre- and post-diet blood samples were compared. Table 2 and Figures 3 and 4 show that the concentration of these

TABLE 2

Effect of Diet on Plasma Cholesterol and Plasma
Triglycerides
Fructose Diet Program Exchanged
100 Grams Fructose for 100 Grams of Other Carbohydrates

SUBJECT CODE	CONTROL DIET CHOLESTEROL mg./100 ml. plasma	FRUCTOSE DIET CHOLESTEROL mg./100 ml. plasma	CONTROL DIET TRIGLYCERIDES mg./100 ml. plasma	FRUCTOSE DIET TRIGLYCERIDES mg./100 ml. plasma
CB	217	181	137	178
LJ	197	205	91	129
IJ	256	243	114	61
MJ	214	216	61	57
GJ	158	183	53	38
JD	193	214	68	78
KK	197	222	151	106
OM	170	195	56	43
JK	186	187	53	49
IN	222	246	46	59
DJ	170	187	76	41
GB	190	235	50	55
GK	232	232	79	70
IM	138	163	35	67
AC	127	148	27	43
SK	173	170	61	73
VO	301	363	84	103
	$\overline{X}$=196.529	$\overline{X}$=211.176	$\overline{X}$=73.0588	$\overline{X}$=73.5294
	S.E.=10.3174	S.E.=11.7584	S.E.=8.2629	S.E.=8.9432
	S.D.=42.5399	S.D.=48.481	S.D.=34.0688	S.D.=36.8784
	F=.876673 (1,32 D.F.)		F=.150008E-2 (1,32 D.F.)	
	Probability=.9999		Probability=.9999	

two blood components did not change significantly as
a result of the fructose diet. There was no attempt in
this research program to regulate the amount of fats
consumed during the diet period or to eliminate all
carbohydrates which might induce the release of in-

sulin. Although the amount of cholesterol and/or triglycerides decreased in some of the test subjects it remained the same or increased in others by the third day of the fructose exchange diet. There is no evidence from this set of tests which would suggest that the fructose exchange diet will directly result in a lowering or an increase in the plasma cholesterol or plasma triglycerides in the participants of such a dietary program.

The effectiveness of fructose in the alleviation of conditions which give rise to the symptoms of psychiatric disorders, migraine headaches, the reduction of the craving for alcohol by alcoholics, and the relief from the nearly insatiable desire for food among some severely overweight persons depends on the ability of fructose to eliminate the stress of an insufficiency of sugar for the nervous system and thereby to prevent the necessity of a stress response which normally would follow such a hypoglycemic condition. Fructose can be expected to decrease only one stress, that of a deficiency of metabolizable sugar to maintain the control of the nervous system cells. No one should expect a decrease in the measurable stress response if the subject has been using sedative drugs, which depress the action of the central nervous system. No reduction in the stress response should be anticipated if the subject has been kept quasi-anesthetized by a continuous consumption of ethyl alcohol. No change in the stress response should be expected if a person has been maintaining a high blood sugar level by a continuous and excess intake of food which has led to a continuous weight gain. Such behaviors may have depressed the stress responses but have led to other detrimental physiological conditions. An effective change in the stress response can be anticipated only if a prior deficiency of blood sugar exists and the nervous system has been operating normally.

A stress of a deficiency of blood sugar, the condition of hypoglycemia, can be created experimentally

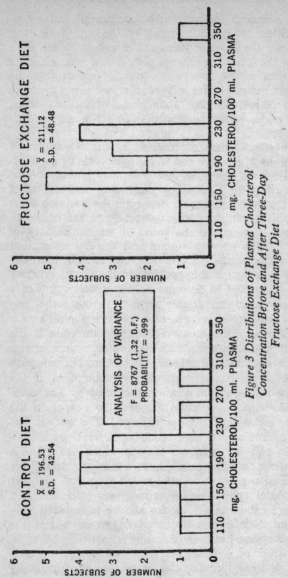

Figure 3 *Distributions of Plasma Cholesterol Concentration Before and After Three-Day Fructose Exchange Diet*

The distributions of the plasma cholesterol concentration show no significant change as the diet is modified from a regular diet to a diet containing 100 grams of fructose exchanged for other carbohydrates.

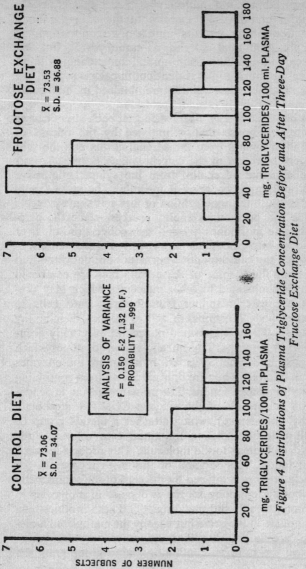

Figure 4 *Distributions of Plasma Triglyceride Concentration Before and After Three-Day Fructose Exchange Diet*

No changes in the plasma triglycerides of 100 grams of fructose for other carbohydrates were found as the result of an exchange hydrates for a three-day period.

by providing a test subject with a diet that is insufficient in carbohydrate calories to maintain the body activities. Many persons apparently require approximately 2000 total calories, as carbohydrate, fat, and protein, to continue their normal functioning without losing weight. If a diet is deficient in caloric supply, the additional necessary calories are obtained by metabolizing glycogen, body fats, and proteins.

It has been amply established that each stress causes a stress response that is initiated by the release of steroid hormones from the adrenal cortex and the subsequent secretion of the catecholamine hormones, noradrenalin and adrenalin, from the sympathetic nerve cells and from the adrenal medulla. The steroid hormones cause the mobilization of fats and some proteins which can be used as energy sources, while the catecholamine hormones trigger the conversion of liver glycogen into glucose as part of their normal actions.

When the catecholamine hormones are delivered into the body fluids some of these molecules are combined with or conjugated to other molecules which may prevent the catecholamines from entering into cells to regulate body functions, or at least reduce their ability to do so. These deactivated molecules eventually accumulate in the urine. The catecholamine hormones which do pass into other cells are modified by the enzymes within the cells. They are thus prevented from continuing their stimulatory actions. The primary enzymatic deactivation is a result of the enzyme COMT (catechol O methyl transferase), which attaches a methyl group (a small molecular fraction containing a carbon and three hydrogen atoms) to the molecule. This process is called methylation. The addition of this methyl group to the catecholamines produced by the cells of the sympathetic nervous system converts the two kinds of molecules to normetadrenalin and metadrenalin. These products can accumulate in the urine but usually the methylated molecules are further modified by other enzymes which remove the nitrogen-containing amino group from the hormone molecules. This is the action of the MAO enzyme (monoamine oxidase). The interactions of these two enzymes convert the original biologically active hormones into terminal excretion products which have no stimulatory action.

The common excretion products of the cathecholamine hormones which escape conjugation can be grouped into two kinds of molecules. One type of terminal molecule is a phenyl glycol, while the most common excretion product is a mandelic acid. Figure 5 indicates the metabolic pathways and the relationships

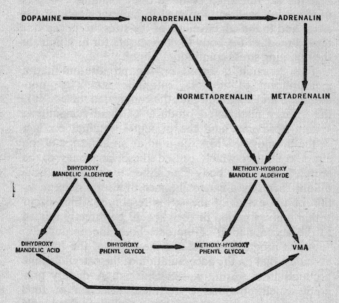

Figure 5 Metabolic Paths and Products of Sympathetic System Hormones

The catecholamine hormones dopamine, noradrenalin, and adrenalin are enzymatically deactivated by the enzyme COMT (catechol O methyl transferase) and MAO (monoamine oxidase). All of the products are excreted in the urine. VMA (vanilyl mandelic acid—3 methoxy 4 hydroxy mandelic acid) is the primary terminal excretion product.

of the sympathetic system hormones to the terminal products. The principal excretion product can be seen to be VMA (3 methoxy 4 hydroxy mandelic acid). All of these terminal and some of the intermediate molecules are excreted in the urine.

Several different test methods are available to determine the concentration of the biologically active as well as the methylated and the terminal excretion products of the sympathetic system hormones. Although no one has published the use of these tests as a measure of the regulated stress response, it is logical to assume that the accumulation of these catecholamine products in the urine is directly related to the magnitude of the stress and to the effectiveness of the stress-response system to readjust the body to compensate for or eliminate the initiating stress condition.

This research is based on the proposition that a measurement of the total catecholamines (free noradrenalin and adrenalin plus the conjugated molecules), the urinary methylated products of these sympathetic system hormones, and the principal terminal product of the hormones, VMA, be used as an indicator of the stress condition which caused these hormones to be secreted into the body fluids. Since the stress conditions themselves cannot be measured, the determination of the extent of the stress responses which occur within a given period of time should be directly related to the accumulation of the catecholamine products.

A test program to evaluate the effect of the fructose exchange diet on the accumulation of the catecholamine products in the urine was established. A dietary program which provided a nutritious selection of food options in three meals and two snacks provided only 100 grams of carbohydrate (400 calories). The 1200-calorie daily diet was adapted from published dietary suggestions of the American Dietetic Association. The control diet provided the carbohydrates as starches and some sucrose. The experimental diet was identical in all other respects except that the sole carbohydrate source was fructose (100 grams) as chewable tablets, beverage sweeteners, salad dressing, and gelatine dessert. The fructose intake was spaced to provide 8 grams of fructose each hour.

A group of 20 healthy adults volunteered to follow the diet as specified and to collect a complete twenty-four-hour urine sample during a day of the control diet and another twenty-four-hour collection while they followed the fructose exchange diet.

The urines were collected in hard glass jugs containing 15 ml. of concentrated hydrochloric acid. Care was taken to insure that all of the bottles were fitted with Teflon-lined caps to prevent possible contamination of the urine samples by cork or paper products. The bottles were kept refrigerated until the analysis was completed within three days of collection. The volume of the twenty-four-hour collection was measured and a portion of the urine was acidified to pH 0.5, transferred to plastic-capped hard glass tubes, and placed in a boiling water bath for twenty minutes to hydrolyze the sample (acid hydrolysis splits up the conjugated molecules) so that the total catecholamine concentration would be determined. The refrigerated, hydrolyzed urine samples were found to be stable for at least one week.

Disposable Bio-Rad Catecholamine Chromatographic Columns were used to separate the catecholamines and the methylated products from the hydrolyzed urine samples. The catecholamines can be determined by the augmented fluorescence of these compounds while the methylated compounds were measured by their ability to absorb ultraviolet light.

After hydrolysis a 5 ml. portion of the urine was mixed with 14 ml. of EDTA solution provided in the Bio-Rad Test Set of chemicals. The pH of the resulting solution was then adjusted to pH 6.5. This entire solution was placed on the top of the disposable columns and allowed to percolate through the resin bed. The columns were then washed with two volumes of glass-distilled water. The original effluent and wash water was discarded. The catecholamines were then eluted (washed off the columns) with 10 ml. of 4.0 N. boric acid. A slight change was made in the original Bio-Rad procedure to provide an internal standard for each determination. The 10 ml. of boric acid containing the catecholamines was divided into four equal portions. Portion 1 was kept as a control in which the normal subsequent treatment which increases the fluorescence of the catecholamines was done in the reverse order of the sequence of the unknown samples. Portion 2 was kept as the unknown. Portion 3 was the unknown concentration of the catecholamines plus 1.0 μg of noradrenalin in a standard solution. Portion 4 contained the unknown concentration of plus 2 μg of noradrenalin. All portions were brought to a standard volume with glass-distilled water. The fluorescence of portions 2, 3, and 4 was compared with the control, using a Turner Fluorometer which was fitted with a high sensitivity adapter.

The data obtained from each of the portions of each of the twenty-four-hour samples were fed into a computer to obtain a least-squares line for the three determinations. The computer was programmed to determine the slope of the line for each sample, identify the intercept of the fluorescence of the unmodified unknown, and provide the computed standard deviation for each sample. The determined values of the sample were multiplied by the amount of urine in the original twenty-four-hour collection to obtain the amount of total catecholamines excreted during the period of the control and the experimental diet.

The enzymatically deactivated methylated derivatives of noradrenalin and adrenalin, which are collectively referred to as the metanephrines, were eluted from the Bio-Rad Catecholamine Columns with 10 ml. of 4.0 N. ammonium hydroxide after the boric acid treatment and a wash of the columns with distilled water. This eluate of ammonium hydroxide and the metanephrines was divided into four portions. Portion 1 was designated as the control. Portion 2 was the unmodified unknown. A 3-μg solution of normetadrenalin was added to Portion 3 and 9.0 μg of normetadrenalin was added to Portion 4. The samples were diluted to equal volume and read at 360 nm on a Beckman DU Spectrophotometer. The absorbence at 350 nm was used to screen the samples for contamination which might influence the values obtained at 360 nm. The same computer program used for the catecholamine determination was adapted for the computations of the methylated derivatives of the catecholamines.

VMA (3 methoxy 4 hydroxy mandelic acid), the terminal product of the enzymatic deactivation of the catecholamines, was determined from the unhydrolyzed twenty-four-hour urine which was collected for the other tests. In two laboratories two different but similar procedures—(1) the Pisano, Crout, and Abraham Method, and (2) the method of Gitlow et al.—were used to determine the concentration of the VMA. Both methods gave equivalent results but in order to prevent bias both the control and experimental diet samples were run simultaneously as blind tests by one procedure or the other. The total amount of VMA excreted during the twenty-four-hour period of the test was computed by multiplying the determined values by the volume of the total twenty-four-hour urine sample.

Tables 3, 4, and 5 and Figures 6 and 7 provide the data of this research program in numerical and pictorial form. In all 20 cases the measured concentration of the accumulated catecholamines in the twenty-four-hour urine sample was higher on the day of the control diet than on the day of the fructose exchange diet. The data obtained show that the decrease in the catecholamine concentration in the urine on the day during which the subjects were following the fructose exchange diet is sufficient to justify the conclusion that this difference would happen as a result of chance less than one time in a hundred sets of determinations. The likeli-

TABLE 3

Daily Excretion of Urinary Catecholamines

SUBJECT	CONTROL DIET VOLUME ml/24 hr.	FRUCTOSE DIET VOLUME ml/24 hr.	CONTROL DIET CATECHOL. ml/24 hr.	S.D.	FRUCTOSE DIET CATECHOL. ml/24 hr.	S.D.
RC	1700	1800	159.4	1.04	132.0	0.52
YJ	1725	1600	87.0	0.59	80.7	0.53
QL	1610	1400	152.5	0.78	104.7	0.78
RJ	1820	2365	282.0	1.68	75.7	0.45
RS	1280	900	175.5	1.46	68.9	1.16
QB	1445	600	125.5	0.89	69.8	1.16
QR	1900	755	154.6	1.15	129.4	1.06
FL	2460	1780	156.9	0.38	83.6	0.36
AE	1230	1360	86.4	0.62	73.4	0.42
UJ	2005	1310	103.9	0.59	72.0	0.82
AW	815	1550	210.6	1.34	75.1	0.33
CB	1420	1700	116.9	0.57	40.9	0.47
SB	1550	1810	236.6	1.55	158.9	0.55
OB	1610	1965	94.2	0.67	74.9	0.54
GB	1020	1230	65.3	1.14	61.5	0.60
HB	710	690	70.5	1.27	45.3	0.76
IB	1800	1810	136.4	0.38	105.7	0.33
QG	1710	1030	195.4	1.20	96.9	1.06
QV	1910	2320	217.8	0.68	125.3	0.27
UC	850	1080	100.8	0.64	73.4	1.17

$$\bar{X} = 146.41 \qquad\qquad \bar{X} = 87.4$$
$$S.E. = 13.26 \qquad\qquad S.E. = 6.77$$
$$S.D. = 59.32 \qquad\qquad S.D. = 30.279$$
$$F = 15.6986 \ (1, 38 \ D.F.)$$
$$Probability = 0.00055$$

hood that the fructose diet significantly decreases the stress response as measured by the amount of catecholamines in the urine is better than 99%.

The VMA concentrations, while not higher in every case on the day of the control diet, nevertheless differ significantly between the control diet day and the experimental diet (fructose exchange) day to demonstrate a decrease in VMA on the day of the fructose-

TABLE 4

Daily Excretion of Methylated Urinary Catecholamine Products

SUBJECT	CONTROL DIET METADR. μg/24 hr.	S.D.	FRUCTOSE DIET METADR. μg/24 hr.	S.D.
RC	1526.5	9.29	1731.5	5.09
YJ	1351.0	8.46	1365.0	9.07
QL	2192.0	7.74	1491.5	10.87
RJ	1571.2	8.96	2165.8	9.65
RS	1369.8	10.75	1847.6	20.80
QB	991.4	6.95	973.0	17.58
QR	1012.0	5.46	945.1	6.61
FL	2190.1	4.85	1552.7	4.45
AE	2098.8	8.57	2018.7	7.78
UJ	1247.6	6.27	1242.0	9.75
AW	2005.8	12.87	1894.8	6.16
CB	1564.3	5.60	1683.4	5.04
SB	2722.9	17.61	2456.0	6.87
OB	1459.1	9.38	1266.0	6.49
GB	814.4	8.34	712.5	6.10
HB	581.0	8.45	432.8	6.68
IB	2367.0	7.18	1627.4	4.63
QG	1747.2	10.80	1232.4	12.18
QV	1648.9	4.64	993.5	2.41
UC	1917.0	12.06	1502.9	14.36

$\overline{X}$=1618.9

S.E.=122.66

S.D.=546.537

$\overline{X}$=1456.7

S.E.=112.21

S.D.=501.809

F=0.951672 (1,38 D.F.)

Probability=0.99999

exchange diet at the 95% confidence interval. In the cases where the VMA concentrations were greater on the day of the fructose diet these samples were obtained from female subjects who were menstruating on the day that this sample was collected.

The urinary accumulation of the total metanephrines, normetadrenalin and metadrenalin, did not differ as a result of the test program. The variations between the result of the two test days would occur as a result of chance 99 times out of 100 determinations.

The conclusions that can be derived from these research data support the contention that the urinary accumulation of the methylated derivatives does not vary with the accumulation of the catecholamines and the VMA in the urine. The data do support the contention that the accumulation of the total (free and conjugated) catecholamines and the urinary VMA shows a statis-

TABLE 5

Daily Excretion of Urinary VMA

SUBJECT	CONTROL DIET VMA mg/24 hr.	FRUCTOSE DIET VMA mg/24 hr.
RC	10.2	7.3
YJ	9.7	9.1
QL	6.0	5.5
RJ	7.6	9.6
RS	4.6	4.1
QB	5.6	2.9
QR	1.8	0.1
FL	9.3	1.6
AE	6.4	4.4
UJ	7.9	6.2
AW	4.3	3.8
CB	5.1	3.6
SB	9.1	5.7
OB	8.0	4.6
GB	3.1	1.8
HB	2.3	1.3
IB	3.8	3.3
QG	6.0	4.3
QV	4.1	2.6
UC	6.4	7.6
	$\overline{X} = 6.118$	$\overline{X} = 4.47$
	S.E. $= 0.553$	S.E. $= 0.572$
	S.D. $= 2.473$	S.D. $= 2.5584$

$$F = 4.01786 \ (1,38 \ \text{D.F.})$$
$$\text{Probability} = 0.0494$$

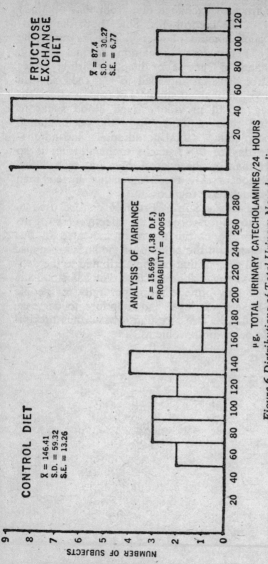

µg. TOTAL URINARY CATECHOLAMINES/24 HOURS

Figure 6 Distributions of Total Urinary Noradrenalin
and Adrenalin on Days of Control and Fructose Exchange Diet

The excretion of the total catecholamines (both free and conjugated) in the urine on the day of the fructose exchange diet is significantly lower at the 99% con-fidence limit than when the subjects were given the control diet containing 1200 calories. See text for details.

tically significant decrease in the stress response on the day of the fructose exchange diet from that obtained on the day of the control diet. Since both diets provided the same amount of energy, both required the use of body energy stores to maintain normal activity.

The exchange of fructose for the other carbohydrates of the control diet was intended to test the one idea that the provision of small amounts of fructose throughout the day would provide enough blood sugar to decrease the stress response. Since the accumulation of the catecholamines (total noradrenalin and adrenalin) on the day of the fructose exchange diet is so much lower than on the control diet day, such differences would occur as a result of chance in less than 1 out of 100 such test programs.

The conclusions are firm. Fructose can be used to reduce the stress response. The effectiveness of its application for all of the disorders indicated in this book will depend on the amount of the stress response of the affected persons that can be attributed to the deficiency in blood sugar. The fructose diet has stood the test. Fructose may provide the opportunity for people to change their stress level and therefore to decrease the necessity for the stress response which has precipitated certain behavioral problems.

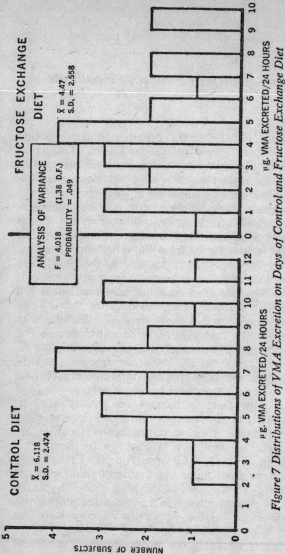

Figure 7 *Distributions of VMA Excretion on Days of Control and Fructose Exchange Diet*

The excretion of this terminal product of the enzymatic deactivation of the catecholamine hormones is significantly decreased on the day of the fructose exchange diet at the 95% confidence limit in comparison to the excretion of VMA when the subject was given a 1200-calorie diet without the fructose. See text for details.

APPENDIX 3

Availability of Fructose Products

Throughout this book the prescription for reducing stress has been based on the exchange of different varieties of carbohydrates. The unique effectiveness of the plan for eating less at a time but more often depends on the periodic inclusion of pure fructose in the diet. Fructose in combination with other monosaccharides in fresh ripe fruits, honey, and sucrose has always been recognized as a very sweet and energy-providing food. Yet it is different from the other simple sugars. As far as is now known, fructose is the only sugar whose molecular structure provides for a slow transport from the digestive tract into the blood and does not cause insulin release while providing for the cells of the nervous system. It is these metabolic characteristics which make the exchange of fructose for glucose (or glucose-producing carbohydrates) so advantageous.

In the United States the market for fructose has until recently been primarily confined to the pharmaceutical industry and as a sweetener for some items in the food industry. Now fructose belongs on grocers' shelves. Unfortunately there is currently no domestic production of pure fructose. Until new production facilities are built it will be necessary to continue to import this sugar from Finland, Germany, Austria, France, and perhaps even from Japan. The price of fructose therefore depends on the costs of shipping in addition to the cost of raw sugar from which most fructose is obtained. The technology for the conversion of corn starch to fructose is now available and may be expected to be commercially advantageous in the future. The cost of

234

separating fructose from other sugars will always be reflected in its price, but the costs and the value to the consumer are not always both defined in dollars. Even though fructose is always higher-priced than sucrose, its distinct benefit for the emotional and physical well-being of those who need to regulate externally their supply of sugar to the cells of the nervous system is almost incalculable.

Although fructose is only a pure food, you can expect many pharmacists to recognize its sale potential and to add fructose to their line of candies and sweeteners. In some areas the distribution of fructose is primarily through supermarkets and groceries. In other places the fructose tablets, crystalline sugar, and syrup will be found on the shelves of specialty food shops and health food stores.

Don't be fooled by advertisements for products which contain fructose but also include glucose, starches, or lactose in anything more than insignificant amounts. The dietary effectiveness in reducing stress, tension, and anxiety depends on the provision of fructose in exchange for other carbohydrates. If you are going to eat fructose together with these other insulin-inducing carbohydrates, it certainly would be preferable to eat sucrose or fresh and dried fruits, which may be just as effective as fructose mixtures. Such foods would also be considerably cheaper than a manufactured product to which fructose has been added for sales promotion. The inclusion of minor amounts of sorbitol and salts of fatty acids in the tablet or candy products will not detract from the value of products which are otherwise pure fructose.

If fructose is not available in your local stores, ask your local health food store to order it for you. In addition, there are a few distributors who will sell their products by direct mail or who can give you information about their dealers. The inclusion of the names and addresses of these distributors of fructose products should not be construed as advertising their particular items nor does it suggest that their fructose is any better than any other. The distributors, importers, and processors listed in alphabetical order below have not commissioned or reviewed this book prior to its publication. They are not responsible in any way for its contents. But they sell the products the book describes and have been contacted about, and consented to, the inclusion of their names as sources of fructose in the United States. If you provide a self-addressed and stamped envelope, they will send you information concerning their products.

A.W.G. Chemical Co., Inc.
450 Park Avenue
New York, New York
    10022

Caleb Laboratory
c/o Ellis Abrahamson
714 Maple Park Court
Mendota Heights,
    Minnesota 55118

North Nassau Dispensary
1691 Northern Boulevard
Manhasset, New York
    11030

Pfanstiehl Laboratories
1219 Glenrock Avenue
Waukegan, Illinois 60085

Vitose Corporation
154 Burlington
P. O. Drawer O
Clarendon Hills, Illinois
    60514

Sunbright Fructose Co.
Box 8443
Lake Street Station
Minneapolis, Minnesota
    55408

APPENDIX 4

Caloric Values of Common Foods

CALORIC VALUES OF COMMON FOODS

The foods listed in this table are grouped to aid in the selection of types of food products. The weights are given for normal-size servings together with the total food energy in calories. The weights of the individual components of the foods—carbohydrates, fats, and proteins—are provided. The values given are based on USDA consumer information and rounded to the nearest whole number. Trace amounts are indicated by tr.

	Weight Grams	Carbohydrates Grams	Fat Grams	Protein Grams	Food Energy Calories
BEANS AND NUTS					
Beans, canned with pork and tomato sauce, 1 cup	255	49	6	16	310
Beans, navy (pea), cooked, drained, 1 cup	190	40	1	15	225
Peanut butter, 1 tablespoon	16	3	8	4	95
Peanuts, roasted, salted halves, 1 cup	144	27	73	37	840

	Weight Grams	Carbo-hydrates Grams	Fat Grams	Protein Grams	Food Energy Calories
FATS, OILS, AND SALAD DRESSINGS					
Butter, regular (4 sticks/pound), 1 stick, ½ cup	113	1	100	1	810
Butter, regular (4 sticks/pound), 1 tablespoon	14	tr	12	tr	100
Butter, whipped (6 sticks/pound), 1 stick, ½ cup	76	tr	67	tr	540
Butter, whipped (6 sticks/pound), 1 tablespoon	9	tr	8	tr	65
Fats, cooking, lard, 1 tablespoon	13	0	14	0	115
Fats, cooking, vegetable, 1 tablespoon	13	0	14	0	110
Margarine, regular (4 sticks/pound), 1 stick, ½ cup	113	1	100	1	815
Oils, salad or cooking, 1 tablespoon	14	0	16	0	125
corn, cottonseed, olive, peanut, safflower, soybean					
Salad dressings, blue cheese, 1 tablespoon	15	1	9	1	75
Salad dressings, French, 1 tablespoon	16	3	8	tr	65
Salad dressings, mayonnaise, 1 tablespoon	14	tr	12	tr	100
FISH AND SHELLFISH					
Bluefish, baked with fat, 3 ounces	85	0	6	22	135
Clams, canned, solids and liquid, 3 ounces	85	2	1	7	45
Clams, raw, meat only, 3 ounces	85	2	2	11	65
Crabmeat, canned, 3 ounces	85	1	2	15	85
Fish sticks, breaded, frozen, 10 sticks	227	15	23	38	400

Food					
Haddock, breaded, fried, 3 ounces	85	5	7	17	140
Ocean perch, breaded, fried, 3 ounces	85	6	13	16	195
Oysters, raw, meat only, 1 cup	240	8	6	20	160
Salmon, pink, canned, 3 ounces	85	0	6	17	120
Sardines, Atlantic, canned in oil, drained, 3 ounces	85	0	12	20	175
Shad, baked with table fat and bacon, 3 ounces	85	0	12	20	170
Shrimp, canned, drained, 3 ounces	85	1	1	21	100
Swordfish, broiled with butter or margarine, 3 ounces	85	0	7	24	150
Tuna, canned in oil, drained, 3 ounces	85	0	9	24	170

FRUITS AND FRUIT PRODUCTS

Food					
Apple juice (cider), bottled or canned, 1 cup	248	30	tr	tr	120
Apples, raw, 1 medium	150	18	tr	tr	70
Applesauce, canned, sweetened, 1 cup	255	61	tr	1	230
Applesauce, unsweetened or artificially sweetened, 1 cup	244	26	tr	1	100
Apricots, canned, heavy syrup, 1 cup	259	57	tr	2	220
Avocados, California, 1 whole	284	13	38	5	370
Avocados, Florida, 1 whole	454	27	33	4	390
Bananas, raw, medium, 1 whole	175	26	tr	1	100
Blueberries, raw, medium, 1 cup	140	21	tr	1	85
Cantaloupe, ½ medium melon	385	14	tr	1	60
Cherries, canned, red sour, pitted, water pack, 1 cup	244	26	tr	2	105
Cranberry sauce, sweetened, canned, 1 cup	277	104	tr	tr	405
Dates, pitted, 1 cup pieces	178	130	1	4	490
Fruit cocktail, canned, heavy syrup, 1 cup	256	48	tr	1	195
Grapefruit, raw, medium, white, ½	241	11	tr	1	45

	Weight Grams	Carbo-hydrates Grams	Fat Grams	Protein Grams	Food Energy Calories
Grape juice, canned or bottled, 1 cup	253	42	1	1	165
Grapes, raw, American type, 1 cup	153	15	tr	1	65
Lemonade concentrate, frozen, diluted, 1 cup	248	28	tr	tr	110
Orange juice, frozen concentrate, diluted, 1 cup	249	29	tr	2	120
Oranges, raw, 1 medium whole	180	16	tr	1	65
Peaches, canned, heavy syrup, 1 cup	257	52	tr	1	200
Peaches, raw, medium, whole	114	10	tr	1	35
Pears, canned, heavy syrup, 1 cup	255	50	1	1	195
Pears, raw, 1 whole	182	25	1	tr	100
Pineapple, canned, heavy syrup, 2 slices and juice	122	24	tr	tr	90
Pineapple, juice, canned, 1 cup	249	34	tr	1	135
Pineapple, raw, diced, 1 cup	140	19	tr	1	75
Plums, raw, 1 medium	60	7	tr	tr	25
Prune juice, canned or bottled, 1 cup	256	49	tr	1	200
Prunes, dried, uncooked, 4 medium	32	18	tr	1	70
Raisins, seedless, 1 cup tightly packed	165	128	tr	4	480
Raspberries, raw, 1 cup	123	17	1	1	70
Rhubarb, cooked, sucrose added, 1 cup	272	98	tr	1	385
Strawberries, frozen, 1 10-ounce carton	284	79	tr	1	310
Strawberries, raw, capped, 1 cup	149	13	1	1	55
Tangerines, 1 medium	116	10	tr	1	40
Watermelon, 1 wedge 4 × 8 inches	925	27	1	2	115

GRAIN PRODUCTS

Bagel, 3-inch diameter, 1	55	28	4	6	165
Biscuits, baking powder, 2-inch diameter, 1	28	13	5	2	105
Bran flakes (40%), dry, 1 cup	35	20	1	4	105
Breads:					
Boston brown, 1 slice 3 × ¾ inch	48	22	1	3	100
commercial breads: raisin, rye, cracked wheat, white, whole wheat, soft or firm, fresh or toasted	25	13	1	2	72
Cakes—from mixes or commercial					
angel food, 1 piece	53	32	tr	3	135
cupcakes, 1 small with icing	36	21	5	2	130
devil's food, 2 layer with icing, 1 piece	69	40	8	3	235
gingerbread, 1 piece	63	32	5	2	175
white, 2 layer with chocolate icing, 1 piece	71	45	7	4	250
Cakes—home recipe					
Boston cream, 1 piece	69	34	7	4	210
fruitcake, dark, 1 small piece	15	9	2	1-	55
plain sheet cake with boiled white icing, 1 piece	114	62	7	4	323
pound, 1 slice ½-inch thick	30	14	10	2	140
sponge, no frosting, 1 piece	66	20	2	5	115
yellow, 2 layer with chocolate icing, 1 piece	75	45	10	3	275
Cookies					
brownies with nuts (from mix), 1	20	13	4	1	85
brownies with nuts and chocolate frosting, 1	85	42	11	4	272
chocolate chip, commercial, 1	10	7	2	1	49
chocolate chip, home recipe, 2½ inch, 1	10	6	2	1	50

	Weight Grams	Carbo-hydrates Grams	Fat Grams	Protein Grams	Food Energy Calories
fig bars, commercial, 1	14	10	1	1	50
sandwich, commercial, chocolate or vanilla, 1	10	7	2	1	50
Corn flakes, added nutrients, plain, dry, 1 cup	25	21	1	2	100
Corn flakes, added nutrients, sugar coated, 1 cup	40	36	tr	2	155
Corn muffins, made with mix, egg, milk, 1 muffin	40	20	5	3	130
Crackers, Graham, 2½-inch square, 4	28	21	2	2	110
Crackers, Saltines, 4	11	8	2	1	50
Danish pastry, without fruit/nuts, 1 round	65	30	17	5	275
Doughnuts, cake type, 1	32	16	7	1	125
Farina, quick-cooking, enriched, cooked, 1 cup	245	22	1	3	105
Macaroni and cheese, commercial can, 1 cup	240	26	11	9	230
Macaroni, enriched, cooked till tender, 1 cup	190	39	1	6	155
Muffins, with enriched white flour, 1	40	17	5	3	120
Noodles, egg, cooked, 1 cup	160	37	3	7	200
Oatmeal or rolled oats, cooked, no sugar, 1 cup	240	23	2	5	130
Oats, puffed, added nutrients, no sugar, 1 cup	25	19	1	3	100
Pancakes, 4-inch diameter, buckwheat mix with egg and milk, 1	27	6	3	2	55
Pancakes, plain or buttermilk mix, egg and milk, 1	27	9	2	2	60
Pie, ⅟₇ of 9-inch-diameter pie					
apple, 2 crust, 1 sector	135	51	17	3	350
cherry, 2 crust, 1 sector	135	52	16	4	350
custard, 1 crust, 1 sector	130	30	17	8	285

lemon meringue, 1 crust, 1 sector	120	45	14	4	305
mince, 2 crust, 1 sector	135	56	16	3	365
pumpkin, 1 crust, 1 sector	130	32	16	5	275
Pizza (cheese), ⅛ of 14-inch-diameter pizza	75	27	6	7	185
Popcorn, commercial, popped with oil, 1 cup	9	5	2	1	40
Popcorn, popped, sugar coated, 1 cup	35	30	1	2	135
Pretzels, Dutch, twisted, 1	16	12	1	1	60
Pretzels, stick, small 2¼ inch, 10	3	2	tr	tr	10
Rice, instant, ready-to-serve, 1 cup	165	40	1	3	180
Rice, puffed, added nutrients, 1 cup dry	15	13	tr	2	60
Rice, white, enriched, cooked, 1 cup	205	50	1	4	225
Rolls, enriched, cloverleaf, home recipe, 1	35	20	1	3	120
Rolls, enriched, commercial, 1	28	15	1	2	85
Rolls, frankfurter or hamburger, 1	40	21	1	3	120
Rolls, hard, round, 1	50	30	1	3	155
Rye wafers, whole-grain rectangle, 2	13	10	tr	2	45
Spaghetti, enriched, cooked till tender, 1 cup	140	32	1	5	155
Spaghetti, meatballs, tomato sauce, home recipe, 1 cup	248	39	12	19	330
Spaghetti, as above, commercial canned, 1 cup	250	28	12	12	260
Spaghetti, tomato sauce, cheese, canned, 1 cup	250	38	2	6	190
Spaghetti, as above, home recipe, 1 cup	250	37	10	9	260
Waffles, from mix with egg and milk, 1	75	27	9	7	205
Wheat, puffed, added nutrients, dry, 1 cup	15	12	tr	2	55
Wheat, shredded, plain, 1 3-inch	25	40	tr	2	90
Wheat flakes, added nutrients, 1 cup	30	24	tr	3	105

MEAT, POULTRY, AND EGGS

	Weight Grams	Carbohydrates Grams	Fat Grams	Protein Grams	Food Energy Calories
Bacon, crisp, 2 slices	15	1	8	5	90
Beef cuts braised, simmered, pot roast, lean and fat, 3 ounces	85	0	19	23	245
Beef cuts braised, simmered, pot roast, lean only, 2.5 ounces	72	0	6	22	140
Beef:					
hamburger, broiled, lean, 3 ounces	85	0	12	23	185
hamburger, broiled, regular, 3 ounces	85	0	20	21	245
roast, oven-cooked, rib, etc., lean and fat, 3 ounces	85	0	38	17	375
roast, oven-cooked, rib, etc., lean only, 1.8 ounces	51	0	7	14	125
roast, oven-cooked, round, etc., lean and fat, 3 ounces	85	0	8	25	165
roast, oven-cooked, round, etc., lean only, 2.7 ounces	78	0	4	24	125
steak, broiled, sirloin, lean and fat, 3 ounces	85	0	31	20	330
steak, broiled, sirloin, lean only, 2 ounces	56	0	5	18	115
steak, broiled, round, lean and fat, 3 ounces	85	0	15	24	220
steak, broiled, round, lean only, 2.4 ounces	68	0	6	21	130
Chicken, breast, ½ with bone, fried	94	1	6	25	155
Chicken, drumstick, with bone, fried	59	tr	1	12	55
Chicken, flesh only, broiled, 3 ounces	85	0	4	20	115
Lamb chop, thick, with bone, broiled, 4.8 ounces	137	0	38	25	400
Lamb, leg, roasted, lean and fat, 3 ounces	85	0	18	22	235
Lamb, shoulder, roasted, lean and fat, 3 ounces	85	0	27	18	285

Food					
Pork, chop, fresh, cooked, thick, with bone, 3.5 ounces	98	0	25	16	260
Pork, fresh, cuts, simmered, lean and fat, 3 ounces	85	0	34	20	320
Pork, fresh, roast, oven-cooked, lean and fat, 3 ounces	85	0	28	21	310
Pork, ham, light cure, lean and fat, roasted, 3 ounces	85	0	22	18	245
Pork, liver, breaded and fried, 2 ounces	57	3	7	15	130
Pork, luncheon meat, boiled ham, sliced, 2 ounces	57	0	2	11	59
Pork, luncheon meat, canned, spiced or unspiced, 2 ounces	57	1	16	8	165
Sausage, bologna, 2 slices	26	tr	8	3	80
Sausage, braunschweiger, 2 slices	20	tr	6	3	65
Sausage, deviled ham, canned, 1 tablespoon	13	0	5	2	45
Sausage, frankfurter (8 per lb.), 1 wiener	56	1	17	7	170
Sausage, pork links (16 per lb.), 2 links	26	tr	12	5	125
Sausage, salami, dry type, 1 ounce	28	tr	13	6	130
Sausage, Vienna, canned (7/5-oz. can), 1 sausage	16	tr	4	2	40
Veal, medium fat, cooked, boneless cutlet, 3 ounces	85	0	12	23	185
Veal, medium fat, cooked, boneless, roast, 3 ounces	85	0	17	23	230
Eggs, scrambled with milk and fat, 1	64	tr	10	7	110
Eggs, whole, without shell, raw or cooked, 1	50	tr	7	6	80

MILK, CHEESE, CREAM, AND RELATED PRODUCTS

Food					
Buttermilk, cultured, made from skim milk, 1 cup	245	12	tr	9	90
Cheese, natural, blue or Roquefort type, 1 ounce	28	1	10	6	105
Cheese, natural, Cheddar, 1 ounce	28	1	9	7	115
Cheese, natural, cottage, creamed, 1 ounce	28	1	1+	4	30
Cheese, natural, cottage, from skim milk, 1 ounce	28	1	tr	5	25

	Weight Grams	Carbo-hydrates Grams	Fat Grams	Protein Grams	Food Energy Calories
Cheese, natural, cream, 1 ounce	28	1	11	2	105
Cheese, natural, Parmesan, 1 tablespoon	5	tr	1	2	25
Cheese, pasteurized processed, American, 1 ounce	28	1	9	7	105
Cheese, pasteurized processed, Swiss, 1 ounce	28	1	8	8	100
Cream, half-and-half, 1 tablespoon	15	1	2+	1	20
Cream, light, 1 tablespoon	15	1	2+	1	25
Cream, sour, 1 tablespoon	12	1	6	tr	25
Cream, whipping, heavy, unwhipped, 1 tablespoon	15	1	6	tr	55
Imitation cream products, powdered creamer, 1 teaspoon	2	1	1	tr	10
Imitation cream whipped topping, 1 tablespoon	4	tr	1	tr	10
Milk chocolate-flavored drink (2% milk), 1 cup	250	27	16	8	190
Milk dessert, baked custard, 1 cup	265	29	16	15	305
Milk dessert, ice cream, regular (10% fat), 1 cup	133	28	6	6	255
Milk dessert, ice cream, rich (16% fat), 1 cup	148	27	26	4	330
Milk dessert, ice-milk type, 1 cup	131	29	7	6	200
Milk dessert, sherbet type, 1 cup	230	58	tr	3	235
Milk, malted beverage (Eastern seaboard type), 1 cup	235	28	11	11	245
Milk, malted beverage (Midwest, ice-cream type), 1 cup	240	30	25	5	340
Milk, nonfat (skim), 1 cup	245	12	tr	9	90
Milk, partly skimmed, 2% nonfat milk solids added, 1 cup	246	15	5	10	145
Milk, whole, 3.5% fat, 1 cup	244	12	10	9	160
Yogurt (made from whole milk)	245	9	9	9	150

VEGETABLES AND VEGETABLE PRODUCTS

Asparagus, cooked, 4 spears	60	2	tr	1	10
Beans, lima, cooked, 1 cup	170	34	1	13	190
Beans, snap, green, yellow or wax, cooked, 1 cup	125	7	tr	2	30
Beets, cooked, drained, peeled, diced, 1 cup	170	12	tr	2	55
Broccoli, cooked, drained, 1 medium stalk	180	8	tr	6	45
Brussels sprouts, 7-8 per cup, cooked, 1 cup	155	10	tr	7	55
Cabbage, cooked, 1 cup	145	6	tr	2	30
Cabbage, raw, finely shredded or chopped, 1 cup	90	5	tr	1	20
Carrots, cooked, diced, 1 cup.	145	10	tr	1	45
Carrots, raw, 5½ × 1 inch, 1 whole	50	5	tr	1	20
Cauliflower, cooked, flower buds, 1 cup	120	5	tr	3	25
Celery, raw, 1 large outer stalk	40	2	tr	tr	5
Corn, sweet, cooked, 1 8-inch ear	140	16	tr	3	70
Cucumber, raw, pared, 10 ounces, 1	207	7	tr	1	30
Lettuce, raw, Boston type, 4-inch diameter, 1 head	220	6	tr	3	30
Lettuce, raw, Iceberg type, 4-inch diameter, 1 head	454	13	tr	4	60
Mushrooms, canned, solids and liquid, 1 cup	244	6	tr	5	40
Onions, cooked, 1 cup	210	14	tr	3	60
Peas, canned, solids and liquid, 1 cup	249	31	tr	9	165
Peas, green, cooked, 1 cup	160	19	tr	9	115
Potato chips, 10	20	10	7	1	115
Potatoes, French-fried, frozen, heated, 10 pieces	57	19	4	2	125
Potatoes, mashed, milk and butter added, 1 cup	195	24	9	4	185
Potatoes, medium, baked, peeled, 1	99	21	tr	3	90
Potatoes, medium, boiled, peeled first, 1	122	18	tr	2	83

	Weight Grams	Carbohydrates Grams	Fat Grams	Protein Grams	Food Energy Calories
Radishes, raw, 4 small	40	1	tr	tr	5
Sauerkraut, canned, drained, 1 cup	150	7	tr	2	30
Spinach, cooked, 1 cup	180	6	tr	5	40
Squash, summer, cooked, diced, 1 cup	210	7	tr	2	30
Squash, winter, baked, mashed, 1 cup	205	32	tr	4	130
Sweet potatoes, baked, peeled, 1 potato	110	36	tr	2	155
Sweet potatoes, boiled, peeled, 1 potato	147	39	tr	2	170
Sweet potatoes, canned, 1 cup	218	54	tr	4	235
Tomato catsup, 1 tablespoon	15	4	tr	tr	15
Tomatoes, canned, solids and liquid, 1 cup	241	10	tr	2	50
Tomatoes, raw, 3-inch diameter, 1 tomato	200	9	tr	2	40
Tomato juice, 1 6-fluid-ounce glass	182	8	tr	2	35
Turnips, cooked, diced, 1 cup	155	8	tr	1	35

Note: Carbohydrate values are total carbohydrate weights. Much of this carbohydrate is not digestible unless cooked. Vegetables that are consumed raw provide bulk, vitamins, and minerals but not the food energy indicated above.

Index